# Top Pay and Performance

# Top Pay and Performance

## International and Strategic Approach

Edited by
Shaun Tyson and Frank Bournois

**ELSEVIER**
BUTTERWORTH
HEINEMANN

AMSTERDAM • BOSTON • HEIDELBERG • LONDON • NEW YORK • OXFORD •
PARIS • SAN DIEGO • SAN FRANCISCO • SINGAPORE • SYDNEY • TOKYO

Elsevier Butterworth-Heinemann
Linacre House, Jordan Hill, Oxford OX2 8DP
30 Corporate Drive, Burlington, MA 01803

First published 2005

**British Library Cataloguing in Publication Data**
A catalogue record for this book is available from the British Library

**Library of Congress Cataloguing in Publication Data**
A catalogue record for this book is available from the Library of Congress

ISBN 0 7506 5919 X

For information on all Elsevier Butterworth-Heinemann
publications visit our website at www.elsevier.com

Typeset by Charon Tec Pvt. Ltd, Chennai, India
www.charontec.com
Printed and bound in Great Britain by Biddles Ltd, Kings Lynn, Norfolk

# Contents

# Contributors

**Frank Bournois** is a Full Chair of General Management at the Université Paris 2 and at ESCP-EAP (European School of Management), where he holds a Chair on Executive Governance.

**Keith Cameron** spent over 20 years as a Human Resources Director for Levi Strauss, Dixons, Storehouse and the Burton Group, latterly becoming an Executive Director of Arcadia Group plc with responsibility for Retail, Logisitics, Property and HR. He is currently a non-executive director of four organizations.

**John E. Core** is Associate Professor of Accounting at the Wharton School of the University of Pennsylvania. He has a BA from Yale University and a Ph.D. from the Wharton School. He has worked as an investment banker for PaineWebber, as a compensation consultant for Ernst & Young, and as an assistant professor at MIT Sloan School. He serves as Associate Editor of the *Journal of Accounting and Economics* and serves on the editorial board of the *Journal of Accounting Research* and the *Journal of Management Accounting Research*. His primary research interest is incentive compensation, but he has also published work in the areas of corporate governance, equity valuation and corporate disclosure.

**Marc Glaeser** is Senior Consultant and International Project Manager of Kienbaum Management Consultants GmbH, Germany and has consulted in companies throughout Europe on HR development and compensation systems and implementation issues.

**Wayne R. Guay** is Assistant Professor of Accounting at the Wharton School of the University of Pennsylvania. He received an undergraduate degree in Engineering and Management from Clarkson University, an MBA from Northeastern University and a Ph.D. in Accounting from the Simon School of Business at the University of Rochester. Wayne has published articles in leading accounting and finance journals on topics such as design of executive compensation contracts, executive and non-executive incentives from stock and stock options, employee stock option valuation and related accounting issues, risk management, equity valuation, and earnings management. He currently serves on the editorial boards of the *Journal of Accounting and Economics*, *Journal of Accounting Research* and *The Accounting Review*.

**David F. Larcker** is the Ernst & Young Professor of Accounting at the Wharton School of the University of Pennsylvania.

**Jean-Pierre Magot** is a Senior Partner at Mercer, France. He specializes in top pay devices for large French multinationals.

**Don McClune** is a Director of MM & K Limited and specializes in compensation and international performance incentive programmes. He has directed many large pan-European peformance incentive projects. Don is a Fellow of the Chartered Institute of Personnel and Development and has extensive experience in personnel management, including as a General Manager Personnel for Tate & Lyle Agribusiness Division. Don is a Visiting Fellow at Cranfield School of Management.

**Paul Norris** has a Master's degree in Law from London University and is a Barrister by profession. He is Chief Executive of MM & K Limited, an independent consulting firm specializing in the design and implementation of business-driven reward strategies for senior executives. Aside from the management of MM & K, Paul advises leading companies about designing executive incentives based on transparent performance targets linked to business goals.

**Sébastien Point** is a lecturer in Human Resource Management and International Management at the Université de Franche-Comté at Besançon in France. He is also Visiting Researcher at Cranfield School of Management.

**Alexander von Preen** is Managing Director and Partner of Kienbaum Management Consultants GmbH, Germany, as well as Director of Kienbaum AG, Switzerland. His area of expertise is the development of HR programmes, specifically compensation and incentive systems for senior to top managers for leading companies in Germany, Austria and Switzerland.

**Shaun Tyson** is Professor of Human Resource Management and Director of the Human Resource Research Centre at Cranfield School of Management.

# Acknowledgements

We wish to gratefully acknowledge the efforts of all our contributors, whose scholarship we are pleased to display in this volume.

We also wish to thank Jayne Ashley, who has made a major contribution to the editing process, and also to express our appreciation to Maggie Smith, our publisher, for her encouragement and patience.

*Shaun Tyson, Cranfield University*
*Frank Bournois, University of Paris*

# 1

# Introduction

Shaun Tyson and Frank Bournois

The twenty-first century has commenced with unprecedented attention to corporate governance in the face of front-page scandals, public pressure and institutional insistence. Whether through diminished deference from employees or shareholder demands for more transparency and accountability, senior executives find themselves having to explain their rewards to sceptical stakeholders. At the same time, increased competition and pressures on costs have put directors under an obligation to perform against tough targets.

Underneath the public face of 'top pay' – where headlines from the tabloids meet column centimetres from the financial broadsheets – there is at a deeper level an organizational drama regularly played out in companies large and small, where rewards are always at the heart of the strategic dilemmas managers face. Top pay is a critical aspect of reward strategy, since the reward systems for senior executives are used to communicate the symbols of success or failure, of being one of the top team, or of not being in the top team. Rewards are the lifeblood of motivation and are the manifestation of a system through which people are motivated to perform, to change, to develop, to remain, to join or to leave the organization.

By rewards we mean more than money, and include in our definition all the methods deployed to energize those who work in and who manage the business. However, money or 'pay' in all its forms is representational,

standing symbolically for the values of approval or disapproval, signi-
fying status and power in most societies.

Public scrutiny and disapprobation, new corporate governance structures and movements in shareholder power therefore bring new pressures into an environment at the top of organizations where the stakes
are high and are personal. High because failure or success at the top
leads to major effects throughout the organization. Personal because
reputation, personal wealth, relationships, lifestyle and perhaps even
the sense of identity are subject to these pressures.

This book is about the fundamental issues raised by these pressures.
A recurring theme we will explore is the extent to which there is convergence across Europe in the corporate governance rules and in the
management approach to director-level rewards. In particular, we will
examine the trends in France, Germany and the UK, and make reference
to the trends elsewhere, to see what is emerging as a common management approach – a common plank in Western Capitalism's supporting
structure. The new corporate governance codes are based on transparency and accountability to shareholders. These are emergent tenden-
cies which may be taken further. Linkages between organization strategy,
performance targets and rewards are regarded as important at a time
when HR strategy is designed to drive business performance. Tests for
the linkages, found in the quality of incentive schemes, are therefore
falling under direct scrutiny. How should director-level remuneration be
decided is an underlying question which this book seeks to address.

Given the explicit and symbolically significant linkages between
rewards and performance, we believe explorations on this topic are
timely. To investigate the field there are two streams of data. First,
consultancy reports, newspaper articles and published surveys are
sources. For example, there are newspaper articles with their data
sources which include corporate annual reports, information from executives and from institutional shareholders and investment analysts as
well as government white papers. The second stream is academic
research into director-level rewards. Here again, a variety of perspectives can be taken: there are empirical and theory building studies, as
well as literature reviews and 'think pieces'. These topics are studied at
universities and business schools in a variety of courses: ethics, finance,
economics, human resource management and industrial relations, for
example.

## Theoretical perspectives to the study of top pay

The study of top-level executive pay brings us into contact with a wide spectrum of subjects. These include the study of corporate governance, and related issues such as boardroom effectiveness and public relations; economic theories of behaviour and rational action; the study of ethics and of power; business strategy and its relationship to reward strategy, as well as practical questions about the design of reward schemes for directors. Not surprisingly, this variety leads researchers to take an eclectic approach to theory.

From the extensive research into top pay we can distinguish five main categories. We will follow these broad headings in our description: economic theory, institutional theory, corporate governance, consultancy prescriptions, and behavioural theories concerning decision-making and the use of discretionary power.

Amongst the economic theories found, agency theory is perhaps the most popular in studying rewards. At its simplest, agency theory argues that the fundamental relationship in which director-level rewards are founded is the relationship between the principal (shareholder or owner) and the agent (director or senior executive). The potential difficulties that arise in this relationship stem from the extent to which the separation of ownership from control has distorted the fiduciary responsibilities of directors, and has affected the risks and opportunism of directors. Such research has been used extensively to explain contingent rewards and executive contracts, and to explore reward alignment with stock performance (e.g. Tosi and Gomez-Mejia, 1989; Jensen and Murphy, 1990; Lippert and Moore, 1994).

An equally instructive theoretical perspective draws upon the study of the corporate governance legislation, which means research into the growth of institutional arrangements to regulate the power relationships in society, including those between stakeholder groups. Different societies and different business systems can therefore be studied to see, for example, whether or not there are convergent or divergent trends in the control of top pay (Cheffins, 2003). We may regard this as an institutional theory version.

Researchers sometimes take the analytical position of examining the influence environments have over organizations, when examining the norms within decision-making for example, and when looking at

3

transparency of reward policy as a device to put pressure on boards to conform. This gives us the opportunity, by making international comparisons, of explaining how institutions produce different organizational responses:

*... it focuses on the ways that different institutional environments generate different kinds of technically efficient business recipes.*

(Whitley, 1992, p. 126)

One danger from this approach might be to foster a deterministic emphasis on the rules and governance structures. Prescriptions from shareholders, such as shareholder interest groups, often see the solution to 'fat cat' problems in the need for more rules and structures to limit the opportunism assumed in senior management – see, for example, Clarke (1998), who sets out the competing stakeholder groups and the influence they seek, and the references to such interest groups as the Association of British Insurers (ABI), e.g. in the consultative documents (pp. 6 and 11, Rewards for Failure, DTI consultative document, June 2003).

These kinds of prescriptions serve the interests of stakeholders, lobbying on behalf of their members. However, prescriptions are also important for consultancies acting in this field. They represent a pragmatic strand in the research on top pay, producing detailed data on reward packages, surveys of rewards, of contracts and pension schemes, as well as summarizing trends (see, for example, Incomes Data Service Reports). All the major reward consultancies conduct salary surveys. There are also 'niche' surveys into rewards covering particular sectors such as financial services or manufacturing, and surveys into specific occupational groups such as finance directors, human resource directors or chief executive officers. The advantages to be gained from data-driven enquiries into rewards come from the fine-grained detail found in these surveys of reward practice. Disclosures, now mandatory, about reward policy and the greater transparency within annual company reports facilitate data gathering for academics and consultancies alike.

The methodologies to assess performance for all the elements within reward packages are also assuming a high degree of standardization. Long-term incentive plans (LTIPs) are very common amongst the top

FTSE companies and measurements such as earnings per share (EPS) or total shareholder return (TSR) are found as target measures for LTIPs in most large businesses. EPS occurs in 40% of the FTSE 100 and TSR in 85% of FTSE 100, as the main performance measures within LTIPs. For share option criteria, the majority of FTSE 100 companies use EPS (72%), with 18% using TSR (IDS, 2003, pp. 24/25). Measurement of the expected value of incentives is now almost always done by means of the Black–Scholes formula, and the emerging common trend towards more pay at risk with proportionately less basic pay is growing, following the typical US director-level salary structure.

A common language in rewards found in Europe and North America has also spread to countries espousing the US ideal. There is a long-standing debate about whether convergence in HRM policies and practices is a result of multinational influence and the spread of consultancy techniques (for example, the Hay job evaluation scheme). Expatriates are also said to spread practices as they move from head office to local offices. The implications for reward research include the question of whether rewards at the top are closer to the style naturally adopted by the parent company, whilst at lower levels employee pay schemes are more likely to reflect local practices, labour market conditions and traditions found in the local country in question. All of these questions show the social and psychological significance of reward policies.

A well-recognized trend in board-level compensation and corporate governance research seeks to establish how boards are structured and how this influences compensation for CEOs and other members. For example, 'insiders' (management executives) are often contrasted with non-executive directors who may represent the wider interests of shareholders (Angbazo and Narayanan, 1997; Cosh and Hughes, 1987; Newman and Mozes, 1999). Other aspects of board structure include the problems of 'duality', where the roles of chairmen and CEOs are vested in the same person (Boyd, 1995), this being a more common practice in the USA than in the UK.

In most studies, behavioural changes or actions by board members are implicit within the hypotheses proposed. Some actions are thought to be universally defined, the meaning behind them unambiguous. A descriptive base is sought by such studies to explain whether and to what extent changes to the structure might impact on performance. This is defensible given a need to establish the nature of the problem.

As has been noted, board structures may be different in the USA from the UK and other European countries, and in the UK, corporate governance changes backed by shareholder groups and given the force of law have been introduced, in the form of The Directors' Remuneration Report Regulations 2002 (SI No. 1986). The Higgs report (2003), also in the UK, proposed a description for the roles of the board, and that half of the members should be independent non-executives. It also recommended a separation of the CEO and chairman roles and described the roles of the non-executive directors. The earlier regulations had already prescribed that the remunerations committee of the board should consist of non-executive directors. Higgs also comments on the differences between the changes to corporate governance in the UK compared to the US. US changes have focused, according to Higgs, on corporate malpractice (following Enron), whereas the motivation for change in the UK had been the poor stock market performance of companies (P12, 1.11), which sparked a debate about 'rewards for failure' (see, for example, the DTI consultative document, with that title, June 2003).

There is evidence on how changes to boards and the extent of managerial discretion are also important. For example, Werner and Tosi (1995) reported that firms with higher levels of managerial discretion paid compensation premiums, in higher salaries and bonus, but that changes in pay were not related to changes in firm performance. Similarly Core et al. (1999) show how CEOs earn greater compensation when governance structures are less effective, and that weaker governance structures are associated with poor performing firms.

CEO turnover and changes to board membership can also affect how a company is regarded by the investment community, depending upon the board's prior performance (Kesner and Dalton, 1994). Fox and Opong (1999) found that although there are short-term effects from these changes, reputations are recovered over time.

In our study of director-level pay we must remember that their behaviour is unlikely to be substantially different from the behaviour of staff in their companies. Much of what can be said about decision-making and motivation will be the same for all employees, since these issues are rooted in the human condition.

*Board members are reluctant to terminate or financially punish poor performing CEOs, for the same reasons supervisors are reluctant to punish subordinates – they personally bear a disproportionately large share of the non-pecuniary costs, but receive essentially none of the pecuniary benefits.*

(Baker et al., 1988, p. 614)

Nevertheless, the study of pay at the top is worthy of special attention, because directors have power to influence their own rewards and to affect the performance of their firms, probably to a greater extent than other employees, at lower levels. They can also manipulate information. In their study of corporate presidents' letters, contained in the annual reports to shareholders, Abrahamson and Park (1994, p. 1329) found evidence of concealment:

*Results were consistent with the claims that accountants and certain types of shareholders and directors prompt officers to reveal negative outcomes, whereas others promote concealment. We also found evidence for the claim that some concealment and its toleration by outside directors may be intentional.*

This fascination with the internal working of boards and those at the top should not prevent us from taking the strategic context into account. Corporate strategies are linked to reward, as argued earlier, and the objectives which trigger variable pay through long-term incentive schemes and bonuses are most likely to be those that reflect desires for corporate success, however defined, for those at the top.

We will discuss later in this chapter the question of whether the new ideas on business and human resource strategy offer a further alternative for the student of rewards to explore, to give us new insights in the field by showing the strategic context where reward policies and practices are used.

The theoretical background to the study of this area is diverse. To see how reward policies and practices may be studied and to take general conclusions from our book means we travel a path through a variety of theories. Merchant et al. (2003) argue that research in the field has become hindered because of the tendency to focus on one theoretical perspective. They suggest organizational incentive schemes are a good example of a system that contains a multiplicity of interdependent elements which can only be researched by using a range of theoretical disciplines – including accounting and economics, but also sociological, anthropological and philosophical ideas and models. In this book, we have sought to offer a number of different lenses through which to observe rewards at the top.

One of those lenses is the institutional and cultural perspective. Legal and institutional norms and rules influence top pay, and we believe an international comparative stance is helpful in revealing how business systems and economic pressures frame the context of corporate governance in regard to top pay.

## International comparative study of top pay

International comparisons within HRM are now virtually essential within any European text on aspects of HRM. The expansion of the European Union from fifteen to twenty-five countries as members, the growing practice of moving work to countries with cheaper labour costs but good quality standards, together with the growth of global brands and marketing, means we are all international now. What could be more natural than to examine HR practices and governance systems within different countries in order to make comparisons? The output from these comparisons informs discussion on cross-border mergers and alliances, investment strategies and business development decisions. There are practical benefits to be found from studies of best practice around the world, and from the descriptions provided. Academic benefits derive from international comparisons by showing if convergence is occurring, the extent to which HR practices reflect different business systems, and the way cultural norms influence human resource management.

There are likely to be significant economic influences on the business systems that arise in different societies. Economies of scale and improvements to their competitive position are drivers for companies who engage in mergers and acquisitions, the development of subsidiaries, and international joint ventures. The structural responses to international challenges can produce complex matrix structures, and accountabilities spread across several countries (Gooderham and Nordhaug, 2003). In practice, large multinationals need to capture all the knowledge and the learning processes which they own into a coherent methodology so that they can foresee new issues, respond quickly to pressures and compete through superior human as well as capital resources. The consequences for HRM from new structural forms can be enormous. The rewards for different levels of boards, for example, are likely to have considerable symbolic significance. Reporting relationships are often fed into grading structures. Complex structures require new competencies to manage them. Complex structures and many levels in the hierarchy affect promotion policies, and subsidiaries offer opportunities for expatriates to develop.

Societies have different cultural norms. HR policies and practices will inevitably follow those norms, and may even help to create them. The 'individualization' of the employment contract in the West, for example, was a feature of a Thatcherite and Reaganite British and American philosophical shift in the 1980s. 'Collectivism' and an emphasis on 'group' behaviours and group norms are often found in Japanese management practices. From the individualist, entrepreneurial culture has come a belief in sharing risk with senior employees – so that bonus and stock option schemes based on long-term organizational performance for senior managers have become very popular.

It is also possible that we value people differently in different cultures. Jackson (2002) argues that societies have a 'locus of human value', a prevailing view about how to value people as humans. He therefore suggests:

*... that there are both tensions between an instrumental locus and a humanistic locus of human value and potential synergies.*

(Jackson, 2002, p. 469)

These two positions seem to be whether, in a given society, people work according to what they receive in a calculating, contractual way or in a less instrumental way, so that whilst still concerned with profit, they seek to humanize the world of work. In this theory therefore, we have prevailing views of the place of humans in the world of work which might result in very different reward strategies. This theory is akin to Williamson's ideas on 'hard' contracts (calculative) and 'soft' contracts (based on mutual obligations and a more 'moral' attachment) – see, for example, Tyson (1999) for a discussion on this. Again, the consequences for rewarding top people are whether or not rewards are seen as entirely contractual or are part of a wider psychological contract between the employee and the company.

This is significant because the nature of the attachment between senior executives and their organization is being described here, which influences the attitude towards bonus, stock options and the reciprocal obligations felt by the executive concerned. The nature of the attachment also influences the extent to which senior management is perceived to be a legitimate source of power and therefore whether they act in their own or the organization's interests.

## The structure of the book

This book is structured so that we begin with the broad and well-known debates on director-level pay and corporate governance, and examine the evidence on transparency and reporting standards across Europe. We look then at detailed descriptions of top pay in France and Germany, before going on to look at equity incentives, reward design and the management of reward structures through remuneration committees and at rewards as part of human resource strategy.

The popular starting point for any discussion on this topic is the debate raging about 'fat cats'. The debate in the press is often emotional in tone, and in exploring this issue we seek to discuss the roles of the various stakeholders, the reality of board-level rewards as opposed to the rhetoric, and the need for a way to deal with the ethics of the various positions.

We go on to look at the legal and corporate governance framework in the UK and in the USA. In particular, Paul Norris takes the shareholder's position, and describes the individual contractual basis for director-level rewards. He examines in detail questions about accounting for share options, and summarizes the importance of realistic targets for directors, from which both shareholders and senior executives can benefit.

Sébastien Point analyses how new rules and corporate governance codes across Europe are showing signs of convergence, and seeks the causes of these trends. His research into company reports gives us an insight into the practices of disclosure in the UK, France, Germany and Sweden, and of the way the rules are applied.

We look in more depth at current trends for directors in France in the chapter by Frank Bournois and Jean-Pierre Magot, and in Germany in that by Alexander Von Preen and Marc Glaeser, where readers will recognize much commonality as well as divergence. Whilst the quantum of pay may be different, and there are inevitably varying effects from the different tax regimes and corporate structures, both chapters reveal justifications for the convergence thesis. For example, there is ample evidence of the integration between director-level pay and corporate strategy, increasing the amount of variable pay, putting more at risk and of the balanced scorecard type of approach. Alongside these trends, we must also note different structures, such as the supervisory boards in Germany.

Equity incentives are a characteristic of director-level reward packages. Wayne Guay, David Larker and John Core, in their chapter, highlight the issues regarding equity incentives and synthesize the academic research, including research on equity incentives and organizational performance, the repricing of options, relative performance evaluation and the expensing of stock options.

The practical questions of how to design a reward package in outline are covered by Don McClune, where he concentrates on the emotional and perceptual issues in the design of the package. Taking a business-driven approach, he suggests reward schemes be utilized to reinforce the cascaded objectives and accountabilities of the senior team.

Remuneration committees now perform an increasingly important institutional role for controlling reward policy. Keith Cameron's detailed account of the role and function of remuneration committees shows a six-point check list for committees to use in assessing reward proposals. He goes on to place the role of remuneration committees in the context of the latest corporate governance rules in the UK.

The book moves from describing the emerging corporate governance context, on through international comparisons, examines the major academic debates on the topic and the strategic questions on reward at the organizational level. In the final chapter, we examine the three main strategic approaches and the consequences for director-level rewards. Human resource strategy is an integral part of business strategy and rewards are central to the strategic purpose of the business and to the long-run competitive posture of the organization. Top pay is important because policy in the area contains the implicit values of the top team and is used as a way to reinforce accountabilities, to reward performance and to support the achievement of the organization's objectives.

# 2

# 'Fat cat' pay

Shaun Tyson

## Introduction

Since the start of the new millennium, most serious newspapers in the UK, and many others in Europe and the USA, have carried stories almost on a daily basis on the excesses of boardroom rewards. These allegations usually contain an account of the pay and benefits received by an executive director, CEO or chairman, and go on to castigate the culprit, without any attempt to explain the actions taken by the directors concerned. The implication, usually left unsaid, is that senior managers act entirely in their own interests, irrespective of the needs of other stakeholders.

A few examples demonstrate the range of headlines found:

### Barclays Chairman's salary quadruples
*... Details of the pay packages contained in the bank's annual report – have emerged just nine days before Barclays is due to close 171 branches affecting 500 staff.*

(*Financial Times*, 30 March 2000)

### Funds furious over RBS bonuses
*The National Association of Pension Funds is to recommend that its members vote against the re-election of two Royal Bank of Scotland directors in protest against the payout to executives of 'takeover' bonuses worth £2.5 million.*

(*Financial Times*, 27 March 2001)

*Big guns act to block C&W fat cat pay off*
*The big battalions of the City today moved to prevent a potential*
*£2 million pay off to the embattled chief executive of imploding*
*telecoms group Cable & Wireless.*

(*Evening Standard*, 12 December 2002)

*Fat cat packages cut as angry US shareholders get set to*
*sharpen claws*
*After a disastrous year for profits, record-shattering bankruptcies*
*and public outrage over fat cat packages, leading US companies are*
*cutting salaries and benefits at the top.*

(*Evening Standard*, 14 February 2003)

In this chapter we explore the intentions and implications behind headlines such as these. At the heart of the issues are concerns for shareholders interest, for employees, and the public or government interest, which bring into play questions about performance management, equity and risk, as well as corporate governance and the needs for transparency.

## Shareholder versus the 'public interest'

In the USA, shareholders, taking advantage of the Securities and Exchange Commission, Shareholder Proposal Rule 14a-8, which permits shareholders to put material in the proxy documentation and for subsequent presentation at the annual general meeting, have proposed resolutions in support of an activist agenda. These shareholder proposals are more likely to be successful if they derive from co-ordinated groups (Gillan and Starks, 2000). Similarly, public pension funds have become active in following their investment strategies, and those firms where there appears to be a breakdown in the negotiation between the firm and the shareholder groups, as evidenced by repeated proposals, suffer a declining performance over time, as reflected in stock prices, compared to those firms where there has only been one proposal in the time period (Prevost and Rao, 2000).

Shareholders have become increasingly vociferous in defence of their own interests on both sides of the Atlantic; this is exemplified in the monograph by Monks and Sykes (2002), published simultaneously in the USA and in the UK, which argued strongly for reform. This proposed

that all fiduciaries should act solely in the long-term interests of beneficiaries, that shareholders should nominate at least three non-executive
directors for each quoted company and that non-executive directors
should control the audit and remuneration committees, amongst other
proposals. These ideas, if implemented, would constitute a 'revolution in
twenty-first century capitalism' according to the preface. The substance
of the powerful argument put forward is that the lack of transparency,
lack of accountability and the failures of institutions caused a crisis in
capitalism and a threat to the equity culture which represented the worst
crisis since 1929. In the wake of Enron, the periodic revelations on 'fat
cat' pay, and the perceived weakness amongst investors and their institutions to deal with the situation, such a position seems to have a strong
evidential basis. As this study pointed out, the USA had come late to deal
with the pay-related corporate governance issues, compared to the UK,
although there was still a felt need by the UK government to do more.

One argument advanced is that managers are thought to have become
obsessed with the maximization of shareholder value in the short term, to
the detriment of societal needs. This implies that the State or government
has been forced to take up the interests of society, to represent the wider
community by creating laws and regulations ensuring transparency and
accountability to shareholders. Indeed, that is the direction policies have
been taking in UK legislation, and in other countries of late.

The assumption that shareholder and State interests are identical is
questionable. Increased regulation restricts decision-making within the
firm, could influence the appointments at director level, and puts further
pressure on CEOs to produce immediately what the shareholders want –
presumably this being increased shareholder value. The context where
decisions are made is of critical importance. For senior managers, balancing the demands of good corporate governance with the needs of customers, in the competitive context as they see it, may result in decisions
being taken which do not seem to be in tune with societal interests, or
those of employees. For example, in the case of the comments on Barclays
quoted earlier, the real bone of contention was not the amount paid to the
chairman. He had been performing a dual role of CEO and chairman tem-
porarily, and the bank had produced record profits. The higher than normal
rewards were a consequence of both more responsibility and good performance. However, the outcry was really because the increased payout
coincided with branch closures. There is a long-standing issue about the

social purpose of retail banking, which is usually the least profitable part of the business. Thus, criticism was levelled at the bank for 'butchering the branch network' in the words of Martin Selter MP, with adverse effects on local communities and on jobs, a decision which drew criticism also from Roy Murphy, the joint general secretary of the banking union UNIFI.

We can see from this case, therefore, that senior managers can be 'damned if they do perform, and damned if they don't', to paraphrase Lorenzo Dow. Shareholder interests and those of the employees, and of the community at large, do not necessarily coincide.

Indeed, shareholder interests are not always clear and, despite attempts by institutions and shareholder groups, and despite the prescriptions intended to codify behaviour contained in voluntary codes, stock exchange rules and government reports, managers are still left to interpret what is expected by the different stakeholders in the business, and to reconcile the different interests.

The development of other stakeholder interests may be at the expense of shareholders. As Clarke (1998, p. 183) points out:

*The attenuation of the shareholder's role in managing the business and the rise of professional management is associated with a growing recognition of the significance of the role and the contribution of other stakeholder groups to the performance of the company.*

He goes on to list the range of stakeholders, including customers, employees and suppliers, as well as investors. As agency theorists would contend, we should expect directors to act on behalf of shareholders, to align their interests with those of the company. However, given the need managers have to preserve their own leadership role, and to respond to the pressure from shareholders, managers may only appear to adopt performance-based reward schemes such as long-term incentive plans (LTIPs), when in fact they use this apparent alignment to corporate needs as a device both to satisfy the conflicting demands they face and to offer a sop to Cerberus, thereby pacifying the shareholders.

*In effect, boards facing the pressures associated with a firm's poor performance may seek to restore their credibility with shareholders by ceremonially increasing control over management. LTIP adoption can provide an opportunity for the firm to arrange stakeholders' impressions about CEO compensation, and the role of compensation in organizational affairs.*

(Westphal and Zajac, 1994, p. 384)

The separation of ownership from control does mean managers must have some latitude to make decisions. They need authority if they are to take responsibility. Senior managers are not just acted upon by institutions, but are themselves actors who have intentions and wants. The research by Westphal and Zajac showed how managers seek to orchestrate the affairs of their corporations. The degrees of freedom to align a manager's interests with the 'interests' of the corporation are also sources of latitude. This is because no one stakeholder can speak with unchallenged authority for the corporate interest.

Corporate governance regulations initiated by governments in Europe and the USA seek to limit this latitude. We describe these new rules in Europe in Chapter 4. For directors, there has never been a period in recent times when no controls were exercised over their behaviour. These were imposed either through statutes covering companies (for example, in the UK, the Companies Act of 1948 and its subsequent amendments, which contained, for example, the requirement on directors to show 'a true and fair view' when publishing the accounts), or through codes of conduct such as the London Stock Exchange's Combined Code produced by the London Stock Exchange in 1998, which covered directors' remuneration.

What is the public interest in top executive pay? For the State and other bodies to seek to regulate rewards for individuals, there must surely be a pressing case. Typical reasons advanced include the State's role in ensuring companies are 'well run', this being a rather general oversight of commercial affairs. Presumably, the government or State wishes to encourage the satisfactory working of capital markets, to encourage investment and to meet international obligations and treaty requirements as in the case of the European Community.

We can see evidence of the British government's reasoning in the prefaces to recent 'white papers' (discussion documents). For example, in the consultative document on Directors' Remuneration of December 2001, Patricia Hewitt, the Secretary of State for Trade and Industry, commented that the area was important because of the significance of executive director motivation for UK productivity, and that the issue was at the heart of the debate on effective corporate governance: 'This is the issue above all others, on which directors face a conflict of interest' (p. 4). She goes on to say that remuneration is important because 'it affects the way in which business is perceived in this country, both by employees and in the community at large' (p. 4).

In the rather controversially entitled paper of June 2003, ' "Rewards for Failure", Directors' Remuneration – Contracts, Performance and Severance', the Foreword from the paper stated that the granting of generous compensation packages to departing company directors where the company had performed poorly was a concern for government. This was because of the need for shareholders to be given a stronger voice and because rewards for failure 'damage the image and reputation of the whole of British business'.

Arguably, there are also tacit reasons for some State controls. For example, to avoid inflationary wage pressures from employees who might otherwise take encouragement from high levels of director reward, to provide a sense of fairness over pay deals and to avoid pressures over taxation levels at the upper end of pay brackets.

The recent scandals which accompanied the collapse of Enron in the USA have given impetus to State initiatives in this area. In particular, the way senior executives at Enron cynically sold their own stock in the company, knowing that the stock would soon be worthless, whilst preventing their employees from trading in their shares, was a cause for concern. As reward packages now frequently include stock options, the need to prevent any form of insider trading is also a reason for intervention.

## Ethics of top pay

Issues behind the 'fat cat' debate include questions of distributive justice – where the apparent inequalities between rewards and effort or performance point to the unfair advantage taken by senior executives, who use their power to their own benefit at the expense of others. A further sense of unfairness might be associated with the view that managers are stakeholders, alongside shareholders, employees and customers. However, it is difficult to decide on the competing claims of these various stakeholders, or to determine which of these has a superior claim (Winstanley and Woodall, 2000).

One implication from the roles of non-executive directors in setting rewards might be that some form of collusion occurs between executive and non-executive directors. This would mean rewards for CEOs and directors would be decided through exchanging favours, or tacit under-standings of personal interest, rather than through any performance measures or rational process. Research studies have not revealed evidence of this kind of 'backscratching', the granting of higher pay levels to CEOs in return for business favours and fees. Hwang and Anderson (1993) found no evidence of backscratching, nor could Angbazo and Narayanan (1997), who concluded there was 'little evidence of mutually beneficial backscratching or collusion'. However, they also state that there was 'a positive relationship between fees paid to the outside directors and the cash and total compensation of the CEO' (p. 2420). But they argue there was no evidence of interlocking directorships or business transactions with the outside directors. Instead, they prefer alternative explanations – such as the need for higher rewards to managers in complex organiza-tions. They also point out that high-quality CEOs who earn high rewards are more likely to recruit high-quality directors to their boards, who nat-urally would expect good levels of reward for their services.

So what is the evidence on the relationship between pay and per-formance for senior executives? There are many famous studies on this topic. Tosi and Gomez-Mejia (1994) argue from their evidence that the monitoring of CEO pay is related to firm performance up to a point where diminishing returns set in: 'once managers have done all they can, increases in CEO monitoring will do little to enhance firm perform-ance' (p. 1003). Yet in terms of compensation strategies, changes in pay for higher-level employees were not always related to changes in firm performance, and firms which gave managers greater discretion were not better performers than other types of firms (Werner and Tosi, 1995). One problem which may account for the many different answers to the questions about firm performance and CEO pay is the difficulty in agree-ing what performance measures to take. This is discussed in more detail in Chapters 5 and 8. However, we may speculate here that the ambigu-ity around these performance measures serves the interests of execu-tives and boards, who can use the confusion to justify compensation packages.

We could see the debate on 'top pay' as a form of discourse ethics, a search for an acceptable process through which the issue of how to settle senior executive pay is debated, and the corporate governance mechanisms decided.

Ethical codes need to be elaborated and discussed in a process of agreement between the parties concerned: 'Codes should be understood more as a process than a result' (Lozano, 2001). The rational dialogue that is required to produce a consensus supports the autonomy of those concerned, and a recognition of their separate and legitimate interests. The discourse is more important than the end-product in this perspective.

The last decade in the UK and in other parts of Europe has seen unprecedented activity in producing new governance rules, codes of conduct and laws. Following the Cadbury and Greenbury reports, prompted by 'fat cat' scandals, the Combined Code was introduced in 1998. The London Stock Exchange made disclosures compulsory from their listed companies. These were according to the requirements of the Code, as stipulated in their governance and disclosures rules. These disclosures were about how the company applied the Combined Code rules and contained confirmation that the company had included the various recommendations, including those on directors' remuneration. For example, Section B.1 of the Code states:

*Levels of remuneration should be sufficient to attract and retain the directors needed to run the company successfully, but companies should avoid paying more than is necessary for this purpose.*

(p. 10)

Rewards, it stated, should be linked to performance, and the details of remuneration for each director should be disclosed. The Code goes on to describe the role of remuneration committees.

Following more scandals, a consultation document issued by the new Labour government in December 2001 set out the case for reform of corporate governance laws:

*In particular, the government wishes to ensure that the regulatory framework promotes transparency and accountability to shareholders.*

(p. 5)

In 2002, 'The Directors' Remuneration Report Regulations 2002' came into force, which stipulated the way remuneration should be set, the extent of disclosure and the role of remuneration committees, as well as the opportunity for shareholders to vote on the remuneration committee report of policy.

The Higgs report of January 2003 concentrated on the role of boards, of the 'chairman' and of non-executive directors, and emphasized the need to ensure the independence and professionalism of non-executive directors. By June 2003, further changes were being proposed in a further consultative document aimed at tightening the rules on termination payments, and pensions, through tackling the directors' contracts.

What we see from these new laws, rules and recommendations are attempts to wrestle with the process by which decisions on remuneration can be taken, which will be seen to be ethical, by all the various stakeholders. The discourse on top pay has, in the UK, taken government into a directive approach: the government is anxious to be in pole position, to be leading opinion. The debate is not so much about the amount of pay, but about the process through which governance is decided. Perceptions of fairness and equity can be seen as paramount, therefore.

## What is the case for high levels of reward for directors?

The almost frenzied attention to directors' rewards by the media may encourage us to ask whether this is based on any factual information. Evidence is not hard to find. Amongst the reliable data are surveys such as those produced by the major consultancies in the field.

If we take UK CEOs' base pay increases for the year to March 2003 (for the FTSE 350), the median salary rise was 8.3%; this was a reduction on the increases in the twelve months to the previous quarter, according to the IDS Management Pay Review (IDS, August 2003). However, the median increase in total cash, including salary, benefits and bonus payments, was 18.5%, a big increase on the previous year. These increases were not repeated lower down the organization, where pay increases were much reduced in percentage terms. The highest increases were in the FTSE 100. The base salary for FTSE 350 lead executives (usually CEOs), as shown in the annual accounts in the period from 1 January to 31 March 2003, was £567 500 p.a. (median) with total earnings of £1 002 377, the difference in the figures being mainly attributable to share option gains or the vesting of long-term incentive plans (LTIPs).

However, there are signs of considerable variation between companies, with some cases where the share options were not triggered, because performance levels were not achieved. Upper quartile earnings for lead executives in the FTSE 100 were £2 130 017 p.a. in 2003 (around £1 million more than the next highest, the finance director). These are similar figures to those produced by Pay Watch (IDS, March 2003), and by the Watson Wyatt World Wide Survey. This latter study showed share option plans as growing in popularity in 2003.

There are several learning points from this account of CEO pay levels. First, pay levels vary between firms – in respect to size of company, performance and share price – and also vary over time, as those factors change. There is a substantial difference between rewards in the FTSE 100 and other companies. Second, base pay increases do not indicate changes to total rewards, where stock option grants can make a major difference to director pay. Third, pay levels at the top do not reflect pay levels lower down. There are always larger differences in pay ranges as one rises in the organization.

Top pay may seem excessive, but we must have a sense of proportion as regards UK senior executives. If we compare UK director rewards to those paid in the USA in top companies, a rather different picture emerges. First, let us take those in the UK who are at the upper end of the director earnings bracket, the extreme cases we may say. For example, according to the *Guardian* survey of July 2003, we can examine chairman and CEO rewards. Including all elements of compensation, the ten highest paid chairmen ranged from £3.456 million p.a. to £1.802 million p.a., the CEOs from £9.156 million p.a. to £3.661 million p.a.

The difference in the structures show varying amounts of pay 'at risk' (see examples in Table 2.1).

These amounts may seem beyond the dreams of most ordinary working people. However, if we compare these with USA total compensation, according to Forbes, top paid chief executives 2002, including salary, bonus, perks and stock gains on exercised options, for the fiscal year 2001 were as follows:

CEOs
Oracle              $706 m
Dell Computers      $201 m
JDS Uniphase        $150 m

**Table 2.1** Survey of rewards for UK chairmen and CEOs

| Company | Base pay | Bonus | Options | Total |
|---|---|---|---|---|
| *Chairmen* | | | | |
| Rio Tinto | 837 000 | 604 000 | 2 015 972 | 3 456 972 |
| Unilever | 940 000 | 1 157 000 | 1 031 986 | 3 128 986 |
| Wm Morrison | 381 000 | 50 000 | 2 024 000 | 2 455 000 |
| *CEOs* | | | | |
| BHP Bilton | 798 842 | 3 365 533 | 499 216 | 9 156 591 |
| Tesco | 916 000 | 1 922 000 | 2 804 000 | 5 642 000 |
| Vodafone | 1 270 000 | 1 626 000 | 1 923 477 | 4 819 477 |

Source: adapted from the *Guardian* executive pay survey. Derived from recent annual reports and accounts of 107 companies in FTSE 100 index companies, or those who were in the index in the last 12 months. Figures include basic pay, benefits, cash bonuses and options granted in previous years and any share-based long-term incentive payments that become due during the year. Includes pay-offs and signing-on fees, but not cash payments into pension schemes. Published in the *Guardian*, 31 July 2003.

The lowest of the top ten earners was Seibel System's CEO on $88 million. UK rewards are clearly not in the same league as those of the USA.

What then are the causes of anger over top executive pay? Envy could be a factor, for example, but the apparent failure to link pay to organizational performance, and the disparity between pay levels for senior executives and the average pay levels for the majority of the workforce are the reasons consistently cited. Accounts of these ratios vary, but for proportions of the average, the figures often quoted for CEOs are around sixty times, and over 500 times more than the minimum wage. Turning to the headlines again, we can see that there are many examples of a generalized sense of injustice and envy, perhaps underscored by emotional content, which may be feelings of unfairness or of powerlessness in the face of privileged power. Frequently, journalists report upon non-base pay elements in the package, such as bonuses, pension fund contribution, golden hellos, farewells and other perks.

The *Guardian*, on 31 July 2003, featured the story of the departure of the CEO of BHP Billiton, who was already allegedly the best paid senior executive of a FTSE 100 company, and who left with a pension 'pot' of £16 million, following the merger of BHP and Billiton, which he led. BHP suffered a 'slump' in profits by 11.5% to March 2003. The story also pointed to the differences in pay between the top executives and the employees, who averaged £24 000 p.a. In this story, which gave more detail than is possible to summarize here, we have all the aspects usually found: big numbers, pay-offs and big pension 'pots' being created. The headlines in the *Guardian* newspaper on the same day reported their own survey with the headline 'shares down 24%, average earnings up 3%, boardroom pay up 23%'.

These reports are in one sense a triumph for the disclosure requirements on the companies' annual reports, where individual rewards and reports by the remuneration committees of non-executive directors would have been less obvious without the legislative requirements for transparency, in the UK and other countries.

The weaknesses of most articles on 'fat cat' pay are in the failure to recognize the complexities of senior executive pay and the tendency to generalize from particular cases. For example, there is a time lag between the allocation of shares and the realization of any profit from their sale, during which time corporate performance may change. Articles such as those quoted also tend to produce an emotional response. This is a paradoxical reaction to management actions for not being rational. Emotions are not always in opposition to reason. Williams (2001) described emotion as: 'The animating principle of sociality and self-hood, the social glue which binds us together yet the force which tears us apart; our lives without emotion would quite simply be not real lives at all' (p. 134). Emotional reactions are to be expected: without emotions we would cease to be human. 'Pay' is an emotive topic because pay levels lead naturally to comparisons, and hence play to our sense of fairness.

One proposal from 'third way' politics is the creation of a new social contract, 'no rights without responsibilities', as a feature of citizenship. This 'has to apply to politicians as well as citizens, to the rich as well as the poor, to business as much as the private individual' (Giddens, 2000, p. 52). This could be taken to be the societal position, but as we have argued, such an egalitarian position is difficult to reach when decisions about allocations of money produce winners and losers.

The causes of anger or envy are not necessarily the amounts of base pay – and we have seen that CEO pay is a mixture of long-term and short-term incentives, perks and benefits, not necessarily in any specific proportion. From the reports in newspapers, pay-offs for contracts, pension contributions at the time of termination, and substantial increases in total rewards, often occasioned by long-term incentive plan payouts or stock option gains, are frequently commented upon.

Some headlines from recent articles illustrate this point:

### Cuckoo in the capitalist nest
*Are share options the best way to reward employees?*
> (*Financial Times*, 11 November 1999)

### M&S disaster boss paid £1.4 million
*City anger as stores chief set for huge bonuses.*
> (*Evening Standard*, 12 April 2001)

### Marconi's property losses mount up
*The outcry over Marconi's dud property deals is set to flare again with the revelation that it has just crystallized a £500,000 loss on the sale of the Buckinghamshire manor house it bought from its former sales chief less than a year ago.*
> (*Evening Standard*, 29 January 2003)

### Kingfisher's Mulcahy pots £15 million pension
> (*Daily Telegraph*, 7 May 2003)

### Railways chief books secret three-year deal
> (*Evening Standard*, 12 July 2001)

### A ghastly year, but Equitable chiefs may get bonuses
> (*Financial Times*, 2 May 2002)

One of the most ironic cases of recent years is Richard Grasso:

### NYSE pays chief $139 m lump sum
*Top US regulators are looking at the details of a $139 million (£88 million) payout received by Richard Grasso, Chief Executive of the New York Stock Exchange.*

*The sum is more than the Exchange's combined net income for the last three years and has provoked outrage throughout corporate America. It comes just as William Donaldson, Chairman of the Securities and Exchange Commission, has said he will target excessive executive compensation.*
> (*Financial Times*, 28 August 2003)

There would seem to be a prima facie case for suggesting that director-level rewards are excessive. Whilst the argument against current levels can be supported by the examples from the headlines, all pointing towards an apparent need for greater control by shareholders and better corporate governance, there is an alternative view. The justification can be found in HRM policies.

Reward levels in organizations are directly related to the financial turnover or size of the business – for example, a high turnover company would typically have higher pay levels. Similarly, large organizations with many levels in the hierarchy need to attract and retain staff, and to offer incentives for promotion. This means, at the top end, salary scales would need to provide headroom for the senior executives. One reason often cited for higher rewards is the need to attract and retain the best senior executives available. Compared to the US, pay in the UK is a fraction of the amounts received by US executives, and yet UK companies such as Marks & Spencer have been successful in attracting world-class top executives. In assessing comparative rewards, we must keep in mind differences between tax regimes, cost of living and lifestyle in the different countries. There is also the question of what are acceptable differentials between senior executive pay and average pay in each country. In the USA, where there is perhaps a greater belief in the marketplace determining pay, there is a greater tolerance of larger differentials between the top-level employees' earnings and those of employees lower down.

Senior executives take risks with shareholders' money and with their own careers, as well as risks which could affect the employees, suppliers and customers. Rewards should reflect the risk taken. There are different interpretations of the relationship between executive compensation and the market value of companies, and changes in profits. For example, Brickley et al. (1985) reviewed stock price reaction when LTIPs were introduced or changed. These plans, it was argued, tended to produce positive market reactions. Lippert and Moore (1994) point to the multiple sources of agency conflict and the effects of various control devices on CEO compensation alignment to performance, and that 'strong alignment may also be sub-optimal because tying a manager's compensation too closely to stock values may result in inefficient risk allocation' (p. 321). Amongst the determinants of CEO compensation alignment, they show that 'idiosyncratic risk' (firm-specific risk) rather than risk in the marketplace generally leads to more costly monitoring and hence

CEOs tend to have compensation contracts with greater alignment to firm performance in these cases. This supports Sloan's (1993) view that incentives based on profit measures help to shield executives from market-wide fluctuations in the value of their firms which are beyond their control. Generalization about how compensation strategies influence risk is not possible. For example, CEO reactions to takeover or merger opportunities are likely to be dependent on many personal factors, such as the amount of stock held, and the potential to improve personal wealth according to the deal on offer.

There is evidence that reward strategies are intended to be aligned with business strategies (for example, through objectives based on performance measures cascaded from the business plan), and that there are therefore good HRM reasons for the design of specific director-level packages, as well as broad trends in what is acceptable in reward packages generally at any one point in time (Bender, 2003).

Complexity is another reason for higher rewards in larger organizations. More complex structures and decision-making are likely to demand more from those who manage in this type of environment. Complexity no doubt requires special skills and abilities, to organize and to lead the top team. There is the possibility that higher CEO pay may be a trade-off against job insecurity. Various evidence exists on this, but there seems to be greater insecurity with higher CEO turnover in Europe compared to the USA, although US compensation is higher (Lucier et al., 2002). We cannot be sure of the reasons for turnover. High pressure on some permanent CEOs might be a source of burnout and stress, whilst some CEOs may be operating to conduct changes at the top or restructuring with an interim management mandate, where short service is built into the contract.

## Conclusions – the consequences for directors

The continuous interest in this subject is evidenced by the long history of reports and newspaper articles. In the UK, a raw nerve was struck at the time when many privatized corporations' directors decided that the move to the private sector offered an opportunity for large-scale pay increases at the top. For example, Hodgson et al. (1999) outlined the issues related to privatization and director-level pay in their pamphlet, and compared the highest paid director and lowest paid workers, showing that directors were

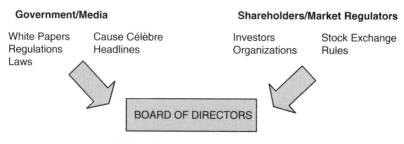

**Government/Media**

White Papers    Cause Célèbre
Regulations       Headlines
Laws

**Shareholders/Market Regulators**

Investors     Stock Exchange
Organizations  Rules

BOARD OF DIRECTORS

Audit and Remuneration Committees

**Figure 2.1** Two sources of pressure.

receiving increases of 10–14%, compared to 3–4% for lower-level workers. The continuous series of reports and media articles about individual cases in the 1990s subsequently bear witness to the importance of the topic. The white papers and reports which are detailed elsewhere in the book chronicle the continuing attempts to reform corporate governance.

Whilst directors were acquiring greater rewards, their reputations suffered. A poll conducted in 2003 by the *Financial Times* showed that four out of five people believed that directors of large companies could not be trusted to tell the truth, and 78% agreed these directors were paid too much (Blitz, R., *Financial Times*, 30 June 2003). This survey also showed a deep sense of distrust over pensions. The lack of trust and the negative opinions about executive pay did not vary according to gender or class. There are even suggestions from senior academics that CEOs are sociopaths – because of their lack of shame (Skapinker, 2003).

The argument in this chapter demonstrates that, underneath the newspaper outrage, there resides a deeper set of issues. There is a debate – where the concern for managerial legitimacy, the separation of ownership from control, and the strong human emotions of envy, feelings of injustice and suspicion are expressed. These powerful issues were fed by the accusations of rewards for failure and large termination payments. A rational process for managing this discourse is required, so that the legitimacy of the different positions taken is acknowledged and where stakeholders can each make their arguments.

Corporate governance reform has had support through these debates from two sources. First, from those in government and elsewhere who regard the inequalities revealed by the top pay debate to be part of wider inequalities in our societies, and who believe corporations should be subject to tight controls. They believe that, by encouraging transparency, pressure will be exerted by public and institutional investors, on both the process by which rewards are decided and the amount of pay. The second source of pressure is from the shareholders and the institutions, who believe managers should align their interest more with the investors, and that the design of packages should reflect that. They welcome more control over remuneration committees and directors.

This chapter has described the importance of the fat cat debate. Performance issues are at the heart of this debate, as indicated by the 'rewards for failure' accusations. Investment is also affected by any misalignment in rewards and organization objectives, as is social cohesion. The personal and reputational aspects of the debate cannot be avoided – the symbolic aspects of rewards and the significance of reputations for directors add to the emotional context in this subject. For all these reasons we have argued that the rules and pronouncements from governing bodies are part of a discourse aimed at adjusting positions in accord with the complexities of the issues raised in this chapter.

We may speculate that corporate governance issues, far from driving the agenda, are by-products of the fundamental issues associated with managerial legitimacy and the control and ownership in companies. The future research into 'fat cats' may shift away from matters related to corporate governance, towards the ethical and relationship issues involved in decision-making, and the human resource strategies of the business.

# 3

# Shareholders' attitude to directors' pay

Paul Norris

## Introduction

Shareholders are increasingly vociferous in their denunciation of pay awards for executives, particularly executive directors. On the face of it, there appears to be a growing rift between investors and the corporate management teams charged with delivering a return to investors. Some might question how a rift can exist if both management and shareholders seek the same end – i.e. a return on their investment. In reality, the nature of the respective investments made by management and shareholders differs, and whilst increased shareholder value is key to achieving both sides' goals, each may look to a different set of criteria to measure success.

The subject of directors' pay must be considered in the wider context of corporate governance. Look no further than the latest manifestation of the criticism aimed at directors, namely payment for failure. In reality, the recent raft of comment has been concentrated (albeit not exclusively) on payment for failure. This refers to the large payments made to departing executives ousted by shareholders for destroying shareholder value. Among other things, this has prompted the UK government to consider legislation to prevent so-called payment for failure. At the annual general meeting of global pharmaceuticals giant, GlaxoSmithKline, held in London on 18 May 2003, nearly 51% of shareholders voted against the remuneration committee's report on directors' remuneration. This vote has the distinction of being the first in which a majority (albeit slender) of shareholders voted against. What infuriated shareholders was the inclusion in the CEO's service contract of terms entitling him, among other things, to continue to participate in incentive plans after termination of his employment.

Moreover, a raft of corporate collapses in the USA and elsewhere has highlighted not only poor governance and accounting malpractice, but also some extravagant pay practices allegedly designed to buy silence or simply to satisfy whim.

Ironically, the very thing that was thought to align the interests of investors and managers is also at the heart of the debate about directors' pay – equity. Share options, for many years an established part of a US or UK executive director's pay package and gaining ground across Europe and the rest of the world as business becomes increasingly global, are increasingly targeted by shareholders. There is also a rising awareness among management teams and their advisers that share options do not necessarily deliver appropriate business-driven incentives for managers – and represent a better deal for managers than for shareholders. The National Association of Pension Funds, a UK investor protection organization, has described options as 'blunt instruments', which reward too much in a bull market and not enough in a bear market.

The question of equity dilution is key to understanding shareholders' attitudes to share acquisition schemes for directors. Typically, option and other forms of share participation schemes involve the issue of new shares to participants. These new shares:

1  increase the amount of issued ordinary share capital, and
2  dilute the shareholding interests of existing shareholders.

UK institutional shareholders have taken steps to reduce the level of dilution caused by introducing share participation schemes for directors and senior executives.[1]

Unless shareholder value increases, the issue of new shares will reduce the value of existing shareholders' equity interests in the business.

---

[1] For further details refer to the Guidelines for Share Incentive Schemes published by the Association of British Insurers.

In straightforward terms, shareholders will want to concentrate on minimizing dilution and maximizing shareholder value.

This chapter looks into the background to the present differences between shareholders and management regarding compensation. It considers payment for failure in more detail and analyses action taken to protect shareholders' interests. This chapter goes on to consider the role of non-executive directors before examining the respective aims of management and shareholders, seeking to identify common measures of performance and proposing some possible next steps.

## Background to shareholders' concern about directors' pay

The strength of shareholders' feelings towards executive pay is difficult to gauge. The British press has recently carried an article about 'thin cats', being those chief executives of large companies whose compensation is recognized as not being excessive. There were many of them. Press coverage of directors' compensation tends to highlight specific cases, thus raising their profile in the public's eye. This can have a magnifying effect, which may encourage the inference that the problem is greater than it is in reality. There is no doubt, however, that shareholders are angry about what is now commonly referred to as payment for failure.

References to shareholders, in this context, are in practice references to institutional shareholders (pension funds, banks and insurance companies). What individual shareholders are feeling is not widely recorded. The reason for this is easy to see. In the UK, generally regarded as having a high level of individual shareholders, the institutions hold about 70% of the shares in UK companies. Typically, across Europe individual shareholders are few and far between. Until a recent change in German capital gains tax law, the majority of the shares in Germany's biggest companies[2] were held by Germany's major banks. Formerly, German tax law discouraged trading in these shares by imposing significant capital gains tax charges. Consequently, in practice the major shareholders in Germany's prime companies might well have objected to corporate practices, but could not vote with their feet without incurring a huge tax charge. Fortunately, throughout the 1990s the

---

[2] Germany's biggest companies comprise the DAX index.

German economy, in common with most western economies, performed well, increasing shareholders' paper gains. The change in the law relaxing the formerly harsh capital gains tax regime came in good time to enable Germany's banks to unload their shareholdings prior to the next economic downturn.

Germany has been relatively slow to embrace wider employee share ownership. Equity participation has not played a significant role in the remuneration of Germany's senior executives. By comparison, French law has, for many years, encouraged individuals to acquire and hold shares. The *plan d'épargne d'entreprise* has long provided a valuable tax incentive to those individuals who choose to save their own funds to buy company shares. However, in common with Germany, equity participation has not played a significant role in the remuneration of French senior executives. Things are changing now.

By comparison with Europe, regulation and best practice has required US and UK companies to disclose details of directors' pay. Companies on mainland Europe have not been required to provide anything like the same level of disclosure and a number of executives have resisted attempts to move towards the US and UK practice. However, the European Commission has indicated that it will press for more disclosure, particularly in relation to individual directors and their compensation.

Since the publication in the UK of the 1992 Cadbury report[3] on good corporate governance, two key words have been 'transparency' and 'disclosure'. The drive towards greater disclosure and the consequent availability of data on directors' pay provide shareholders with unprecedented knowledge about this subject. This higher level of knowledge has come at a time when economies and markets have turned down, thus highlighting to shareholders the opposite directions taken by the value of their investments on the one hand and directors' pay on the other. When this is coupled with the uncertain future for corporate earnings growth and associated implications for the value of equity investments, it is clear to see why shareholders are looking closely at directors' compensation packages.

---

[3] The first in-depth report and recommendation on corporate governance in the UK based on the findings of an independent committee chaired by Sir Adrian Cadbury.

## Payment for failure

This aspect of perceived corporate excess has done more than any other to anger shareholders and cause them to challenge directors' compensation policies and practices.

A direct result is increasing pressure to reduce the notice periods contained in directors' service contracts to not more than one year. This pressure has increased in the wake of well-publicized corporate failures (e.g. Marconi), following which senior directors departed with large payments and enhanced pension pots whilst shareholders were left holding an investment worth a fraction of its original value. One of the consequences of this increasing pressure and a major reason for the incidence and size of some of the reported termination payments to departing executives has been a corresponding increase in the incidence of 'liquidated damages' clauses in directors' service contracts.

A typical clause provides that if the director's contract is terminated, otherwise than for cause, he or she will continue to receive:

- salary
- benefits (including pension contributions)
- a payment in lieu of bonus and any cash long-term incentive.

Depending on seniority, these payments may continue for up to two years and, in addition, any outstanding share options, restricted shares or deferred entitlements to shares also vest on termination. In exceptional cases, the executive may be allowed to continue to participate in incentive plans, as in the case of Jean-Pierre Garnier at GlaxoSmithKline.

The existence of such a clause entrenches a contractual right to receive on termination what might well be a significant amount, which has no connection with performance.

The existence of a liquidated damages clause significantly reduces the value of the notice period, almost to the point at which the notice period simply provides a period within which to put things in order on the termination of employment.

A reason given for the emergence of liquidated damages clauses is that they simply represent a fair reflection of the amount to which an executive should be entitled on termination of employment. However, the majority of bonus and incentive plans are expressly excluded from service contracts (typically, plan rules contain a provision to the effect that the plan does not form part of the participant's contract of employment and participation shall not be taken into account for the purposes of determining any compensation or damages on the termination of employment for any reason). The liquidated damages clause can therefore be used to impose a liability on the employer (where one may not otherwise exist) to the advantage of the director.

What can be done to reduce the incidence of payment for failure?

Some employers are reducing notice periods in directors' service contracts without any attendant consideration, although these reductions have tended to be from 24 months down to 12 months. This process has had to be managed carefully to avoid the possibility of expensive litigation, which would defeat the object of the exercise. It is likely to be easier in practice to introduce shorter notice periods for new recruits, although there are examples of companies that have successfully reduced notice periods of 24 months down to 12 months, in some cases without paying additional compensation. There is no evidence that public companies are looking to reduce directors' notice periods to below 12 months.

Circumstances will have a material bearing on the best way to tackle this issue. For example, negotiations to recruit a new and formerly successful CEO into a company that has fallen on hard times might legitimately need to consider carefully the individual's view of the risks associated with taking on the new role. On the other hand, an incumbent director in a sector where job prospects are weak may agree to a shorter notice period and no cash compensation, particularly if the alternative is termination.

The executive's and the company's perception of and attitude to risk are key factors in arriving at a successful outcome. An additional factor is the individual's obligation to mitigate his or her loss in the event that the service contract is breached by the employer. Age, nature of work and market job prospects are all relevant to determining the issue of mitigation but, ordinarily, an individual cannot rely on a court awarding him or her a termination payment commensurate with the unmitigated length of his or her notice period.

One straightforward way to deal with payment for failure is not to agree to the inclusion of liquidated damages clauses in service agreements. Depending on the circumstances, this may not be easy to achieve. In addition, if directors' bonus and incentive plans are based on transparent targets linked to the delivery of strategy, it should be clear whether a bonus is or is not payable. This may be significant, as the English courts have tended to include in their assessments of the level of termination awards an amount in respect of bonus, especially if it can be shown that a history of bonus payments exists. The existence of transparent targets and the ability easily to determine if and the extent to which they have been achieved should assist employers, shareholders and the courts.

Another way to deal with this issue would be for directors' service contracts to provide for payments on termination of employment to be phased over time and to cease if the director finds another job before the end of the relevant period. Apart from the practical disadvantage that this potential solution provides no incentive for the director to find another job before the end of the relevant period, it does avoid a one-off non-recoverable payment by the company. If the making of phased termination payments was also contingent on the future performance of the company, there would be at least some justification for payment on the grounds of affordability. On the downside, it could be argued that a director held responsible for failure would continue to benefit from the skills of the remaining or new management in digging the company out of a hole.

A third way might be to include in service contracts clauses permitting the employer to terminate in the event that the director fails to meet specified levels of performance. This, however, raises a number of potentially difficult questions:

- Would the employer be justified in terminating the contract if in any year the executive failed to achieve the required level of performance?
- If the executive is charged with meeting both short- and long-term performance targets, what would be the consequence of failing to meet short-term targets whilst remaining on track in respect of the long term?
- Who decides if the executive has failed to perform?
- If the achievement of performance targets is to become embedded in service agreements, what are the consequences for those incentive plans expressed to be 'discretionary'?
- What if the director's failure is due to the failures of others or to factors outside his or her control?
- How in practice would changes in strategy requiring corresponding changes to performance targets be dealt with?

This is unlikely to be a practicable solution. The problem is difficult to resolve because it is not simply a matter of linking pay to performance. There are legal, contractual considerations to take into account. The threat of costly and time-consuming litigation is high and that risk increases with the amount of compensation payable. A route worth considering might be to recognize that a contractual right exists, but to gear the amount of compensation to the changes in the enterprise value of the business over the director's period of tenure. For example, if the unrestricted contractual entitlement is to £1 000 000 but at the end of the director's term the enterprise value is only 75% of the enterprise value at the start of the period, then the amount payable would be £750 000 phased over three years.

The UK government, having threatened legislation, indicated it did not feel that legislation was the answer, preferring industry to find its own solution. In practice, it is likely that, in the absence of legislation, the solution in any particular case will reflect the relative negotiating positions of the parties. It is not difficult to see what needs to be done, but it is difficult for one company to reach a practical solution unless others follow suit.

On the upside, there is a clear and strengthening wave of feeling against payment for failure. Shareholders will vote against compensation policies that include provisions in directors' service contracts that are perceived to make it more attractive to fail than to succeed. Even successful and highly respected companies such as the food retailer, Tesco, and WPP, the advertising giant, have been criticized by shareholders for the termination provisions available to the CEO should he be asked to leave the company.

Whilst the courts will continue to reach decisions based on the law as it applies to the facts before them, they too cannot ignore the current wave of antipathy towards those executives who, having failed to deliver, continue to benefit at the expense of the company.

## Action taken to protect shareholders' interests

In the USA, listed companies must produce information about directors' compensation in a detailed proxy statement. Proxy statements include current and historical details of cash and equity compensation, including details of option exercise prices, current market price, the estimated cash value of equity compensation and details of performance measures used to determine the level of incentive compensation. In addition, proxy statements must also include a performance graph showing the company's total shareholder return compared to relevant market indices (e.g. Standard & Poor's 500 index, or relevant industry sector index).

The UK has developed a code of best practice regarding disclosure of directors' compensation. This has recently been extended and developed by new regulations concerning the disclosure of directors' compensation and the company's compensation policy (The Directors' Remuneration Report Regulations 2002).

There is some evidence that the themes of transparency and disclosure, which the regulations seek to promote, are being adopted in Europe. Regulatory authorities in Germany have threatened legislation if the country's major companies do not adhere to a voluntary code to publish details of directors' compensation.

The UK has not gone so far as the USA, which has introduced legislation in the form of the Sarbanes Oxley Act, designed to curb malpractice of the kind witnessed in the Enron affair. For example, it prevents companies from taking compensation advice from the consulting arms of their auditors.

## The UK best practice code

Derived from the final report from the Committee on Corporate Governance and from the earlier Cadbury and Greenbury reports (1992 and 1995 respectively), the former best practice code set out guidelines on directors' pay under the following headings:

*The link between remuneration and performance*: levels of remuneration should be sufficient to attract and retain the directors to run the company successfully but companies should avoid paying more than is necessary for this purpose. A proportion of directors' remuneration should be structured so as to link rewards to corporate and individual performance.

It was for the remuneration committee to ensure that the company's remuneration policy and practices:

- aligned the interests of management and shareholders, and
- encouraged high levels of performance to enhance the value of the business.

Specifically, the remuneration committee was required to:

- decide the overall remuneration policy
- be fully aware of competitive pay practices

- decide on the appropriateness of bonus schemes and long-term incentive plans (which should have performance conditions attached)
- be mindful of the wider implications of their decisions ('knock-on' effects throughout the company, pension plan costs and termination of employment costs)
- restrict directors' notice periods to 12 months.

*Transparent procedure*: companies should establish a formal and transparent procedure for developing policy on executive remuneration and for establishing remuneration packages of individual directors. In particular, no director should have any part in determining or deciding his or her own level of remuneration.

Listed companies should appoint a remuneration committee comprising independent, non-executive directors who should have access to professional advice on compensation matters. Membership of the committee should be reported to shareholders.

*Disclosure*: the company's annual report should provide a statement of the remuneration policy and the details of the remuneration of each director.

Disclosure should be made annually, specify the remuneration policy, give details of the individual directors' salaries, bonus payments, share option awards, long-term incentive awards and the value of benefits in kind. The annual disclosure should also explain any items that were above the recommended levels.

### The new regime

In December 2001, the UK Department of Trade and Industry (DTI) published a consultative document entitled 'Directors' Remuneration'.

To quote the Secretary of State for Trade and Industry:

*More than six years ago, the Greenbury report[4] set out three fundamental principles in this area: accountability, transparency and performance linkage. The government agrees that these are*

---

[4] A report of the committee on corporate governance chaired by Sir Richard Greenbury, the second of a trio of reports (known as the Cadbury, Greenbury and Hampel reports respectively) on the same subject.

*the right principles, but it does not believe that the best practice framework has been successful in achieving adequate levels of compliance. Although many quoted companies have complied fully, this is not an area where so patchy a performance is acceptable.*

*It is not for the government to take a view on the appropriate level of remuneration for executive directors. That is a matter for companies and their shareholders. But it does intend to legislate to ensure that corporate governance framework delivers proper transparency and accountability.*

(Patricia Hewitt, December 2001, Foreword to the
Consultative Document)

The UK government enacted legislation with a view to promoting transparency and accountability to shareholders. This legislation, which affected companies that had a financial year-end falling on or after 31 December 2002, requires companies to:

- publish a report on directors' remuneration as part of the annual reporting cycle
- disclose within the report details of the individual directors' remuneration packages, the company's remuneration policy, and the role of the board and remuneration committee in this area
- put an annual resolution to shareholders on the remuneration report.

The regulations apply only to companies that are incorporated in the UK and listed on the London, New York or NASDAQ stock exchanges, or in a member state of the European Economic Area. They do not apply to companies listed on the Alternative Investment Market (AIM). The reporting requirements for unquoted companies remain unchanged and they will continue to have to report in accordance with Part 1 of Schedule 6 to the Companies Act 1985.

Under this new legislation, company directors must publish an annual report for the previous financial year specifying:

- *The role of the remuneration committee.* The legislation does not require the establishment of a remuneration committee. Instead, it anticipates that shareholders will wish to see this happen. Where a remuneration committee has considered matters in relation to directors' pay, the report must:

- state if external consultants were appointed to assist with directors' pay and confirm whether the consultants were/are retained elsewhere within the company, and
- describe the role of the remuneration committee and the board in determining directors' pay.

■ *A forward statement of policy relating to directors' remuneration*, to include:

- details of performance conditions attached to awards under long-term incentive and share option plans (including an explanation of why they were chosen) and any significant proposed amendments to a director's entitlement under such plans
- details of any comparator groups used to measure performance
- an explanation of the relative importance of the performance elements for each director's contract
- an explanation of awards made under share option and long-term incentive if performance conditions are not required
- a statement of the company's policy on the duration of directors' service contracts, notice periods and termination payments.

■ *A review of directors' remuneration for the previous year*, to include:

- the amount of each director's salary, fees, bonuses, taxable expenses and non-cash benefits (especially accrued pension entitlement)
- the amount of any termination payments made to any directors during the previous reporting year and any sums paid to third parties in respect of a director's services
- a performance line graph comparing the company's total shareholder return (TSR) over the past five years with that of companies comprising a named broad equity market index (stating the reasons for the selection of that index)
- details of share options and awards under long-term incentive schemes.

Auditors are required to audit the disclosures other than the graph.

Each company must put a resolution approving the directors' remuneration before shareholders at the AGM. The results of the shareholder vote will not be binding on the company but the results will have to be published.

The British government has also amended the Summary Financial Statement regulations to require that parts of the directors' remuneration are included in the Summary. For example, all listed companies must disclose their five-year comparative TSR performance (in much the same way as US corporations are required to disclose similar data in their proxy statements), whether or not their incentive plans are linked to TSR. This may be justified on the basis that TSR is a good measure of the value of an investment. It is not necessarily a good measure of management's performance – not least because share price is influenced by factors other than management's or the company's performance.

Additional reporting requirement should be viewed alongside the:

- extra work that will be needed to account for the cost of share options (see below), and
- proposals contained in the recent EU Prospectus Directive that companies should issue a prospectus every time they issue shares.

The accounting proposals in respect of share options and other forms of share-based payment are of direct relevance to shareholders' attitudes towards directors' pay, not least because, as a result, company profit and loss accounts must include a charge for the cost of the options or other equity awards.


## Accounting for share options

This controversial issue is entering its closing stages (Norris and Mills, 2002). Arguments rage for and against, and the dissenting voices include those of influential sceptics. Former SEC Chairman, Harvey Pitt, commented that Enron collapsed not because it failed to account for stock option grants through its profit and loss account. 'If we start with the issue of expensing stock options instead of focusing on the issues of how we make them serve the public investor, we will take a simplistic solution to a complex problem,' he said.

Whatever the IASB finally decides, it is a widely held view that there should be a common form of accounting for stock options. It is directly relevant to the debate that there is a new EU regulation requiring the use of International Accounting Standards from 2005 by all EU companies listed on a regulated exchange.

In July 2000, the UK Accounting Standards Board (ASB) published a Discussion Paper entitled 'Share-based Payment'. The foreword noted that implementing the proposals would result in a significant change to accounting practice, in particular by requiring a charge to the profit and loss account in respect of the grant of employee stock options.

In September 2001, the IASB reissued the Discussion Paper inviting additional comments. However, it had already tentatively agreed that:

- share-based payment transactions involving the purchase of goods and services with payment made in shares or options should be recognized in the financial statements, resulting in the recognition of an expense in the income statement when those goods or services are consumed
- in principle, these transactions should be measured at fair value of the shares or options issued
- where an observable market price does not exist, an option pricing model should be used to estimate the fair value of share options.

The IASB received many additional comments both for and against its proposals.

### US experience

In the early 1970s, the Accounting Principles Board issued 'Opinion No. 25' on 'Accounting for Stock Issued to Employees' stating that compensation in the form of stock issued through options should be measured by the quoted price of the stock at the measurement date less the amount, if any, that the employee is required to pay. The 'measurement date' is the first date on which both:

- the number of shares that the option holder is entitled to receive, and
- the option or acquisition price, if any are known.

If the option is subject to performance criteria, the 'measurement date' will normally be the vesting date, at which time there may be an intrinsic value in the option. Accordingly, there is a requirement to expense performance-related option grants by accounting for the estimated cost over the vesting period.

ELSEVIER

# enews

Register for **eNews**, the free email service from Elsevier Science and Technology Books, to receive:

* **specially written author articles**
* **free sample chapters**
* **advance news of our latest publications**
* **regular offers**
* **related event information**

...and more

Go to **http://books.elsevier.com**, select a subject, register and the eNews will soon be arriving on your desktop!

If you would prefer to register by post, complete and return this card to the address overleaf.

## http://books.elsevier.com

## Select the subjects you'd like to receive information about, enter your email and mail address and freepost this card back to us.

**ARCHITECTURE AND THE BUILT ENVIRONMENT**
- [ ] General Architecture
- [ ] Architectural Practice Management
- [ ] History of Architecture
- [ ] Landscape
- [ ] Sustainable Architecture
- [ ] Urban design
- [ ] Planning and Design

- [ ] BUILDING AND CONSTRUCTION

**BUSINESS & MANAGEMENT**
- [ ] Accounting/CIMA Publishing
- [ ] Finance
- [ ] Hospitality, Leisure and Tourism
- [ ] Human Resources and Training
- [ ] Pergamon Flexible Learning
- [ ] Operations Management
- [ ] Management
- [ ] Sales and Marketing
- [ ] IT Management/Computer Weekly

**COMPUTING & COMPUTER SCIENCES**
**Computer Weekly:**
- [ ] IT Management and Business Computing
**Made Simple Computing:**
- [ ] Introduction to computing and programming

**Computer Science:**
- [ ] Computer Sciences
- [ ] Artificial Intelligence
- [ ] Computer Graphics
- [ ] Computer Architecture
- [ ] Human Computer Interaction
- [ ] Information Security
- [ ] Information Systems/Databases
- [ ] Networking
- [ ] Operating Systems
- [ ] Software Development
- [ ] Information Systems

**Professional Computing:**
- [ ] Data Management
- [ ] Information Security
- [ ] IT Management
- [ ] Networking
- [ ] Operating Systems
- [ ] Software Engineering
- [ ] MCSE Certification
- [ ] Security

- [ ] CONSERVATION AND MUSEOLOGY

**ELECTRONICS AND ELECTRICAL ENGINEERING**
- [ ] Communications
- [ ] Control and Instrumentation
- [ ] Electrical & Power Engineering
- [ ] Electronics and Computer Engineering

**ENGINEERING**
- [ ] Bioengineering
- [ ] Environmental Engineering
- [ ] Industrial Engineering
- [ ] Materials Engineering
- [ ] Mechanical Engineering
- [ ] Optical Engineering
- [ ] Petroleum and Petrochemical Processing

- [ ] FORENSICS

**MEDIA TECHNOLOGY**
- [ ] Film/TV/Video Production
- [ ] Postproduction
- [ ] Scriptwriting
- [ ] Lighting
- [ ] Computer Graphics and Animation
- [ ] Gaming
- [ ] Photography/Imaging
- [ ] Audio
- [ ] Radio
- [ ] Broadcast and Communication Technology
- [ ] Broadcast Management and Theory
- [ ] Journalism
- [ ] Theatre and Live Performance
- [ ] Special effects/Make up

- [ ] SECURITY

Name: _____

Job title: _____

Email address: _____

Mail address: _____

Postcode: _____  Date: _____

Signature: _____

I would like to receive information by Email [ ]  Post [ ]  Both [ ]

Science and Technology Books, Elsevier Ltd. Registered office: The Boulevard, Langford Lane, Kidlington, Oxon OX5 1GB. Registered number: 1982084

---

Jo Blackford

Data Co-ordinator

Elsevier

FREEPOST - SCE5435

Oxford

OX2 8BR

UK

This accounting principle has inevitably led US corporations to grant non-performance-related full priced options to executives. (In the bull market of the 1990s, US executives were granted large numbers of share options on this basis that delivered wealth based solely on the rising stock market. The executives might argue that both they and shareholders saw their wealth increase during this period, so where is the problem?) Major problems for shareholders and all those concerned about long-term corporate growth are that:

- Shareholders suffered dilution at levels far in excess of the UK maximum permitted levels of 10% in 10 years.[5]
- US incentive compensation was driven primarily by short-term performance measures principally related to financial accounting targets (e.g. earnings per share or return on capital). There was no incentive for executives to be concerned about the long-term sustained generation of shareholder value. Consequently, when the economic downturn hit, many management teams were unprepared. Those with a 'parachute' were also unconcerned because their downside was, unlike that of their shareholders, protected.

Subsequent debate about the right way to treat share options resulted in Statement of Financial Accounting Standards No. 123 – Accounting for Awards of Stock-Based Compensation to Employees (FAS 123), which encourages all companies to adopt a fair value method of accounting for stock options or similar equity instruments.

FAS 123 also allows companies to continue to measure compensation cost of options using the intrinsic value method of accounting prescribed by the old APB Opinion No. 25, provided they make pro-forma disclosures of net income as if the fair value-based method of accounting defined in FAS 123 had been applied.

Key issues raised in FAS 123 are:

- The measurement date for determining the fair value of a stock option should be the grant date (whether or not the option is performance related).

---

[5] This is the maximum level of dilution permitted under the Guidelines for Share Incentive schemes referred to in note 1 of this chapter.

- The fair value should be recognized over the service period, which is usually the vesting period.
- The total amount of compensation cost recognized for an award of a stock option shall be based on the number of shares that eventually vest.
- No compensation cost should be recognized for forfeited awards, either because they fail to satisfy a service requirement for vesting, or because a performance condition is not achieved.
- Previously recognized compensation cost shall not be reversed if a vested employee stock option expires unexercised.
- For performance-related options, initial accruals for compensation costs shall be based on a best estimate of the outcome of the performance condition and shall then be adjusted for subsequent changes in the expected or actual outcome up to the vesting date.

FAS 123 (combined with APB Opinion No. 25) remains the current generally accepted accounting principle for the accounting of stock options in the United States at the time of going to press.

## UK experience

The current UK position is contained in Urgent Issues Task Force (UITF) abstract 17 'Employee Share Schemes', issued by the UK ASB in May 1997. This states: 'The intrinsic value of share options granted (i.e. any difference between the exercise price and the market value at date of grant) should, as a minimum, be charged to the profit and loss account.'

UITF 17 does not preclude companies from applying a more onerous accounting treatment based on a fair value methodology, and some UK companies (e.g. Kingfisher and South African Breweries) have begun to account for stock options using a modified Black–Scholes model. This model produces an estimated fair value of an option by replicating what an investor would be willing to pay today for the opportunity (derived from holding the option) of upside potential over the option period. The model was designed to value traded options and needed modifying to make it applicable to employee options because:

- traded options have a much shorter lifespan than employee options (typically three to nine months instead of at least three years)

- employee options are not tradable
- the exercise of employee options may be performance related.

In contrast to the US ABP Opinion No. 25, UITF 17 does not distinguish performance-related from non-performance-related options. The operative date is the date of grant in each case.

In addition, UITF 17 exempted savings-related share option schemes, although it admitted that there was no good technical reason for this. This type of option is peculiar to the UK but is similar to the all-employee US 401(k) plan and the French *plan d'épargne d'entreprise*.

### The current position

The UK and International Accounting Standards Boards have recently published all but identical new draft accounting standards (known as 'Exposure Drafts') on 'Accounting for Share-Based Payments'. The Exposure Drafts require companies that deliver equity-based compensation in any form to charge such payments to their profit and loss accounts based on the fair value at the award date. Interested parties were given 120 days starting on 7 March 2003 to comment.

For share options this means that the grantor company must value the share options at the grant date. This value is to be discounted to reflect any performance conditions on the exercise of the options and the possibility that the options may not vest owing to termination of employment. The company will be required to expense the discounted value through its profit and loss account over the vesting period of the option. This is typically three years.

Strangely, to some observers, if the option is never exercised (because the performance targets are not achieved or because the market price of the underlying shares never exceeds the option exercise price), the Exposure Drafts nonetheless require the expense to appear in the profit and loss account and do not permit the expense to be reversed (but see below).

A difficulty for shareholders and anyone else trying to ascertain the financial impact of a company's option grant policy is that whilst the Exposure Drafts advocate a uniform approach to the calculation of fair value, they leave the choice of pricing model up to each company to decide. Even if all companies choose the Black–Scholes model (as selected by Boeing, Citigroup and Disney, among others), the required modifications as referred to above are likely to reflect a subjective view of what is best for the company concerned.

Coca-Cola has recently decided to address option fair value in a new way. Instead of using a Black–Scholes model, Coca-Cola determines the fair value of its employee stock options by averaging firm price quotes from two investment banks for options with features identical to those of the employee stock options. History does not relate the method adopted by the banks to produce their quotes, but it must be possible that they too use an adaptation of the Black–Scholes model!

In February 2004, the IASB published IFRS2 on share-based payment. It contained no major U-turns but one slight surprise was produced by the UK ASB, which has given UK-based unlisted companies an extra year's grace in which to prepare for options and other share-based payments expensing through the profit and loss account.

The following main points come out of IFRS2 and the announcement by the UK ASB:

- All listed companies must account for the 'fair value' cost of share options and other share-based payments with effect from 1 January 2005. Fair value is measured at grant date and charged over the vesting period.
- The new accounting treatment applies to all shares or share options granted by listed companies after 7 November 2002 and which are due to vest after 1 January 2005.
- Any conditions on vesting or exercise are to be disregarded unless they are market-based conditions. Instead, the existence of such conditions is to be taken into account by adjusting the number of the shares included in the measurement of the fair value cost so that, ultimately, the amount recognized as the 'fair value' is based on the number of shares that eventually vests, a concept known as 'truing up'. If no shares vest, then there will be no cost and any previous charges should be reversed.
- Market-based conditions, such as a target share price, upon which vesting or the ability to exercise is conditional, are to be taken into account when estimating the fair value of the shares or share options granted. Where market-based conditions exist, there shall be no 'truing up' if a lower number of shares or options actually vests owing to the failure to meet the market-based vesting conditions.

■ The IASB has given only very limited guidance on how to calculate the fair value of options. However, it does identify some common factors in many share option schemes which might preclude the use of the (somewhat inflexible) Black–Scholes formula and the circumstances in which other types of valuation models would be more appropriate.

■ Despite pressure, there is no exemption from the new accounting treatment for all-employee share schemes or for unlisted companies.

■ The UK ASB has confirmed that it will introduce an identical UK accounting standard which will apply to all UK companies preparing accounts under UK GAAP, although unlisted companies will not have to implement the new standard until 1 January 2006. However, entities applying the Financial Reporting Standard for Smaller Entities (FRSSE) will be exempted from the new standard.

This new accounting standard is likely to have its greatest effect in relation to executive and all-employee share option schemes. In consequence, more and more companies may consider switching their plans to those delivering value to participants through whole shares, unlike share option schemes, which deliver value based on the difference between the exercise price and the option strike price.

The lack of clear guidance on how to calculate the fair value of share options means that companies can adopt varying valuation methods, resulting in inconsistency between sets of accounts. Companies and their advisers are likely to choose the valuation techniques best suited to their particular circumstances.

The decision to differentiate between market-based vesting conditions and other vesting conditions causes complexity. The permitted adjustments where vesting conditions are not market based are likely to steer most companies towards non-market-based conditions, placing the continued use of TSR as a performance criterion further into question.

Any company thinking about introducing a new share scheme or about making a new grant under an existing scheme must understand the financial and accounting consequences of doing so. The ability to model a range of 'what if' scenarios will be an essential skill for designers and operators of employee share incentive schemes.

Arguments continue for and against the proposals to expense the cost of share-based payments. The Accounting Regulatory Committee, which advised the IASB on the 'public good' arguments, has argued that share options are not a form of compensation that should be expensed through the profit and loss account – contrast this with Warren Buffett's now famous pronouncement that options are clearly compensation and should be expensed through the profit and loss account. The Accounting Regulatory Committee argument is that by authorizing companies to grant options to employees, shareholders are sharing part of their equity in the company with employees as stakeholders.

## Non-executive directors

Non-executive directors find themselves front and centre on the parade ground of directors' pay. They are the instruments through which best practice codes are operated and managed. Best practice codes require remuneration committees to comprise exclusively independent non-executive directors. The role of the non-executive director and the links between non-executives and shareholders have been highlighted recently by the publication of the Higgs report (2003). The report's recommendations have been diluted after much debate and the revised recommendations are included in the combined code on corporate governance.

The UK introduced regulations (referred to above) requiring, for accounting periods ending on and after 31 December 2002, all fully listed companies to publish as part of their annual report and accounts a separate report on directors' pay from the remuneration committee. Current best practice codes state that remuneration committees should have access to professional advice on directors' pay. The report on directors' pay in the annual report and accounts must name the firms providing such advice and state the areas in which advice is given. In the USA, recent primary legislation limits the sources available to remuneration committees in as much as compensation advice cannot be provided by the same firm that audits the company's books. Whilst similar legislation does not exist in the UK, the practice of separation is growing among major corporations. In the Euro zone there is increasing pressure for more disclosure about directors' pay, and so it is likely that European companies will follow in due course the lead set by their US and UK counterparts both in terms of disclosure and as regards obtaining professional advice.

The non-executive director is the creature of the unitary board system as operated in the USA and the UK. Under this system, a single board comprises both managers (executive directors) and non-executives who have no management role and who invariably hold a number of non-executive directorships. Consequently, the non-executives on the board tend not to work full-time for one company. The non-executive's role is to provide perspective based on experience in other fields and with other companies. An important part of the role is to both challenge (constructively) and support management's plans for the business.

In some other European countries such as Germany, a two-tier board structure is favoured in place of the unitary system. In this model, companies operate through a management board and a supervisory board. As the name implies, the management board is responsible for the day-to-day running of the business. Supervisory board members include those who would be the non-executives in the unitary system but the supervisory board also includes elected workers' representatives. Major strategic decisions (e.g. a significant disposal) cannot be implemented without the consent of the supervisory board.

The relative merits of the two systems are increasingly debated. One view is that the two-tier system clearly distinguishes the formulation of strategy from its implementation and that a similar (although not the same) result is achieved by a number of major companies operating under the unitary system which have established a management committee, comprising executive directors and heads of functions not on the board, to run the business. Another view is that the two-tier system is cumbersome. As the supervisory board is separate from the management board and is largely comprised of a different membership, it is remote from those factors currently affecting the business. Consequently, delays can arise and competitive advantage lost, while the supervisory board is brought up to speed.

In practice, the boards of listed companies in the USA and the UK operate through a number of committees, typical among which are:

- a nominations committee – to vet and approve senior appointments
- an audit committee, and
- a remuneration or compensation committee.

Therefore, in a unitary board regime, the non-executive directors are directly involved in approving and setting the remuneration levels of the executive directors, including the CEO. In theory, the executives should not take part in decisions regarding their own remuneration. More importantly, perhaps, as far as shareholders are concerned, the non-executives sitting on the remuneration committee approve the design of incentive plans, including share options, where the linkages between pay and performance are most critical.

At the heart of the differences between shareholders and management as regards directors' pay is not so much the amount that is paid, but rather the absence of a transparent link between the amount paid and performance. When considering a CEO's compensation package, it is as relevant to ask what the company is paying for as it is in respect of the compensation for any other employee. If incentive compensation is directly linked to transparent performance targets based on the delivery of the business strategy, the question of amount should be irrelevant. The single most important role of the non-executive directors on the remuneration committee is to ensure that a robust and justifiable link between pay and performance exists.

## Reaching the same destination by different routes

Both management and shareholders are the key cast members in any company. Both invest in the company. Shareholders invest their capital. Management invest their time and skills. Management and shareholders alike expect a return on their investment. Shareholders' return is a function of capital appreciation and dividend. The return on management's investment is the pay package.

The company has an existence separate from either management or shareholders. This explains how companies can contract with third parties for the supply of goods and services, and it is essential to the principle of shareholders' limited liability in the event of corporate failure. The principle was firmly established in a much criticized decision of the English House of Lords in 1897. Lord Macnaghton said:

*The company is at law a different person altogether from the subscribers ... and, though it may be that after incorporation the business is precisely the same as it was before, and the same persons are managers, and the same hands receive the profits, the company is not in law the agent of the subscribers or trustees for them.*

Whilst shareholders are sometimes thought of as owners of the business, each shareholder is not a part owner of the undertaking. No shareholder can point certain tangible assets and claim legal title over them. Other stakeholders, for example, revenue authorities and creditors, rank above ordinary shareholders in the event of a winding-up.

However, a shareholder has rights in the company, sometimes referred to as a share or equity interest. Thus, a shareholder's interest in the company is different from, say, that of a debenture holder, who has rights over the company's assets. Moreover, unless specified in the company's articles of association (or by-laws), shareholders have no right to manage the business.

Whilst it is true that, in addition to their rights in the company, shareholders also have obligations towards the company, those obligations are financial and are limited in practice to paying up calls on their shares. On the other side of the coin, a shareholder's liabilities are limited to the amount paid up on his or her shareholding interest in the company, a fact that places ordinary shareholders in a limited liability company at a significant financial advantage over equity partners whose liability in respect of their partnership is unlimited.[6]

Some clues start to emerge as to why shareholders are very interested in the behaviour of management. Shareholders invest their capital but generally have no right to manage the business. This is left to the board of directors. The company exists separately from its shareholders, but clearly needs an 'agent' through which to take actions. The 'agent' is, once again, the board of directors. The board of directors, albeit through a committee of non-executives, also sets executive directors' pay. At this point you might say alright, but is it not the case that directors are under a duty to act in the best interests of the company? Yes, of course, but for a long time it was established law in the UK that directors owed no duty to individual shareholders. Contrast this with the USA, where directors are in a fiduciary relationship with all those who have dealings with the directors in relation to the company's securities. That fact has not, however, prevented some spectacular abuses and corporate collapses.

Directors also need to take account of the interests of stakeholders other than shareholders. It has been argued that the continued existence

---

[6]But partners can now effectively limit their financial liability by forming limited liability partnerships.

of a corporation depends on its financial relationships with all stake-holders, namely employees, suppliers, customers, debtholders and share-holders. Notwithstanding the undoubted voracity of that argument, it is important to understand why companies exist in the first place.

Companies exist to create wealth and prosperity. This is not a philo-sophical argument. In a capitalist (Western) environment, the primary economic role of a corporation is to create value for its shareholders. That companies should act within best practice guidelines and adopt ethical practices does not detract from that goal. The key drivers of wealth and prosperity are shareholders' capital and management's skills. Without the introduction of shareholders' capital, initially to back and subsequently to provide continuing support for commercial ideas, pro-viders of other forms of capital will flee and corporations will fail. If management cannot continuously convince shareholders of the value of their commercial ideas (corporate strategy), shareholders' capital will eventually flee and the company will fail. Without the initial support of shareholders, no company will ever be in a position to develop and man-age the financial relationships with other stakeholders referred to above.

Of course, once a company is established and has established rela-tionships with customers, employees, suppliers, debtholders and the like, a failure to manage successfully any of those relationships can have a cat-astrophic effect on the business. But, in the beginning, it is the sharehold-ers' capital that gets the business off the ground and which underpins the company's ability to acquire additional capital to grow. Consequently, the key relationship in any corporate venture is the relationship between the company and its shareholders. As companies employ executive direc-tors to manage the business from day to day and to deliver shareholder value, management and shareholders should enjoy a close relationship. Both should pursue the same goal, i.e. wealth creation. Yet the current strength of shareholders' complaints against management excesses sug-gests that, if that is true, there may be a difference of view about how to achieve that goal. Put another way, shareholders and managers may have very different views about what constitutes and how to measure performance (Black et al., 2000; Rappaport, 1997).

One of the reasons for this divergence is attitude to risk. Shareholders can balance the risk of their investment in the company against a broadly spread portfolio of equity and other investments. It is unusual (and most employment contracts expressly forbid it) for executive directors to hold more than one job at one time. Moreover, shareholders can withdraw their capital and continue to earn a return on their investment by reinvesting in another corporation. Executives can withdraw their labour but will not continue to earn a return on their investment of time and skills until they get another job. However, given the size of some of the termination payments to recently departed executives, numbers of them are unlikely to need to re-enter the job market. Nonetheless, executives whose future is not underwritten by a substantial termination deal will tend to want their performance measured by reference to factors over which they have, or they feel they have, a high degree of control.

By and large, the market price of an ordinary share in the company is not high on the list of factors over which executives believe they have control. However, for shareholders, measuring the performance of their investment in the company is straightforward and there is a common performance measure for all shareholders. All shareholders are interested in capital appreciation (as reflected in the market price of their shares) and the dividend stream paid in respect of their shares.

Investment performance is a function of share price and dividend stream. These are the two constituents of total shareholder return or 'TSR' referred to above. A great deal of attention has focused on TSR whilst, particularly in relation to executive pay and the way in which shareholders think about executive pay, arguably not enough attention has been focused on the drivers of capital growth and dividend streams, which together deliver TSR.

Suffice it to say at this point that whilst there may be little argument from either management or shareholders that wealth creation (TSR to shareholders) is the goal, there is some argument about whether TSR is an appropriate measure by which to gauge the performance of management. One of the problems is that share option schemes, regardless of the performance conditions attached to grant or exercise, are dependent on the value of the underlying share on a specific day. If the market price of the underlying share is higher at the date of exercise than the option strike price, it is beneficial to the optionholder to exercise the option because there is an inherent gain.

You might argue that typically an option is exercisable over a period and so the optionholder can wait until the share price makes it attractive to exercise the option. This is true, up to a point. But it does not change the fact that unless the market price of the underlying share at the chosen exercise date is higher than the option strike price, it is unlikely that the optionholder will exercise. Share incentive plans that are not dependent on the market price of stock on a specific day (or on the relationship between the market prices of a share on an opening date and a closing date) remove this problem, and afford both management and shareholders an opportunity to concentrate on performance measures that demonstrate a transparent link between success in doing what needs to be done to deliver increased shareholder value and executives' pay.

## Conclusion

The present and future ability of a company to generate cash, combined with an analysis of the risk to the company's ability to continue to generate cash, are central to an evaluation of the value of the business. The value of assets shown in the balance sheet gives a moment-in-time snapshot assessment of present value (but based on historical cost). To an investor, however, the present value of assets is a factor in deciding whether to commit capital, but far more important are the return that the company can generate from the commercial use of its assets and the risk that the company will be unable to maintain that return.

Consequently, investment decisions taken by the board should produce a return that is greater than the cost to the company of making the investment, for the company to be able to demonstrate that it is adding value to shareholders. Companies are financed through a combination of debt (in a variety of forms) and shareholders' equity. The relative proportions of debt and equity will fluctuate from time to time and from company to company.

At this point it would be easy to stray into an in-depth examination of performance and the cost of capital, but that would be outside the scope of this chapter. Throughout the book there are detailed comments on the linkages between pay and performance, especially in Chapters 2, 5, 7 and 8. Suffice it to say here that all companies must generate cash to survive and grow and to create shareholder value, i.e. to deliver a return to shareholders that will encourage investors to buy the company's stock. Those companies that generate enough cash to invest in their future growth and to pay increasing amounts of dividend to shareholders are currently in favour with fund managers. Such companies are best placed to survive the kind of economic downturn experienced in the early 1990s and again at the start of the twenty-first century.

Companies can make accounting profits yet run out of cash. Earnings per share may increase but shareholder value may decline. Cash is a factor to which both shareholders and management can look for an indication of a company's ability to generate future value. The current economic outlook for the UK and Europe can be summarized as low profits growth, low inflation and low interest rates (and the same may be said of the USA if the threat of deflation can be averted). Against that background, fund managers believe that the dividend element of total shareholder return will assume a greater importance. In other words, a company's cash flow, its ability to generate cash in the future and the risk that it might not be able to maintain current or better cash flows are likely to figure highly in analysts' assessments of value.

Management incentive plans which take the company's share price as their principal performance target serve the best interests of neither management nor shareholders. It is argued by management that they cannot control the market price of a share. This may be true in the long term, but management behaviour can influence market sentiment in the short term. Regular and open communication is essential. Management can, however, control a number of factors, including cash flow, which the market takes into account when assessing corporate value. Incentive compensation linked to these factors and delivered in shares should go a long way toward bringing management and shareholders together.

The codes are being used in the context of the latest and sensible development, namely the notion of 'comply or explain'. This concept is at the heart of the much criticized Higgs report in the UK on the role of non-executive directors. It is also behind moves in Germany to ensure that the country's major companies publish separate details of individual directors' compensation packages. According to the *Financial Times*, only eight out of the 30 constituents of the DAX index of Germany's largest corporations publish separate details of the CEO's pay. Comply or explain makes sense because each company's circumstances are different and change from time to time. No legislation or set of guidelines can keep pace with the speed of change. It is, however, useful to have a set of guiding principles of best practice to use as a basis for discussion between a company and its shareholders. This is particularly relevant in the area of directors' compensation, where there is a move away from comparative performance measured around an average towards incentive compensation based on transparent targets linked to the delivery of strategy.

Shareholders are exercising their votes to make clear their feelings about directors' pay. In response, companies are conducting reviews and entering into dialogue with their shareholders. It is also the case that numbers of companies are talking to their shareholders in advance of a potentially embarrassing and highly visible vote to explain their proposals. The increasing dialogue between management and shareholders suggests that the doctrine of comply or explain can work and is working.

An advantage of comply or explain is that companies must think through their proposals fully in advance. It is, however, incumbent on institutional shareholders to ensure that those of their representatives with whom companies must discuss their compensation plans understand the company's business and do not see the best practice guidelines as a rigid set of rules.

Under this approach, good governance in the context of directors' pay is not a box-ticking exercise. For many institutional shareholders a company's plans regarding directors' compensation fall to be dealt with as a compliance issue. Investment teams, who must understand the company's business in order to make informed investment decisions, do not get involved in the discussions.

Both management and shareholders need some time to get used to the environment of comply or explain. Ultimately, both management and shareholders want the same thing – a successful company. Consequently, it makes sense to encourage regular dialogue and communication. Legislation is not an answer because its existence immediately places the parties in confrontation.

# 4

# Accountability, transparency and performance: comparing annual report disclosures on CEO pay across Europe

Sébastien Point

## Introduction

A growing interest in corporate governance codes and rules has appeared in Europe. Corporate governance involves using mechanisms by which a company is directed and controlled. It both encompasses the relationships between different stakeholders and refers to the set of rules that frame private behaviour (Stilpon, 2001). A corporate governance code is a set of principles, standards or best practices relating to the internal governance of a corporation. Most European countries have today established their own governance codes, which tend to increase transparency in the way companies are directed and controlled on a daily basis. Executive directors' compensation is increasingly subject to transparency. As CEO pay has often become front-page news, and given the recent accounting scandals in the United States, CEOs are expected to examine their corporate principles and focus on full disclosures. Thus, pay disclosures appear as an essential part of directors' accountability to their shareholders. Sensitive and taboo, top executive pay disclosures remain contentious in many European countries.

Heidrick & Struggles (1999), consultants in executive search, rated 10 European countries in terms of quality and transparency of corporate information disclosures on board governance.[1] The United Kingdom was described as one of the best-performing countries, whereas Germany was seen as needing some improvements in corporate governance disclosure rules. France and Sweden, although offering large variations from one company to another, were rated at the European average. Revisited every two years, the survey identified far-reaching changes within four years. Germany and France markedly improved their position, becoming respectively on the European average and the third best performing country. Both countries showed marked improvements in their respective corporate governance environment. For instance, an average of more than one in 10 companies in France voluntarily disclose information about top executive pay (Davis Global Advisors, 2000). In addition, still in 2001, the United Kingdom remained the best performer, whereas Sweden maintained its average ranking. The review in 2003 embedded the position of these countries.

The 1999, 2001 and 2003 surveys showed that companies in France, Germany, Sweden and the UK performed differently. That is the reason why we focus on these four countries within this chapter. Even more important is the fact that the British, French, German and Swedish legal systems are based on four distinct foundations. Consequently, when companies do publish information on CEO compensation, disclosures are expected not to be uniform across these four countries. For instance, Swedish companies are legally required to disclose the total compensation awarded to the chairman of the board and the managing director. These requirements on individual disclosures are on a par with new regulations designed by the French government (the New Economic Regulations – NER – Act). This also tends to converge towards British corporate governance rules, which, through the Greenbury report and the Combined Code, required more transparency in this matter. In contrast,

---

[1] The disclosure level takes into account the company director's age, tenure, main executive position, other board positions, company shareholding, compensation and the detailed list of board committee members.

Germany is often seen as not easy to compare with its European counterparts, given its specific legal and institutional framework.

The aim of this chapter is to investigate to what extent companies disclose information (if any) about CEO pay within their annual reports. Furthermore, we highlight how the corporate governance rules affect top CEO pay disclosures within these documents in different European countries. To achieve this aim, we analysed 58 company reports from four countries – France, Germany, Sweden and the UK (see Table 4.3).

The first part of the chapter highlights an historical view of corporate governance in each country during the last decade, in terms of pay disclosures within company annual reports. Since 1992, corporate governance rules and codes have been multiplied to increase transparency in response to the 'fat cat' debate. As an illustration, the comparative survey of corporate governance rules and codes published by the law firm Weil, Gotshal & Manges (2002) counted no more than 25 codes established across Europe from 1997. That is the reason why we decided to conduct a longitudinal survey, analysing company annual reports from 1997 to 2001 to highlight changes (if any) during the last decade. The second part discusses the impact of corporate governance recommendations by analysing in detail the amount of information published within company annual reports. The favoured approach to improving corporate governance is to increase the light cast on corporate practice, with mechanisms such as remuneration committees (Jackson and Carter, 1995). The questions we wish to address are as follows: what is the impact of corporate governance codes and rules on CEO compensation disclosures? How do companies depict mechanisms relating to compensation issues? How do companies favour transparency within their annual reports? How do they legitimate directors' pay level? How do companies link performance and executives' compensation? Do annual reports highlight performance criteria? Does the approach to disclosure show convergence among British, French, German and Swedish corporate reports?

## Directors' pay disclosures: 1992–2002, the critical years

Before starting our analysis of CEO top pay disclosures, this part summarizes all corporate governance rules and codes implemented in the

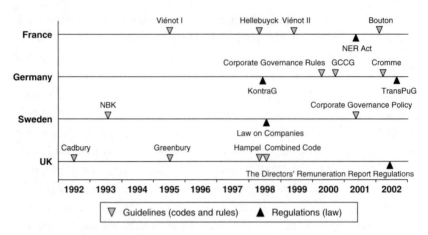

**Figure 4.1** Main corporate governance codes and regulations influencing CEO compensation disclosures in France, Germany, Sweden and the UK.

last decade. As mentioned in the introduction, a corporate governance code is a set of principles, standards or best practices relating to the internal governance of a corporation. However, within this chapter, we focus only on codes dealing with CEO compensation disclosure issues.

Among European countries, the UK was amongst the first to be concerned with CEOs' pay transparency. Willingness to improve transparency in France came later, in the mid-1990s. The corporate governance debate, launched in Europe by American pension funds seeking both transparency and performance, appeared more recently in Germany, partly due to the German co-determination principles. Sweden was the only European country where such disclosures were legally required within corporate annual reports. However, given the increasing concern for top pay transparency, two pan-European codes also emerged, identifying some common elements among the existing guidelines that underlie 'good corporate governance'.

## The UK: have early concerns fired the 'fat cat' debate?

In the UK, the Cadbury report (1992) was aimed at improving remuneration transparency and shareholders' power as key corporate governance issues. The Cadbury report remains important historically. Often presented in the literature as one of the leading explanations of what good governance entails (in response to several scandals in the late 1980s, such as Blue Arrow, Guinness and Maxwell), it has been highly influential in the UK and abroad. In terms of CEO pay publication, it suggested the disclosure of separate figures for salary and performance-related criteria (today widely recommended across Europe). Furthermore, the Greenbury report (1995), also in the UK, emphasized accountability, transparency and the link to performance as the three fundamental principles governing directors' remuneration. It also encouraged the remuneration committee to report details of remuneration packages as well as the company's policy in this matter. In fact, the Greenbury Committee demanded a closer link between company and individual performance. Both Cadbury's and Greenbury's governance rules were theoretically designed to improve the perception of CEO pay and make high pay levels acceptable. This was particularly the case for the Greenbury report, recommending full disclosures of directors' remuneration to ensure accountability to shareholders and to reassure the public.

In the UK, the Hampel report (1998), built on Cadbury and Greenbury, but did not bring radical changes in CEO compensation disclosure requirements. Nevertheless, the main recommendations from the Cadbury, Greenbury and Hampel reports were taken in account in the Combined Code (1998). According to the Combined Code, the annual report and accounts must contain a report on directors' remuneration, including the remuneration policy and the amount of each element of the remuneration package (the amount of stock options and long-term incentive schemes included). Moreover, as a listing condition, companies should explain in their annual reports whether they fulfil or not corporate government requirements.

The specificity of the British corporate governance codes is to rely on a disclosure ('comply or explain'), as discussed in Chapter 3. In other words, when a company does not comply with a code (or partly complies), it must highlight the item(s) with which it has not complied and, above all, give reasons for any non-compliance. Even though the Cadbury, Greenbury and Hampel reports had a substantial influence, the Combined Code seems to be the main reference for corporate governance guidelines in the UK. Furthermore, section 1 of the Combined Code was introduced into the listing rules of the London Stock Exchange on a disclosure 'comply or explain' basis. Not surprisingly, in our survey, the 'comply or explain' rule is explicit in most British annual reports (i.e. mentioning clearly they comply with the Code provisions set out in the Combined Code or London Stock Exchange Listing Rules). The COB (the French commission for transactions on the CAC 40) judges the Combined Code as the most efficient (COB, 1999).

Although more disclosures may have increased pay levels and fired the 'fat cat' debate, the Directors' Remuneration Report Regulations (2002) appeared as even more demanding in the UK. Designed to complete the Companies Act 1985 (the main UK law foundation), the new regulations required more disclosures about CEO top pay. The regulations aim at ensuring greater transparency and, above all, at strengthening the links between performance and pay. Among other issues, their concerns are:

- the content of remuneration reports
- how information should be set out within annual reports
- the approval and signing of directors' remuneration reports
- the improvement of comparisons by providing performance graphs and new regulations on long-term incentive schemes.

In fact, the UK government believed that there was an acceptable level of transparency in respect of the disclosure of individual directors' remuneration package, but not about remuneration policy (Department of Trade and Industry). Thus, aimed at strengthening disclosure requirements on directors' pay, the regulations suggested more comparisons to highlight pay convergence among competitors. Even more important, these new governance rules should give more power to shareholders, with the right to vote on directors' compensation levels. Although there has been a modest increase in the number of companies choosing to put their remuneration report or their remuneration policy to a shareholder vote (Department of Trade and Industry and Pricewaterhouse Coopers, 1999) (as suggested by the Greenbury report for all new long-term incentive schemes), the new regulations required an annual resolution to be put to shareholders on the directors' remuneration report. In a way, the UK government asked shareholders to give their opinion about the quality and the content of disclosures made by the directors in the remuneration report. Consequently, for London Stock Exchange listed companies with financial years ending on or after 31 December 2002, it became compulsory to put a resolution approving the remuneration report to the vote at the company's annual general meeting. Hence, the

Directors' Remuneration Report Regulations oblige listed companies not only to publish a complete and detailed report on director's remuneration, but also to obtain shareholder approval of the report.

## France: CEO pay should no longer be kept secret!

'Only eight CEOs agree to reveal their fortune.'[2] This was how the famous French newspaper *Le Monde* presented the reluctance to disclose directors' remuneration in France, at a time when no legal requirements existed. The article regretted this lack of transparency and highlighted some tricky practices aimed at keeping directors' wealth secret. As an example, even though annual reports disclosed the number of stock options held by executive directors, no information was given about the date of valuation and the price of shares. Furthermore, subsidiaries were entities where stock options were sometimes generously distributed.

The COB already requires quoted companies on the French stock exchange to publish the total remuneration for the board in annual reports; 1995 brought new hopes on the French international scene when the Viénot report appeared. However, these first French governance guidelines failed in encouraging detailed CEO pay disclosures within company annual reports. According to Marc Viénot,[3] 'revealing it would help rival companies attract French CEOs away with better packages'.[4] In fact, this reluctance to disclose CEO pay, especially when the second version of the Viénot report came out (i.e. Viénot II) was depicted as 'voyeurism' rather than transparency, and hence was seen as a form of discrimination against this socio-economic category of managers.[5]

In November 2003, a new report was published in France. The third chapter of the Clément report encouraged further top pay transparency.

---

[2] Seuls huit PDG acceptent de révéler leur fortune. *Le Monde*, 8–9 July 2001, p. 15.

[3] Marc Viénot is the former chairman of the French company Société Générale. He also headed the corporate governance committee that implemented the first recommendations in 1995.

[4] France: a CEO's pay shouldn't be a secret. *Business Week*, 9 August 1999, p. 47.

[5] Salary disclosures in France: transparency or 'voyeurism'? *Financial Times*, 26 July 1999, p. 2.

The report mentioned that, during the years 2000, 2001 and 2002, investments lost an average 65% of their value, whilst top pay increased by 36% in 2000, 20% in 2001 and 13% in 2002, so that French directors became higher paid than their British counterparts. Before the report was published, French directors were concerned by the implementation of legal rules concerning corporate governance mechanisms and top pay disclosures. Indeed, the Clément report could have suggested that the remuneration report or the remuneration policy be put to a shareholder vote (which was the major concern for directors), as has been the case in the UK since 2002. However, the report only recommended that the whole remuneration package should be attested by chartered accountants, published and presented to the annual general meeting. Stock option plans should also be implemented at fixed dates. In this way, the Clément report converges towards other European countries by emphasizing the link between pay and performance that is required.

In all European countries, disclosing directors' pay within official documents is regarded as the only true way for shareholders to be properly informed. Otherwise, it was feared that the shareholders often received little useful information. That may be the reason why, in 2001, the French government voted in a new law called *la loi sur les nouvelles régulations économiques* (the New Economic Regulations Act). Amongst other aims, this law seeks to improve shareholders' rights and transparency about top executive compensation and responsibility, as well as reporting on the social and environmental consequences of the company's activities. Indeed, these regulations required the company to reveal the type and the amount of the package paid to each member of the board within the management report. Pay levels and all kinds of perks should be known to shareholders, as such data have to be disclosed within company annual reports (15 May 2001 Act, article L, 225-102-1). Consequently, from the fiscal year 2002, annual reports should disclose information (at least more than they already do) about the environment, social responsibilities and directors' pay. The detailed remuneration package and the amount of stock options paid to CEOs should no longer be kept secret. In practice, being aware that their pay level remains still lower than famous French football stars such as Zinedine Zidane, Thierry Henry and Marcel Dessailly, some CEOs are believed to have had few reservations about disclosure of their overall pay within annual reports.

Even though the decade of the 1990s was an important period for corporate governance in France, the first years of the new century appear even more turbulent. As serious scandals occurred in France, the Bouton report (the code that appeared at the end of 2002) may be seen as the French response to the crisis that shook confidence in international financial markets in 2002.

## Germany: the co-determination principle slows down the emergence of governance codes and rules

Since 2000, Germany had not had any self-regulation concerning corporate governance comparable to the various codes in the UK (Cadbury, Greenbury, Hampel) or France (Viénot I and II). The Act on Control and Transparency (KontraG) entered into force in 1998. Despite the need for German companies to be more strongly oriented towards shareholder value, the KontraG did not highlight any significant issue concerning CEO compensation.

German corporate governance principles have already been defined through the 1998 law on Control and Transparency in Business. However, Germany got its first code (GCCG) in 2000 and laid foundations for another one, through a review in 2002 (Cromme). These codes were designed later than all the other countries reviewed in this chapter, which may be explained by the co-directorship principle established in Germany and by the dominant role of banks. Under the specific co-determination regime, employees and trade unions elect some members of the supervisory board. In addition, the dominant role of the banks in a complex system of cross-shareholding (owning shares in 24 of the DAX 30 companies) aims at cementing long-term relationships between firms and leads to a system of interlocking directorates: a company with a significant ownership stake in another company usually has a representative on the supervisory board of that company (Jürgens and Rupp, 2002). Consequently, Germany is often cited as a classical case of 'non-shareholder value orientation'. As a result, the need for more transparency seems to be less urgent to top managers in Germany.

Apart from the emoluments of the total management board, the GCCG suggested that the company should disclose the fundamentals of the system for remuneration. Executive board compensation is to be disclosed in the notes to the consolidated financial statements, broken down individually by fixed salary, performance-based compensation and long-term stock-based components. Theoretically, the German code aimed at making companies and their governance as well as the remuneration of board members and performance reviews transparent to investors.[6] In Germany, reporting and transparency seem to be increasingly concerned with the structure and disclosure of performance-based compensation.

The Cromme Code (2002) anticipated the Transparency and Disclosure Law (Transparenz und Publizitätsgesetzes – TransPuG). The Code, considered as a 'soft law', supplements the so-called 'comply or explain' rule (see above): '*The recommendations of the Code are marked in the text by use of the word "shall". Companies can deviate from them, but are then obliged to disclose this annually*' (p. 2). The Transparency and Disclosure Law, which came into force on 26 July 2002, laid the legal foundations for the application of the Code. Furthermore, the TransPuG created, inter alia, a new section 161 in the AktG (the German stock corporation law). Consequently, the executive and supervisory boards of listed companies would be required to declare whether they comply with the recommendations of the code and whether to publish such a declaration. This law was expected to be '*enacted as quickly as possible so that the "comply or explain" regulation can be applied to the fiscal year following publication of the code and the Transparency and Disclosure Law*'.[7] Consequently, since 2003, any German listed company unwilling to comply with the provisions of the Cromme Code has had to issue an express declaration to this effect each year and explain their decision within their annual report. In terms of directors' remuneration, the Code suggested, when issued, that figures be disclosed individually. Indeed, the Code distinguished recommendations ('shall') from suggestions ('should', 'can'). Individual disclosures belong to the latter. However, given, for example, the reluctance of Jürgen Schrempp (Chairman of the DaimlerChrysler Group) to disclose its remuneration levels during the annual general meeting, the Cromme Committee

---

[6] Statements of Dr G. Cromme, Chairman of the Government Commission German Corporate Governance Code on the publications of the draft, 18 December 2001, Düsseldorf.

[7] Statements of Dr G. Cromme, at the press conference following the handing over of the German Corporate Governance Code on 26 February 2002 in Berlin.

decided in May 2003 to make an amendment of the Code, making individual remuneration disclosures compulsory.

## Sweden: legal requirements to disclose directors' total pay

Early contributors to the corporate governance debate in Europe (published one year after the Cadbury report), the Näringslivets Börskommitte (NBK) required the disclosure of individual information for executives having a special position in a company. Apart from total remuneration and other benefits, reports were expected to indicate at what age the executive was entitled to retire with a pension and the level of the pension in relation to his or her salary. The Swedish Companies Act (1975), which made ownership and control highly transparent in Sweden, aimed at providing better information about the total amount of remuneration and other compensation paid to the board and to the managing director. Even though the Swedish Companies Act has been changed and updated on a regular basis since it entered into force in 1975, companies' duties about CEO compensation disclosures remain unchanged. The new and more recent guidelines (Corporate Governance Policy, 2001) reinforce the Shareholders' Association principles presented in 1993. The NBK recommendations have been reduced to meeting the need for information concerning benefits for senior executives. Hence, Swedish companies quoted on the Stockholm stock exchange need provide only information about the chairman of the board, the group chief executive and the managing director's total compensation and individual benefits within annual reports. These recommendations have been confirmed by the Swedish Industry and Commerce Stock Exchange Committee in August 2002. However, the committee emphasized that individual disclosures should be confined to the company's top management.

## Pan-European codes: creating principles embracing different models

Three pan-European codes aimed at developing a set of corporate governance standards and guidelines have been created in conjunction with national governments. For instance, in 1999, the Organization for Economic Cooperation and Development (OECD) published its general principles on corporate governance. Even though these principles did not aim at detailed prescriptions for national legislation, the OECD identified

some common elements that it believed underlie good corporate governance throughout the existing rules and codes in Europe. The principles
build on these common elements aimed at embracing all the different
models that existed until 1999 (the date of the OECD guidelines creation). Especially in terms of CEO compensation, the code was an aggregate of all the existing ones. It suggested that: *Companies are generally
expected to disclose sufficient information on the remuneration of board
members and key executives (either individually or in the aggregate) for
investors to properly assess the costs and benefits of remuneration plans
and the contribution of incentive schemes, such as stock option schemes,
to performance'* (p. 20). Issues about CEO compensation disclosures
appear more ambiguous than in any 'national' code. Moreover, for some
countries the principles represent minimum requirements, whereas for
others they might represent a source of inspiration (Stilpon, 2001).

The Euroshareholders Corporate Governance Guidelines (another pan-
European code) are based upon the same principles. However, the guidelines appeared more specific and detailed for each country: *As far as the
different national legal structures allow, Euroshareholders has tried to be
as specific as possible in describing its view on the various corporate governance issues'* (p. 1). However, no recommendations were suggested in
terms of compensation disclosures, except that the principles upon which
the remuneration are based should be published in the annual report.

There is another code: the European Association of Securities
Dealers (EASD) created a Corporate Governance Committee, which
was charged with preparing the 2000 corporate governance Principles
and Recommendations. EASD's *aims include providing its members
with a forum for the exchange of views and reflection, setting pan-
European market standards and fostering changes in regulations and
rules that inhibit pan-European securities trading'* (document preface).
The code embraces most recommendations designed within the UK
guidelines, mainly upon the CEO compensation package. However,
nothing is mentioned about top pay disclosures.

## The impact of the corporate governance recommendations on disclosures

Looking closer at annual reports, the current trend is to devote a whole
section to CEO compensation issues. The Hampel report (UK) clearly

**Table 4.1** UK, French, German and Swedish corporate governance principles and rules, as well as regulations dealing with CEO compensation issues

| Country | Laws and governance codes, principles and rules |
| --- | --- |
| *Pan-European* | OECD Principles of Corporate Governance (1999) <br> EASD Principles and Recommendations (2000) <br> Euroshareholders Corporate Governance Guidelines (2000) |
| *France* | Viénot I report (1995) <br> Viénot II report (1999) <br> Recommendations on Corporate Governance (Hellebuyck report) (1998, 2001) <br> The New Economic Regulations Act (NER) (2001) <br> Promoting better Corporate Governance in listed companies (Bouton report) (2002) |
| *Germany* | Corporate Governance Rules for Quoted German Companies (2000) <br> German Code of Corporate Governance (GCCG) (2000) <br> German Corporate Governance Code (Cromme) (2002) |
| *UK* | Cadbury report (1992) <br> Greenbury report (1995) <br> Hampel report (final report) (1998) <br> The Combined Code (1998) <br> The Directors' Remuneration Report Regulations (2002) |
| *Sweden* | Recommendations of the Näringlivets Börsfommitte (NBK) (1993) <br> Law on Companies (1998) <br> Corporate Governance Policy (2001) |

recommends each company has a remuneration committee report, covering both details of the packages and the company's remuneration policy ('*a statement of remuneration policy*' for the Combined Code). Consequently, only UK reports provide a whole and distinct section within their document, known as the 'remuneration report'. Furthermore, three British documents clearly mentioned the goal of such a report. For example, the BOC Group, in its 2001 report, insists on the fact that '*where appropriate, in order to improve clarity, voluntary disclosures are also given*'.

French reports give little information, mostly restricted to the existence of the remuneration committee (often renamed as the appointment and remuneration committee) within a section devoted to the company's governance rules. This is not really in line with Viénot II guidelines, which recommend the publication within annual reports of a whole chapter dedicated to CEO compensation issues. However, in 2001, the trend was to provide a larger amount of information, given the new regulations (NER Act) implemented for the financial years ending on or after 31 December 2001.

The German Corporate Governance Code (2000) underlines that the rules, their acceptance, implementation and respective adjustments to the specifics of the individual company shall be communicated in the annual report. Surprisingly, no part of the report offers such disclosures. It also recommends that executive board compensation issues should be disclosed in the notes to consolidated financial statements. Hence, German annual reports do not contain any specific part relating to governance rules (unlike French ones). One or two exceptions publish an 'executive pay scheme' section in their report. Usually, following the notes to the consolidated income statement, a brief paragraph on the total remuneration of the supervisory board and the board of management is issued.

Despite legal requirements to publish the total amount of directors' remuneration, there is no obligation for Swedish companies to provide individual information. The growing concern in Europe about executives' benefits favoured the creation of two main codes. They recommend Swedish companies should provide information about executives' compensation benefits. However, neither code is explicit about the nature or the extent of information the companies should provide within their annual reports. Nevertheless, all the reports reviewed here give some details about directors' remuneration in the accounting section, and five (about half of our sample) give more details within a narrative portion through a note to accounts (of about one page length).

## I. Recommendations about remuneration committees

Even though three out of four countries do not recommend the presence of any remuneration report within company annual reports, all countries are concerned with the creation of a remuneration committee (as recommended in most governance codes – see Chapter 9). In the UK, both Cadbury and Greenbury reports favoured the establishment of a remuneration committee. Furthermore, both the Combined Code and Hampel require the remuneration committee to develop a policy on executive compensation. Other European governance codes (Bouton, Viénot I and II in France; Corporate Governance Rules for quoted German companies, GCCG and Cromme in Germany; Corporate Governance Policy in Sweden; EASD, Euroshareholders and OECD, pan-European) also favour the appointment of remuneration committees (sometimes named compensation or personnel committees, or merged with the nomination/appointment committee). This section highlights two problems relating to the remuneration committee disclosures: whether annual reports detail the role and the composition of the committee.

### Is the role of the remuneration committee specified among corporate reports?

To our knowledge, none of the reviewed governance codes or rules in Europe deals with the obligation to discuss the role of the remuneration committee within the director's report (or anywhere within annual reports). In the UK, the new regulations require companies to include the role of the board's remuneration committee (for 2002 annual reports). However, most of the surveyed UK and French documents (with one exception) give some explanations. Surprisingly, such information remains rare in German and Swedish reports (with respectively one and three companies concerned).

Chapter 9 of this book reports the remuneration committee's role. The latter is clearly mentioned within most British and French documents. Moreover, 27% of the British and more than half of the French reports detail how many times the committee met during the year. These range from once to six times a year. The French standard seems to be twice a year.

French annual reports (a third of our sample) explain why the remuneration committee met during the year. Providing more explanations about the role of the committee is in the spirit of the Bouton report (which came into force in late 2002). The latter recommends publishing some information on remuneration committee activities for the given reporting period. Consequently, we should expect even more disclosures in the coming years. Furthermore, the L'Oréal 2001 report highlights the satisfaction of the chairman towards the committee's work: '*The Chairman [...] expressed his satisfaction with the quality and complete independence of the work carried out by the two Committees, and indicated that he wished them to increase the scope of their activities in the future*'. What we should note is that so few companies mention when the CEO compensation has been reviewed. At most, three documents give such details. Stipulating that *'executive salaries are reviewed annually by the committee'*, only two companies are precise about when the latest CEO package revision has occurred.

## Do companies mention the composition of the remuneration committee?

In line with all governance codes, most reports detail the membership of the remuneration committee. Since 1992 and the publication of the Cadbury report in the UK, the governance rules have required detailed information on the membership of the remuneration committee. Most rules emphasize that the remuneration committee should be in a majority (EASD Principles and Recommendations, pan-European; Hellebuyck and Viénot II, France) or exclusively (Cromme, Germany; Greenbury and Hampel, UK) composed of non-executive directors or independent directors. The goal is to prevent directors deciding their own remuneration levels. Consequently, all the surveyed British reports highlight the non-executive composition of the remuneration committee (the quality of information has improved, from 67% in 1997–98 to 100% in 2001). What is more surprising is that none of the French, German and Swedish reports in our sample was doing so. The number of non-executives within the committees is reported in 60% of British and French documents.

Remuneration committees range from two to six members (with a trend of three in France and six in the UK). What we might note is that companies do not systematically discuss the independence of the board members in the reports. It is quite difficult for the reader to guess whether the members of the remuneration committee are independent non-executives or not (for example, ex-employees, etc.).

Consequently, none of the reviewed reports discuss, when mentioned, what 'independence' means for the remuneration committee members (as widely debated within French and UK governance rules and codes). Even though Viénot I (France) strongly highlights the potential lack of credibility created by cross-directorships, none of the French reports discusses or mentions the need for independence or the need for non-conflicting interests among the committee members. In France, the recent number of privatizations has favoured cross-interests among companies and has raised potential conflicts of interest.

In the UK, the TUC (Trades Union Congress) believes that independence is not compatible 'with the current make-up of remuneration committees' (TUC, 2000). In fact, most non-executive directors are executive directors or CEOs from other companies. The TUC emphasized that 46 of the top 50 *Financial Times* companies shared at least one member of their remuneration committee. This creates a situation where the same pool of executives sitting as non-executive directors on other companies' boards are setting each others' pay! That may explain why five of the seven British companies emphasize that the '*Non-Executive Directors of the Company have no personal financial interest in matters to be decided, no potential conflicts of interest arising from cross-directorships and no day-to-day involvement in running the Company*' (stating exactly the A4 code of the Greenbury guidelines!).

A typical concern from 2001 annual reports, and especially from British reports, is to state whether or not the chairman of the company attends the remuneration committee meetings. Usually, '*whilst the chairman, the deputy chairman and the chief executive are not members of the committee, they attend the meetings for discussions but are not present when their personal remuneration is discussed and reviewed*' (clearly mentioned within 40% of British reports). This complies with most UK codes, recommending that executive (or non-executive) directors should not participate in the decisions on their own remuneration. In contrast, we may emphasize that the Corporate Governance Policy (Sweden) suggests that the chairman of the board should also be on the committee, but the members should not be employees of the company (i.e. they should be independent non-executives). Unfortunately, the reviewed Swedish reports do not deal with this question, nor do the French or German reports. Even though a third of the French reports mentioned that the chairman attends meetings, a few (three French reports) added that the chairman and CEO do not take part in the committee's proceedings when the matter under review concerns them personally.

## II. Towards more directors' remuneration transparency

Transparency is one of the guiding principles of all the codes in Europe. Furthermore, it may be considered as the favourite metaphor of governance (Jackson and Carter, 1995). Each country establishes corporate governance rules and codes for better control and transparency for the shareholders. However, given the different laws and regulations in each country (NER Act, France; KontraG, Germany; law on companies, Sweden; Directors' Remuneration Report Regulations, UK), corporate governance guidelines do not always succeed in improving transparency. This section questions whether companies disclose a specific CEO remuneration policy and whether the individual remuneration is clearly mentioned within the documents.

### Does the report mention the overall remuneration policy?

As already mentioned, the Hampel report (UK) encourages the establishment of a remuneration committee to develop a policy on remuneration, whereas, to our knowledge, none of the codes from other European countries reported in this survey did so. As the Greenbury and Hampel reports recommend: *'the remuneration committee must provide the packages needed to attract, retain and motivate directors of the quality required but should avoid paying more than necessary for this purpose'*. Consequently, 14 out of 15 British companies clearly state having an overall policy, which enables them to attract and retain the highest calibre executives. However, we may note with surprise that the text is sometimes exactly the same in 1998 and 2001 annual reports (see Table 4.2 as an illustration).

In addition, the objective of the policy is to align the interests of directors and shareholders (see the British Greenbury guidelines), and remuneration in shares, states Hampel (UK), can be a useful and legitimate way of aligning the directors' interests with those of the shareholders (see Chapter 2). All British companies (except two in 1998) clearly mentioned the willingness to align *'the interests of directors and shareholders and to motivate the highest performance'*. Even though policy implementations remained a major issue for UK guidelines, only two French companies disclosed the same preoccupations in their 2001 annual reports.

Three British reports also emphasized that the pay and benefit packages were competitive. Furthermore, two British reports emphasized that their practices are aimed at attracting high performing directors:

*Taking all of this into account, a high performing executive ... can expect to be in the top 50 per cent, and in exceptional cases in the top 25 per cent, of the range for comparable jobs in other companies.*

(BOC, 1998)

**Table 4.2** Duplicated annual reports

|  | *1997 or 1998 annual reports* | *2001 annual reports* |
|---|---|---|
| *Allied Domecq* | 'In order to attract and retain management with the appropriate skills to provide shareholder value for the future, the group aims to ensure that its pay and benefit practices are competitive; that they motivate employees at all levels; and that they recognize and reward high standards of performance.' | 'In order to attract and retain management with the appropriate skills to provide shareholder value for the future, the group aims to ensure that its pay and benefit practices are competitive, that they motivate employees at all levels and that they recognize and reward high standards of performance.' |
| *Hanson* | 'To continue to compete successfully it is essential that the company attracts, develops, retains and motivates the highest calibre executive directors in the best interests of shareholders.' | 'To continue to compete successfully it is essential that the company attracts, develops, retains and motivates talented and high-achieving executive directors in the best interests of shareholders.' |
| *Pilkington* | '*Key objectives of the remuneration policy* are to ensure that salaries and incentives are aligned with the performance of the Group and the interests of shareholders and to enable the Group to attract, retain and motivate the highest calibre of executive on a worldwide basis.' | 'The objectives are to ensure that salaries and incentives are aligned with the performance of the Group and the interests of shareholders and to enable the Group to attract, retain and motivate the highest calibre of executives on a worldwide basis.' |

*[The company] believes that its remuneration policies and programmes represent a competitive advantage and best practice through a heavy emphasis on pay for performance and 'at risk' compensation for its top executives.*

(GSK, 2001)

*To involve senior executives more closely in the growth and development of [the company's] business, their variable bonuses represent a greater proportion of their total remuneration package than is the practice among other industrial groups.*

(Schneider, 2001)

### Is individual remuneration clearly mentioned?

As reported in the introduction of this chapter, Swedish companies were early concerned with individual disclosures, being required to report pension schemes individually. However, our analysis emphasizes that all other components of the remuneration package remain aggregately disclosed, except for chairmen and managing directors. Viénot II (France) mentions that the total executives' pay should appear in the annual report of the company. Even though the disclosed sums remain global, the code recommends distinguishing the fixed from the variable parts, as the Corporate Governance Rules (Germany) suggest. Even though the NER Act (2001) makes individual remuneration disclosures compulsory for French companies, Michelin provided only aggregate figures for directors' pay (as also highlighted by *Le Monde*, 17 December 2002). Although legal requirements were to start in 2001, full and individual disclosures were expected to appear in all French reports from the 2002 fiscal year. In the UK, since the Greenbury recommendations, British reports should include full details of the remuneration package of each individual director by name, such as basic salary and benefits or bonuses. All the UK reports surveyed provided individual figures. As Figure 4.2 reports, individual remuneration disclosures are being suggested or required in many countries.

## III. Directors' pay legitimacy throughout annual reports

The link between performance and rewards is the primary tenet of the CEO compensation system and the justification which organizations give for granting large increases in CEO compensation (Miller, 1995; see also Chapter 8 of this book). The current fashion for French magazines is to assess CEOs' performance (sometimes in a subjective way) compared with their remuneration level.

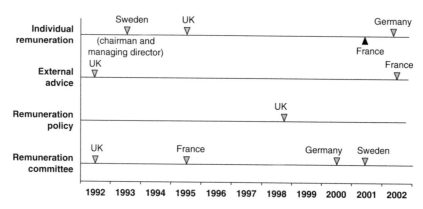

**Figure 4.2** The improvement of directors' remuneration transparency throughout the decade in France, Germany, Sweden and the UK.

French newspapers gave large media coverage to Jean-Marie Messier. For the fiscal year 2001, Messier's overall remuneration increased by 80% to 2.38 million Euros (perks included),[8] whereas, at the same time, the performance of the company produced a loss of 13.6 billion Euros (never seen before for a French company).[9] As Holland et al. (2000) report, most research in the UK or in the USA suggests little or no relationship between CEO compensation and organizational performance. For the authors of the reports, in response to poor performance, the board must provide a significant premium to attract the calibre of person required to change the organization's fortunes. In fact, Jean-Marie Messier's variable pay seems to be based on the operating results, which did not take into account asset deprecations as well as financial losses for the pay evaluation. Therefore, considering the depreciation of Vivendi's investments for 2001, the rise of financial fees reduces the net income level of the company and the shares of the company, but certainly not the CEO pay level!

This part highlights the remuneration policy, e.g. the principles for distinguishing fixed and variable pay components, as well as

---

[8] Le salaire du PDG a progressé de 80% en 2001. *Le Monde*, 17 April 2002.
[9] Vivendi Universal paie la facture de son expansion. *Le Monde*, 7 March 2002.

attribution rules of bonus. It deals with the hottest CEO compensation issues:

1 How does the company justify the CEO pay level?
2 Does the company publish performance criteria within its report?

### Does the company seek to justify directors' pay levels?

CEO pay packages contain basic pay, bonus, benefits and LTIPs (see Chapters 7 and 8). Only British company reports in our sample mentioned criteria determining CEO basic salary. Various criteria are taken into consideration, such as performance (100%), experience (54%), responsibility (47%), market value (40%), contribution (27%) and competitors (20%). But the current debate, among all European companies, concerns the variable part of directors' pay.

It has been widely acknowledged that CEOs should be paid the necessary incentives to retain their talent. European corporate governance recommendations suggest that the remuneration package should attract, retain and motivate directors, and give directors keen incentives to perform at the highest level, as most company remuneration policies highlight within annual reports (see above). Furthermore, in the UK, the Combined Code underlines that the committees should perform the balancing act between attracting high-quality directors and not paying more than is necessary, and take responsibility for ensuring performance-related elements form a significant proportion of executives' pay.[10] All corporate governance codes and rules argue for an increase in the relationship between pay and performance.

The Greenbury report (UK) states: '*remuneration committees should consider factors which measure company performance relative to a group of comparative companies*'. Even more important, the Directors' Remuneration Report Regulations (still in the UK) require more additional information on performance linkage, including graphs for instance. Because the new regulations came into force for financial years ending on or after 31 December 2002, none of the analysed documents, in this chapter's research to date, provided any diagrams. Consequently, 80% of the British companies mentioned that executives' pay is competitive

---

[10] Top rewards under scrutiny. *People Management*, 7 February 2002, p. 19.

by reference to other global companies, similar in terms of size, geographical spread and complexity of business. Two French reports highlighted comparisons aimed at legitimating the level of directors' pay. Contrasting with their British counterparts, such information may be more to legitimate pay levels rather than to comply with international corporate governance guidelines.

*Remuneration of Group officers are set with a dual aim, on the one hand placing them on a par with remuneration levels in comparable industrial groups and on the other structuring them in a way that ensures that the personal work of these officers contributes to growth in the Group's results.*

(Saint Gobain, 2001)

*To fix the pay level of the chief executive officer, the Human Resources Committee has referred to a survey based on large American and European companies in the communication sector.*

(Vivendi Universal, 2001)

### Is a performance measure clearly mentioned?

The variable part of directors' remuneration is significant and even more important than the fixed part. It has been widely acknowledged that CEO top pay should be linked to clear performance standards. In the UK, the early Cadbury report suggested that reports should provide information about salary and performance-related elements, giving the criteria on which performance is measured. Still in the UK, the Greenbury report clearly mentions that the company should show '*how performance is measured, how the performance measures relate to company objectives and how the company has performed over time relative to comparative companies*'. The Department of Trade and Industry appointed Pricewaterhouse Coopers in 1999 to monitor compliance by listed companies with the best practice framework on directors' remuneration set out in the Greenbury Code of Best Practice and the Combined Code (Department of Trade and Industry and Pricewaterhouse Coopers, 1999). As main results, most companies (74%) report through text in the annual report how performance is measured. However, a small majority (52%) did not disclose how rewards were related to performance. Few reports showed how performance measures related to long-term company objectives (5%) or how the company had performed over time relative to companies in the same sector (3%).

Within our survey, 10 companies (of which seven were British, two French and one Swedish) emphasized the necessity to implement bonus schemes within directors' remuneration packages. They all agreed that this annual performance-related bonus was designed to reflect both the group's performance and the executive director's contribution to it. Moreover, the bonus was expected to link individual performance with business plans. They also emphasized that performance bonuses for the CEO were based against demanding financial targets and individual accomplishments against objectives. Three French (20%) and most British annual reports (87%) provided criteria to assess this short-term performance.

These targets were based on earnings per share (EPS) in five reports (one French) and also return on capital employed (ROCE) for one British company (two annual reports). In other cases, performance criteria ranged from economic profit (EP), economic value added (EVA), return on investment (ROI) and total shareholder return (TSR) to growth in profit before tax. Most French companies were vague in terms of performance criteria disclosures. As an illustration, one mentioned that the variable bonus was based on three corporate financial criteria, without specifying which criteria were used for that purpose. For five British and two French companies, the personal performance against strategic business goals was also a key component in the calculation. Sixty per cent of British annual reports stated that the remuneration committee usually sets performance targets and key management objectives annually. Unfortunately, only one company detailed the conditions of bonus attribution: '*the performance condition requires EPS to equal, or to exceed, a target arrived at using an RPI + 3 per cent growth factor*'. Five British and one French document revealed the bonus levels. Sometimes, companies highlighted the level of maximum pay-off, sometimes they (rarely) underlined how rewards related to performance: '*the bonus payable to participants was the equivalent of 7% of their annual basic salary for every 1% of real growth in the company's earnings per share*'. Finally, two British companies mentioned the existence of a discretionary and exceptional bonus aimed at rewarding individual performance.

Most UK reports (54%) and two French companies underlined that the long-term incentives were aimed at aligning executive interests with those of shareholders (see Chapter 2). '*Long-Term Incentive Plan is designed to encourage participants to focus their attention on the longer-term growth in shareholder value by providing them with a deferred performance related award in Ordinary Shares.*' The long-term remuneration vehicles were aimed at giving incentives to participants to promote the long-term success of the business. All the UK reports but one (i.e. 94%) explained how performance was measured for LTIPs. Awards made to executive directors were often conditional upon total shareholder return performance (40% of British reports) over a three-year period or earnings per share growth (27%) relative to an increase of the UK retail price (27%), or to a comparator group of companies (40% of reports), but rarely with named companies (only three reports). Nevertheless, only 50% of the British documents mentioned how rewards of the LTIP were related to performance.

## Conclusion

Due to the various legal systems, institutional parameters and traditions, there is presently no internationally accepted universal model for corporate governance. Moreover, there is no single model of good corporate governance. However, there is an emerging trend of an internationally accepted benchmark on corporate governance (Stilpon, 2001): apart from the creation of pan-European codes, most countries tend to converge towards similar guidelines, i.e. the appointment of remuneration committees or detailing individual remuneration. Among the reviewed countries (France, Germany, Sweden, the UK), two favour the 'comply or explain' rule. So as far as the CEO compensation topic is concerned, German and British reports should converge in the coming years. French and British reports sometimes raise the same issues, and also in the coming years French disclosures will probably be similar to the Anglo-Saxon model. 2001 and 2002 have been prolific years in terms of corporate governance rules and regulations, especially as regards CEO compensation disclosures. All countries surveyed in this chapter have been concerned with creating new rules: France (the Bouton report), Germany (Cromme and TransPuG), Sweden (Corporate

Governance Policy) and the UK (the Directors' Remuneration Report Regulations). Consequently, disclosure changes were likely to expand in annual reports after the financial years ending on or after 31 December 2002 or 2003. We agree with Stilpon (2001), who stated that, across OECD countries, the accountability of directors and executives has been strengthened, shareholder rights enhanced and disclosure improved within the last five years. Consequently, as codes are being harmonized, a significant degree of uniformity about CEO compensation disclosures has appeared across Europe.

The provision of more transparency to CEO remuneration levels worldwide may highlight the fact that French CEOs are not paid as well as their counterparts (especially from Anglo-Saxon countries). Given stock options figures, nowadays disclosed within company annual reports, we have an overall idea of the 'generosity of some companies' (*Le Monde*, 2002c). Hence, we can only assume the amount of CEO capital gains, as company reports do not tell whether CEOs sold their stock options immediately or not. When there is a sharp fall of stock markets, most CEOs certainly expect to earn even more money. As Holland et al. (2000) mentioned, the paradox in this process is that it provokes a 'domino effect', where CEO compensation becomes focused on comparative data as a source of benchmarking rather than company performance. Moreover, the COB emphasized that when companies are required to disclose their own corporate governance practices, they compete with one another in terms of providing transparency. Simultaneously, full disclosures of individual compensation packages have increased the pressure on remuneration in a competitive field. As Hampel noticed, *'remuneration disclosures are often excessively detailed, to the point where the essential features of remuneration packages have been rendered obscure to all but the expert'* (p. 37).

The unanswered question is, to quote Bartlett and Chandler (1999), whether the disclosures meet the needs of the annual report readers. As the authors conclude: *'the aim should be to provide shareholders with information they can understand, that is knowledge'*. Few of the narrative sections are likely to be understood by most unsophisticated readers, since the style of these sections usually goes beyond the level of comprehension of the public. The 'comply or explain' rules produce corporate annual report standards and oblige companies to disclose the same narrative portion whatever company, sector and size the company belongs to.

**Table 4.3** Annual reports sampling over four years

|  | Company | 1997 | 1998 | 1999 | 2001 |
|---|---|---|---|---|---|
| *France* | Elf TotalFina | x (Elf) | | | |
|  | | x (Total) | x | | x |
|  | L'Oréal | | x | | x |
|  | Michelin | x | | | x |
|  | Renault | x | | | x |
|  | Saint Gobain | x | | | x |
|  | Schneider Electric | | x | | x |
|  | Vivendi Universal | | x | | x |
| *UK* | Allied Domecq | | x | | x |
|  | BOC Group | | x | | x |
|  | Diageo | | x | | x |
|  | GlaxoSmithkline | x (Glaxo Wellcome) | | | x |
|  | | x (Smithkline Beecham) | | | |
|  | Hanson | | x | | x |
|  | Pilkington | x | | | x |
|  | AstraZeneca | | x (Zeneca) | | x |
| *Germany* | BASF | x | | | x |
|  | Bayer | x | | | x |
|  | BMW | x | | | x |
|  | Henkel | x | | | x |
|  | Siemens | x | | | x |
|  | Volkswagen | x | | | x |
| *Sweden* | Electrolux | x | | | x |
|  | Ericsson | x | | | x |
|  | SCA | x | | | x |
|  | Scania | x | | | x |
|  | Skankas | | | x | x |
|  | Ssab | | | | x |

This depersonalization of annual reports should, on the one hand, benefit the comprehension of the reader. Nevertheless, on the other hand, such depersonalized approval clearly favours unthinking publication by mentioning compliance but no more. Moreover, the complexity of duties (which implies more responsibility, especially for a company's success or failure) and the CEO's contributions to a company's success may also legitimate top executives' pay level (Nichols and Subramanian, 2001). Consequently, the close link between CEO compensation, corporate reputation and CEO image should be considered in the future. As the Hampel report emphasized (section 4.2), *'now that details of individual directors' remuneration are disclosed, they are liable to have an impact both on the company's reputation and on morale within the company'*.

# 5

# Director performance standards and rewards in France

Frank Bournois and Jean-Pierre Magot

## Introduction

In this chapter, we outline some of the key issues in top executive pay in France. We do not intend the account here to be a comprehensive review. The complexity of the subject makes this impossible, and readers can draw on Chapter 4, where cross-European corporate governance regulations on director-level pay are described. This chapter concentrates on performance standards and the measurement of performance typically found at this level, together with the related trends in variable pay for directors.

The proportion of variable pay for lead managers on executive committees has substantially increased over the last 10 years among French multinational companies. It is now between 30% and 40% of the base annual salary when objectives are met and can reach a maximum of 60–100% of the base.

Furthermore, the development of stock options over the long term has boosted the weight of variable pay within the overall remuneration package; the amount of options attributed annually in the majority of cases is equivalent to between 100% and 300% of the base annual salary, and can be even greater.

The factors that have contributed to this development are, in our view, the following:

- The propagation of the Anglo-American model (particularly through the tendency to benchmark remuneration packages against UK/US comparators and through mergers of French companies with British and/or American companies) and even comparisons of practices within a single company (a form of internal benchmarking) have led to a readjustment towards the more dynamic modes of remuneration.
- The awarding of limited increases in the base annual salary as a result of low inflation.
- A trend towards the more favourable fiscal treatment and a greater social acceptance of substantial earnings from stock options.
- The determination to bring remuneration more closely in line with the company's performance.

Can we deduce from this trend that remuneration actually is more closely correlated to company performance and, in particular, to shareholder objectives? Across all sectors, no survey or study in France has shown that remuneration practices are very closely related to shareholders' interests over the medium to long term. This central point calls for attention because it conditions not only executive packages, but also the deployment of a strategy concerning the remuneration of all employees, and necessitates sustained consideration of the choice of performance standards.

## The definition of performance standards: choosing indicators

Performance standards are set using several types of measures:

- Monetary (these comprise revenues, costs, margins, results, turnover, return on capital employed).
- Quantitative (these are measures of various kinds, such as those concerned with productivity).
- Qualitative (such as delays in projects, satisfaction of internal and external clients, the development of cross-team projects).

- Internal (these are usually related to the company's scorecard, that is the bundle of measures mixing financial and non-financial targets on which the company has decided its performance should be measured).
- Market-related (values of company, e.g. share price or total shareholder return according to the financial markets).
- Comparative performance (relative to the direct comparison of competitors).

## The normal method for performance management in France

A recent French law, aiming to increase transparency, requires making public the remuneration offered to lead managers in companies listed on the stock exchange. Thus, reliable information concerning key performance indicators can be analysed for the majority of the French companies of the CAC 40.

The following are the indicators most frequently used for the annual bonus: First,

- net earnings
- earning per share
- cash flow.

Second,

- the relative performance of the share compared to the CAC 40 index
- return on capital
- operating income.

Third, on a more occasional basis,

- EBITDA, operational profits, market share, EVA (economic value added).

Most companies use several indicators for their executives.

The conditions for exercising options also vary. Fewer than 25% of CAC 40 companies have established conditions for exercising some or all stock options.

The following indicators are used as a basis for conditions placed on exercising some or all stock options:

- the profitability of the equity base
- value creation
- the operating income divided by the turnover
- the relative performance of the company's shares compared to an index
- a minimum share price to be reached.

## Levels of criteria

There are a number of levels at which performance can be measured:

- group level
- director level (if responsibility is functional) or business unit level (if it is operational).

## Term of performance measurement

The period over which performance can be measured is also a variable. Performance standards can be assigned:

- an annual term, generally within the framework of the budget
- a term of two to three years, linked to strategic development objectives
- a term of four to five years, aimed at evaluating performance (growth/ profitability) on the market over the medium term.

On this basis, the types of performance measures can also be defined according to their origins. Performance standards can be classified under two headings, according to a financial and a managerial logic.

## Financial logic

Performance standard indicators can derive from:

- An economic and firm performance basis, involving turnover, margins, revenues, costs, operational profits and consolidated cash flow.

- A logic based on value creation – that is, where the consumption of capital is taken into account. Indeed, operational results can be reformatted so that they can be compared to the return on the capital committed by shareholders and banks. This leads to a new way of educating executives and managers about the modalities governing current-production and investment decisions. Far from being a simple issue, this logic hinges on research being undertaken showing a significant correlation, over the medium to long term, between value creation and stock-level evolution. As such, this logic is fully in line with the assessments of financial analysts and tends to be included increasingly often in the executive's company scorecard.

## Managerial logic

Managers apply a certain 'logic' to their decisions and actions, based upon how they are educated, trained and their experience. Different managerial logics are involved in the elaboration of performance standards.

These include a logic of the MBO (management by objectives) type focused on performance within a given function. This approach, which has shaped the behaviour of several generations of managers, is illustrated by the following mechanism: each manager or executive is given objectives relative to his or her missions to be achieved during the reference period, and the result, compared to the objective, indicates the level of performance.

There is a recent trend where a logic which takes other stakeholders into account, that of the balanced scorecard, opens the way to another approach to valuation. Multidimensional performance measures combine financial- and customer-driven performance standards as well as factors contributing, over the short and medium term, to the meeting of other performance standards, such as internal organizational-learning processes.

Most systems used in France combine these two logical approaches. In future, we anticipate systems will soon incorporate social rating indicators, measuring, for example, the degree to which a business group is involved in sustainable development, and the formation of human and social capital.

## The impact of performance standards and the components of a remuneration package

Performance standards are an important part of short- and middle-term bonus systems, as well as systems involving stock options, which are usually seen as longer term systems, delivering rewards against results achieved in time frames of around five years.

To provide an example, performance standards, broken down by elements of variable remuneration, can be seen in the trends illustrated in Tables 5.1 and 5.2.

The art of the 'executive compensation policy' lies in adjusting the choice of performance standards to the shareholder and strategic context, which is one of the central roles of the remuneration committee.

This adjustment has recently led to substituting, in place of the restricted notion of the EBITDA (earnings before interest, taxes, depreciation and amortization), more comprehensive profitability indicators, particularly in industries with high capital consumption. Frequently, this leads to placing conditions upon both the allocation and the exercising of stock options, bringing the interests of management more and more closely in line with those of shareholders by means of indicators such as TSR (total shareholder return).

Holders of stock options do not run any risks: when they face a potential loss of capital, they simply do not exercise their options, unlike the ordinary shareholder, who is at risk immediately when he or she acquires stock. Furthermore, the recent rise in the volatility of financial markets

**Table 5.1** The case of an executive committee member in a French multinational company

|  | *Weight in the bonus* |  |
| --- | --- | --- |
| Annual bonus | 40–50% | Corporate-level financial/monetary indicators (operational profits, ROCE,* turnover, market share, etc.) |
|  | 50–60% | Specific objectives linked to the sphere of activity, including objectives based on managerial logic |

*ROCE = Return on capital employed.

**Table 5.2** The case of a managing director or business unit director

| | *Weight in the bonus* | |
|---|---|---|
| Annual bonus | 20–30% | Corporate-level financial/monetary indicators |
| | 50–60% | Financial/monetary indicators at the business unit level |
| | Around 20% | Specific individual objectives, mostly qualitative in nature |
| Middle-run bonus | – | A percentage of the value created (or destroyed) is credited to (or debited from) a bonus account |
| Stock option plan | – | A recent trend has led to making the exercising of some or all stock options conditional upon meeting (or surpassing) 'profitable growth' or shareholder objectives (net earning per share, total shareholder return) |

**Table 5.3** Stock option conditions of performance

| *Internal* | *Comparative* |
|---|---|
| Minimum price for exercising options | Evolution of the valuation as compared to a peer company |
| Evolution of the price since allocation of the option | |
| Minimum ROCE level for exercising options | Compared TSR |
| TSR level over three months | |

has led to value creation no longer being correlated with stock price (which, moreover, reduces the value of stock options as an incentive for beneficiaries). Stock options are thus not a remuneration device correlated with value creation, but they should be correlated with shareholder objectives, which supposes other types of performance standards.

Adoption of this system should be all the easier due to the fact that, in the context of low stock prices, the allocation of stock options can lead to an almost guaranteed profit when the options are exercised.

## The quantification of performance standards

The choice of the type of indicators reflects the priorities of shareholders and the strategic priorities of management, upon which lead managers' incentives (e.g. the CEOs) – and, by extension, those of the rest of the company's leadership – will be based. But how are these indicators to be quantified in a context involving a shorter economic cycle and political instability, resulting in the propagation of risks and uncertainty concerning forecasts and expectations?

This quantification is traditionally carried out by establishing annual objectives. However, this can prove to be of little use in determining levels of performance against each indicator by comparing what is achieved with the objectives set, because these are generally set during the budget process (i.e. in the previous year). Hence, companies try to diversify their measurement approaches for performance standards by incorporating into each indicator a comparison between the minimum and maximum results, or by combining an objective with a measurement of progress made over the last one, two or three years.

Although compensation levels are still typically established on an annual basis, some French multinational firms quantify (or would like to quantify) indicators in order to bring a renewed dynamism to their systems; this dynamism is linked to a desire to improve the flexibility of their strategy. In fact, the period of time over which compensation levels are set can differ according to the indicators, thereby increasing the flexibility of the systems.

## The relationship between the level of remuneration and performance standards

The relationship between remuneration and performance can be:

1 linear
2 progressive
3 central

according to the different logics being applied (see Figure 5.1).

A linear relationship has the advantage of being easy to explain. A progressive one provides incentives for better performance. Centred logic

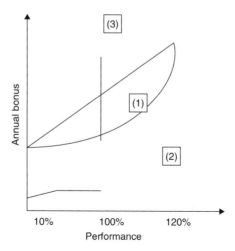

**Figure 5.1** Relationship between bonus level and performance.

focuses executives' attention on those zones of performance that are to be given priority.

Although the linear mechanism has been mostly discussed thus far, this policy tends to be offset by the two other approaches. Indeed, adopting the linear relationship amounts to affirming that going from 90% to 91%, from 99% to 100% or from 103% to 104% represents the same growth in value by the company and requires the same attention on the part of the beneficiary, which is obviously a questionable assumption as we can see from Figure 5.1.

## System adjustment: identifying adjustment needs

The need for adjustments can be linked to changes corresponding to:

- New shareholder priorities, particularly as linked to a change in the nationality of major shareholders, leading to a redefinition of the remuneration package and thus of performance standards.
- Strategic objectives (such as diversification, internal/external growth, etc.).
- Managerial change due to a management buy-out or the introduction of a balanced scorecard system.
- The analysis of the cost of the system by comparing, on the one hand, the costs of (annual, or middle-term) bonuses and stock options with, on the other, shareholder value creation over one, two or three years.

- The trends observed in the competitiveness of executive remuneration packages.

**Table 5.4** Impact of factors and interrelationships

|  | Shareholder imperatives | Strategic objectives | Managerial evolution | Cost/ benefit of systems | Competitiveness |
|---|---|---|---|---|---|
| Level of criteria | *** | *** |  |  |  |
| Term of criteria | ** | ** |  |  |  |
| Logic of performance | *** | ** | *** |  | ** |
| Quantification of performance standards | ** | *** | *** | *** |  |
| Remuneration/ performance relationship |  |  | *** | *** |  |

***Very significant impact.
**Some impact.

The impact of these different factors can be synthesized as shown in Table 5.4.

This analysis constitutes an essential part of the preparation for an effective remuneration committee meeting.

## The top pay committee in French companies

The so-called remuneration committee (*comité de rémunération*) plays an increasing role in the elaboration and monitoring of top pay policies and practices for directors, as opposed to other managers whose salaries are mostly regulated by collective agreements on pay levels. In the recent context of information transparency, a new law of 2001 (loi du 15 mai 2001 sur les Nouvelles Régulations Economiques (NRE)) in its article 225-102-1 makes it compulsory for public companies to disclose the precise amounts paid to directors (including fringe benefits of all kinds) coming from the mother company, as well as from companies under direct and indirect control. This transparency is intended to help make investors more aware of correlations between share price evolutions and top directors' pay.

Usually, the remuneration committee members have to deal with the amounts paid to the CEO and his or her number two, the managing directors (*directeur-général et directors-généraux délégués*). They may also define the pay policy of all senior directors, the employee profit-sharing schemes policy, and the more general directions for stock option plans and retirement packages.

In France, the legal role of the remuneration committee is strictly speaking of an advisory nature and it is not a decision-making body. Remuneration committee members meet between one and four times a year, and have between three and five members. In the majority of cases, the committee also plays the role of appointment committee (*comité de nominations*) for the very senior positions in the company.

In the French CAC 40, 95% of companies had a top pay committee in 2004 versus 50% back in 1995. This is a clear indication of the growing pressure of corporate governance rules.

## Parliament initiatives failed to go further into top pay limits

Naturally, this obligation to disclose top pay figures has not been well accepted by company leaders, who claim that it is an intrusion into their private life. Political party members, including those on the right, have even suggested that maximum amounts of director-level pay should be set by law.

A parliamentary fact-finding commission on company rights was led by Pascal Clément (Member of Parliament). In its report, it highlighted some of the contradictions that have stirred up the commission members. The French case shows that the base income is significantly smaller (16%) than that of European counterparts like Germany (33%) or the UK (40%), hence prompting successful leaders to go and work abroad.

The question was actually triggered after a very tense national debate on the severance pay received by Jean-Marie Messier, Vivendi Universal's ex-CEO, and incomes that were considered to be too high, allocated to some of the company executives of the CAC 40 when their companies were losing money.

**Table 5.5** Comparisons of income for company executives in the USA, UK, Germany and France

| | Elements of the company executives' incomes* (figures are % of total income) | | | | | |
|---|---|---|---|---|---|---|
| | Base income | Yearly bonus | Medium-term bonus | SARs† | Free shares | Stock options |
| USA | 12% | 11% | – | 17% | 15% | 45% |
| UK | Almost 40% | 17% | 13% | – | 8% | 22% |
| Germany | 33% | 24% | – | 7% | – | 36% |
| France | 16% | 14% | – | – | – | 70% |

\* Companies listed on each country's stock exchange: CAC 40 for France, FTSE for the UK, DAX 30 for Germany and S&P for the USA.
† Stock appreciation right.
Source: Clément report, reprinted in *Les Echos*, 26 November 2003.

The Clément parliamentary fact-finding commission report on company rights finally did not recommend legislation on the company executives' incomes and it barely accepted that the shareholders general assembly is totally free to accept or to refuse to vote on justifying information related to incomes. In France, out went the idea defended by some people – and actually studied in the UK – of a special shareholders' general assembly vote on the company executives' incomes. To bring the general assembly down to a battleground seems counterproductive considering the relationship that the French have with money, explained the report written by Pascal Clément (right-wing MP), president of the laws committee.

The conclusions allowed for a few legislative and regulatory adjustments aimed at reinforcing the information to the shareholders and to re-establish confidence. The report states neatly the contradictions that have shaken the members of the fact-finding mission. On the one hand, it *does not take the Enron crisis and the Vivendi, France-Telecom or Ahold scandals as the result of isolated failures*, but as the signs of a structural lack of confidence: *the whole system itself has failed*. On the other hand, it refuses to *condemn the company executives as it may entice them to relocate, which would not be in the national interest*. In fact, it denounces *the teenage crisis of financial capitalism* and *the poor running of the board of directors*.

Pascal Clément was frequently interviewed by the press, and made some interesting remarks concerning the French environment:

*The shareholders are not aware of the overall incomes paid to company executives, especially because of the bonuses and premiums 'which amounts and recipients' are sometimes not disclosed. Yet, shareholders have the right to know if the head of the company could, for example, benefit from insurances, in the case that he could not cash in on his stock options.*

*At the European level, the harmonization of accounting standards is greatly advancing. It will be necessary that, in the long run, financial markets establish common European rules, but we have not reached this stage yet.*

Answering a question about the UK, where the head of a company's income is approved by the shareholders' general assembly, the French position is explained:

*I do not wish it to happen, as General Assemblies will then concentrate on this income issue rather than on business strategy, which is more important. On the other hand, I suggested that the Financial Market Authorities (AMF) gather the information on the CAC 40 company executives' incomes and make them public. The report of the fact-finding mission also suggests having an auditor certify the accuracy of the information regarding the individual incomes with all their components.*

## When CEOs feel concerned by equitable treatment

As in many other European countries, CEOs are blamed for the increase of their incomes, especially when their income does not follow the evolution of the share price. The following extract from *Le Figaro Economie* is highly illustrative of the French climate on this issue. We have chosen to illustrate this with the CAC 40 companies, i.e. the largest companies in terms of capitalization. As HR specialists, we regularly benchmark the best HR policies and practices of large companies and the CAC 40 companies are highly representative of what is happening in terms of new management trends (see Bournois et al., 2003).

Under the headline 'The incomes of the CAC 40 company CEOs have increased by 18% in two years', Nicholas Daniels reports on substantial pay rises received by France's CEOs in *Le Figaro Economie* on 16 May 2004. The headlines here are similar to those, for example, in the *Guardian* and the *Financial Times* in the UK, as shown in Chapter 2. The French article points out that, after 2001 and 2002, when there was a recession, 2003 showed a rise. To quote from the article:

*Years are going by and look alike when it comes to company executives' incomes. The constant rise in incomes in 2001 and 2002, at the time of an economic recession, had caused a certain turmoil. In 2003, it continued even further, but this time was shown as part of the profit increase. This shows a direct link between the company results and the company's management incomes.*

*Of course, irony seems easy but the figures published these last weeks confirm a fast increasing inflation. The average is at 1.97 million Euros in 2003 against 1.67 million two years earlier. This is an increase of more than 18%!*

The highest paid CEOs were at L'Oréal, Michelin and Vinci, although these companies are nowhere near the USA *Fortune* 500 CEOs' salaries and options.

He goes on to explain the relevance of this for the Clément report. In particular, the positive response to the call for greater transparency is noted, although this is dependent upon the legal structure of the company. For example, Michelin, being a 'société de commandite par actions' does not have to reveal certain company details. In addition to substantial base pay increases, CEOs are often accused of receiving massive gains from stock options. Stock option gains are linked to stock market improvements, of course, as well as to the amounts of stock distributed. Some considerable gains were recorded, for example, at Vivendi Universal, AXA, Aventis and Alcatal. Perhaps of greater significance are the remarks in the article which suggest that conflicts of interest occur in the remuneration committees. This, it is argued, is because the members have other connections with the company, showing that members of committees in the CAC 40 are either providing services to the company themselves for a paid reward, or are also members of another company which itself has a commercial relationship with the organization of whose remuneration committee they are members. This seems to support the 'back scratching' hypothesis.

The Clément report was intended to alter this situation and produced 15 proposals, which were designed to reassure CAC 40 company executives, rather than to threaten them with shareholder interventions. The proposals (which have some similarity to those found in the UK's 'Combined Code') are listed below, in outline form.

**For the shareholder**

- To provide for certification by the statutory auditor of the accuracy of the individual information on incomes, so the shareholders'general assembly, according to the vote it issues on the annual accounts as per article L.225-100 of the Commercial Law, will be free to accept or to refuse to vote on the accounts, based upon the justification of the information related to incomes.
- To oblige institutional investors to indicate their vote policy to the companies in which they invest.
- To remind shareholders that they have the right to ask a judge for consequential damages, these being different from social damages, in case of mismanagement, with the obligation for the company executives to face the consequences.
- To seek to improve the quality and the accuracy of the financial information provided by the bank analysts by including the Chinese wall principle in the law.

**For the board of directors to provide a sense of responsibility**

- To publish the board of directors' rules of procedure in the annual report.
- To provide total transparency integrated in the rules of procedure, on the transactions made by the banks represented by the board of directors and on the orders given to them.
- To establish mechanisms of free share transfers with the obligation to keep these shares in the medium term, to make the executive directors part of the development of the company.
- To limit the number of directors to a maximum of 14.
- To oblige the board of directors to dedicate a specific session on the nominating project of any director or otherwise, after the meeting of

the nominating committee, and on the day of their appointment, obligation for the nominated directors to be present and to introduce themselves to the general assembly which nominated them.

**To clarify the practices on incomes**

■ To clarify the legal obligation to publish the incomes in order to emphasize the link between performance and incomes (indicate whether they are fixed or variable, amounts and criteria, fringe benefits, retirement plans).
■ To state, in the annual report, the company policy regarding stock options and detailed information on the distribution of stock options, with an impact study, especially with regard to capital dilution.
■ To authorize – predetermined by the general assembly – the plans for the application for shares at fixed dates.
■ To prohibit, under the control of the financial market authorities (AMF), subscriptions for plans when there is a break in stocks.
■ The enactment by the AMF of a standard form on the income statement rules.
■ The publication by the AMF, for example on their internet site, of up-to-date tables summarizing the SBF 120 company executives' incomes with, on the opposite page, the results of the years $n - 1$.

## Conclusion

There are signs of convergence in the problems of director-level pay and in the solutions proposed. The central issue remains the linkage between pay and performance. The problems are not the amounts of money which are paid out, but rather the justifications for the rewards paid to those at the top.

The choice of performance standards within executive remuneration systems should be part of a consistent approach.

Accordingly, given the necessity of performance standards to be the criteria according to which executives will be evaluated, performance standards are at the very heart of the board's concerns. The rapidity with which they are aligned and adjusted becomes a competitive advantage for both the company and its shareholders, and makes it possible to

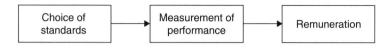

**Figure 5.2** Alignment of pay to standards.

motivate staff on the basis of clear opportunities for reward according to performance.

This rapidity is all the more decisive for executives due to the fact that their term of office at the top of their company has become considerably shorter, both in France and in Europe as a whole.

A new trend concerning lead management stock plans consists of adding or substituting a stock plan modelled on practices in the UK and the USA, which involves the following mechanism:

■ The allocation of stocks free of charge to reward the presence of the beneficiary on a predetermined date (generally three years before).
■ The allocation of stocks free of charge on a given date (generally three years before) in proportion to:
 – the fulfilment of internal objectives (primarily profitable growth)
 – the attainment of a certain level of stock market performance (total shareholder return) compared to competitors or companies in related fields.

These mechanisms make it possible both to align the interests of lead managers more closely with those of shareholders (that is, to ensure a clear 'line of sight' between managers and the corporate performance goals) and to avoid the shortcomings of stock options, many of which are 'out of the money' or 'below the water' in the jargon of compensation experts – that is, their value in the marketplace is lower than the price at which they were allocated.

Our brief discussion on performance-based pay and performance management in France has shown the significance of a close relationship between variable pay and the performance management system in a company. The principles of rewards seem to have a universal appeal. Not only are we facing convergence in corporate governance, but also in the practice of HRM and reward policies, particularly throughout Europe.

# 6

# Developments in top-level compensation in Germany

Alexander von Preen and Marc Glaeser

## Introduction

In Germany, the topic of compensation and associated benefits and perquisites has traditionally been regarded as a confidential personnel issue. This was particularly the case for senior management and top executive compensation packages. Over the past 15 years, this has changed at an increasing rate. The reasons for this include not only the further internationalization of German companies, but also, more importantly, the changes to the German market itself. The consensus within the German economy continues to be that success depends on a prosperous and expanding world economy (Jacobi et al., 1998, p. 193). Developments relating to the creation of the Single European Market and European integration in a wider sense have resulted in a concentration of capital in which German companies have been instrumental. Take-overs, mergers and the creation of multinational corporations in Germany (e.g. DaimlerChrysler, Deutsche Bank, Allianz, Deutsche Telekom, Deutsche Post, to name just a few) have created even larger, globally active interlinked companies. The global reach of such companies is also seen, for example, through their ambition to be listed on the New York Stock Exchange. In addition, the traditional backbone of the German economy, the 'Mittelstand', with some 3 million enterprises, has expanded internationally.[1] This greater interaction beyond the national boundaries has resulted in fiercer exposure to market and capital competition. This has directly fuelled corporate governance discussions and developments for corporations both in Germany and abroad. In addition, overall shareholder expectations from the globally active institutional investor community have been influential in a change towards greater transparency.

At the individual company level, this has resulted in greater cost sensitivity and strategic orientation. Compensation and benefits packages have therefore also gained importance due, firstly, to the increasing focus on costs, specifically personnel costs, which generally represent one of the largest single factors of importance due to increased competition. Secondly, packages are of significance for a company executive wanting, and in many instances needing, to align the human resource strategy and within this specifically the company compensation policy with overall company strategies and market positioning (Von Preen and Blang, 2003). This is closely associated with an altogether more demanding economic environment, which has led companies to review and to discuss the various compensation elements of such packages to a much greater extent. Traditionally, reward policies sought to keep compensation packages within adequate limits – thereby, for example, focusing on internal equity. Increasingly, therefore, the effectiveness of the compensation policy and its actual influence upon individual compensation packages are becoming more important for companies. This development is fuelled by a number of questions. Is internal equity more important to the company than being market competitive? Within a defined market, where do we as a company want to position our compensation and benefit levels (at the lower quartile/25th percentile of the market or the median/50th percentile or the upper quartile/75th percentile)? Should this positioning be the same for all employee and management groups?

Not only are these issues and the overall market developments raising questions about the company compensation policies and levels, but such

---

[1] While the term *Mittelstand* is often translated into small and medium-sized enterprises (SMEs), this definition neglects the basic convictions and attitudes in the socio-economic and political process that are represented by this sizeable group of companies in Germany. Even when only considering those with more than 12.5 million Euros annual turnover, these alone represent over 30 000 German enterprises (Hauser, 2000).

issues are also drawing attention to the different compensation elements (base pay, bonus, benefits, etc.) and their respective relationship within the overall compensation package. This has resulted in compensation packages in Germany no longer being predominantly concerned with monthly base pay, for instance (Anderson and Klasen, 2003), but instead has encouraged companies to introduce and expand elements of variable compensation (both on a short-term and a long-term basis[2]) to differentiate benefits and perquisites for employees and especially for management groups. While the academic and professional debates continue in respect of the need and usefulness of rewarding extrinsic motivation in contrast to supporting the individual's normally existing intrinsic motivation levels, there is an overall development that may be observed. Let us leave to one side for the moment the uncontentious view that there are areas such as research and development departments that may be less prone to such pay incentive-driven approaches (Schwertfeger, 2003). This overall development is the underlying acceptance on the part of companies that improved overall compensation packages (both in terms of quality and quantity) do provide for increased work effort and motivation by their managers. The management groups in Germany are the focus of this chapter. At this stage, it is important to note that this refers to those individuals who are managing employees (*Leitende Angestellte* – LA) and top executives or board members (*Vorstände*). These, as well as the general exempt employees (*Außertarifliche Mitarbeiter* – AT), are not usually governed by tariff and collective bargaining agreements. This allows for greater flexibility when addressing issues relating to personnel – for example, compensation packages.

The first main part of this chapter outlines the developments within senior management compensation levels and the main package elements, as well as considerations for the package design, in Germany. This is a country which is not only important economically for the other European Union members, but also its central European geographic location and its overall international importance were underlined by being named in

---

[2] With respect to compensation, generally short term refers to performance or objectives that have been achieved within one year, while long term refers to performance or objectives that have been achieved over a three- to five-year period so to underline sustained performance. This long-term period is defined by a company and is then applicable for the company as a whole.

2003 as the world's largest exporter: a recognition received several times over the past 10 years. The second part of the chapter addresses some of the essential developments with respect to top executives and their compensation packages. In addition, issues of general corporate governance relating to compensation in Germany and the associated implications are briefly outlined before coming to a careful prognosis of continued changes and developments.

## Compensation developments and elements in Germany

Compensation in Germany was originally based on fixed components both in terms of base pay as well as variable payments. Annual incentives (short-term variable pay) were paid typically without any specific rules or objectives governing their payout. Generally, the manager's superior determined the amount of the bonus on a discretionary basis. This has changed since the mid-1990s. There are three predominant trends that can be detected within the design of compensation packages for managers in Germany, each of which will be elaborated further below. First, the variable component of compensation packages has increased for managers. Second, the objectives for variable compensation are increasingly determined and tied or aligned to company strategy and broken down into individual target management processes. Finally, the design and the content of what companies are offering their management as compensation packages is now more often seen, presented and developed as part of a total compensation approach. These three trends are undoubtedly all closely interrelated.

Before elaborating the trends as well as the essential compensation elements, we need briefly to define several reoccurring terms. The phrase *base compensation* refers to the monthly payment that a manager or executive receives. It is traditionally paid to administration trainees in 13 instalments, while the higher in the organization one goes the more prevalent is payment in only 12 instalments. For those receiving 13 months base compensation, in addition to the regular payments, half of one month's salary is usually paid mid-year and the remaining half at the end of the year. In many instances, this is replacing or reflecting the basic tariff-related vacation and Christmas bonus. *Variable compensation* refers to the compensation a manager or top executive receives for the performance achieved and objectives realized, on a discretionary basis or simply as a guaranteed part for short-term pay, specifically the last 12 months. *Long-term variable compensation* refers to equity- and performance-based compensation, or more specifically incentive stock options generally defined in a formal programme, rewarding achieved performance and realized objectives, which is granted for a period greater than 12 months (generally for periods of three to five years). These programmes may include such incentive plans as stock options, stock grants (restricted stock), stock appreciation rights, phantom awards of stock or performance shares/units. *Total cash compensation* refers to the sum of base compensation plus all variable compensation earned in one year. *Total compensation* refers to the sum of total cash compensation plus long-term variable compensation plus any benefits and perquisites received in one year. To arrive at this sum, the long-term variable compensation as well as benefits and perquisites are valued using different valuation methods (e.g. Black–Scholes for long-term compensation).

## Increasing variable compensation potential

Compensation levels have, over the past several years, continued to increase to a modest degree. This has, however, been mainly the result of an increase of possible variable compensation components. This overall increase is caused by, on the one hand, a relatively marginal increase of base compensation levels over the past several years for management groups and, on the other, by a greater need (with respect to costs, and the corporate aim, in terms of working environment) for overall flexibility. Average base pay increases for senior management functions have been stagnant for the past five years, ranging from 3.5% to just over 4%. The projections for the coming years also do not indicate any significant increases.

Flexibility is achieved through variable pay, which varies according to the chance or risk of the performance achievements and objectives being met. Even though variable compensation is something which cannot be introduced straightforwardly in companies with no such tradition due to legal restrictions in Germany, the far greater obstacle is persuading managers to accept the chance of receiving greater compensation levels due to variable compensation. Such convincing often needs to be very comprehensive and needs to outline fully the probability that the compensation levels will actually increase (the up-side) if and when the

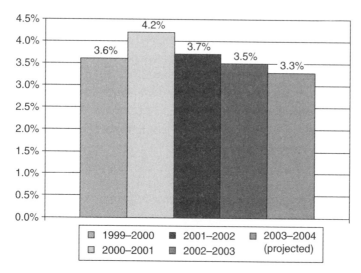

**Figure 6.1** Average base pay increases over the period 1999–2003 and projection for 2004 for senior management functions in Germany.

objectives are met or overachieved. As meeting objectives is increasingly volatile because of the economic situation, the degree of performance or the degree of success with objectives are harder to achieve (the down-side). Variable compensation allows companies to pay variable compensation if objectives are met and thereby the overall performance may support such costs. Good performance is no longer simply rewarded on an individual discretionary basis.

Short-term variable compensation, which normally varies according to the hierarchy and management level, now represents between 25% and 45% of base compensation for management functions. This represents an almost two-fold increase over the past 15 years. This is also a trend, of course at lower percentages, which can be seen for lower management and employees at exempt levels. Very recently, the discussion with respect to variable compensation has also been introduced at collective bargaining agreement negotiations for tariff employees. Currently, short-term variable compensation is increasingly determined on the basis of some of the following predominant criteria: the assessment of performance and target achievement, the relative market changes and individual assessments by superiors. Systematic procedures such as the application of salary increase matrices or competence-based evaluations are less prevalent but nevertheless are used.

The need for flexibility, overall fixed cost reduction and the wider acceptance that money is a key motivation factor are certainly the main underlying reasons for an increasing variable compensation component for management functions. Nevertheless, the criteria with which the possible payout levels are achieved and the mechanics/criteria used for determining this connection are expected to link to the company strategy. This is the second trend found in the development of compensation packages for German managers.

## Variable compensation and company strategy

Leading companies in Germany are increasingly aware of the importance of the personnel or the human resource strategy within their company strategy and therefore of the need for both to be aligned. Within the now increasingly aligned human resource field, compensation has developed from an indirect steering instrument (*Führungsersatzinstrument*) to an integral human resource and thereby company strategy steering method (*Führungsinstrument*) (Femppel, 2002). In a survey conducted in the summer of 2003, this was further underlined when over 80% of the companies replied that for them there is a high or significant impact of company strategy on the design of the company compensation system (Kienbaum/Hewitt, 2003). The compensation system and its programmes are therefore predominantly seen as programmes that should support the achievement of company targets effectively, by supporting a performance- and results-oriented corporate culture, by retaining key talent, as well as by increasing overall employee and management satisfaction and thus acting as an instrument of motivation. In addition, a cost-effective design of compensation programmes is also seen as essential.

Terminology and concepts such as performance- and value-based management have led companies to re-evaluate their compensation systems. Since managing performance effectively requires companies to subscribe to the need for clear objectives, this means they need also to introduce and maintain straightforward systems and processes which convey the right messages while at the same time also aligning and differentiating compensation to support the achievement of objectives. Therefore, the alignment between company strategy and compensation has resulted in a move away from tying variable compensation solely to the individual, based on qualitative objectives. Instead, companies now orient their compensation towards financial and quantitative objectives and overall company performance. The classic target management system is increasingly being replaced with consistent company or corporate target cascades and key performance indicators (KPIs). Based on recent market developments from the top 100 companies in Germany, 80% have or are in the process of redesigning their compensation systems (Von Preen and Blang, 2003).

This has also led to the expectation and increasing requirement of the compensation policy to be in line with market practice, which therefore requires companies to define properly their relevant market, i.e. comparator companies against which one would like to evaluate one's own system, as well as compare the compensation level and overall package. Defining the relevant comparator group is also a critical decision for the implementation and realization of a compensation strategy. In practice, leading German companies consider the relevant market to be with companies of comparable size in related industries.

It is actually the size of a company which is the most important determinant for the compensation levels for senior managers. 'All empirical studies show a positive correlation between compensation and company size' (Kienbaum, 2001, p. 15). 'Company size' is defined according to annual turnover and the number of employees. This underlines one of the key relationships between compensation and responsibility, whereby a larger company represents greater functional complexity with wider responsibilities, as well as reflecting the required individual capabilities.

The relevant market can be further defined, emphasizing the point that determining the competitive position is essential. Table 6.1 illustrates this, based on a survey conducted last year amongst some of the leading companies in Germany, where they would like to position themselves within the relevant market for the different compensation components (Kienbaum/Hewitt, 2003).

These results also draw attention to an interesting development for German companies, specifically relating to the relative decreasing importance of base compensation levels. One can clearly see a difference between the desired positioning for base compensation versus both total cash compensation and total compensation. This is also an aspect of the third trend, discussed later in this chapter.

Base compensation levels continue to represent the majority of the total compensation package for managers. This is partly because compensation

**Table 6.1** Market positioning for different compensation components within a defined relevant market

| Positioning within relevant market | Base salary (%) | Total cash compensation (%) | Total compensation (%) |
|---|---|---|---|
| 90th percentile (upper end of market) | 11 | 15 | 15 |
| 75th percentile (upper market quartile) | 18 | 30 | 30 |
| Between 50th and 75th percentiles | 14 | 21 | 23 |
| 50th percentile (middle of market) | 26 | 11 | 12 |
| Average | 14 | 5 | 5 |
| Below 50th percentile | 5 | 5 | 5 |
| N = 45 | | | |

Sample drawn from top 250 enterprises in Germany.

levels are no longer solely subject to the job an individual holds or to the person holding the position, but are increasingly calculated from a combination of the two approaches (pay the job or pay the person).

The determination of base compensation levels in Germany are also driven by professional experience, as well as the match between job requirements and the capabilities an individual brings to a specific function. In addition, short-term as well as overall medium-term (two to three years) performance provides a further degree of differentiation between individuals at a similar level within an organization. For short-term and long-term variable compensation, the performance at an individual level, as well as the company or corporate results, play a key role. During reward reviews, the short- as well as medium- to long-term objectives for which managers are responsible are closely monitored.

The findings of a recent study illustrate that individual target achievements remain the key criteria for determining variable compensation (Kienbaum/Hewitt, 2003). Additionally, organizational performance at different levels is measured and accounts for short-term variable compensation when it is determined. These organizational targets are most often the overall profit followed by developments or targets of operating income, profit before tax and adjustments, and overall turnover.

**Table 6.2** Predominant criteria used for senior management variable compensation

| Criteria | Senior management (%) |
| --- | --- |
| Individual target achievement | 86 |
| Group-related target achievement | 64 |
| Legal entity target achievement | 50 |
| Division/business unit-related target achievement | 43 |

Percentage total exceeds 100%, indicating multiple responses.

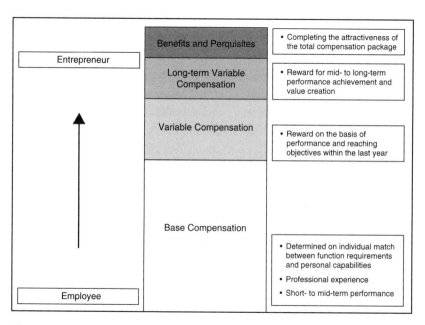

**Figure 6.2** The transition from employee to entrepreneur within a company through the total compensation perspective.

## Development of a total compensation approach

The third trend observed over the past several years in Germany is that of considering the total compensation package for managers. This observation is supported by a multi-year study and review process of a working group dealing with compensation within the German person- nel association (*Deutschen Gesellschaft für Personalführung* – DGFP), which has concluded that there is clear trend away from reliance solely on a base rate emphasis in compensation policy towards a total compensation approach (Femppel, 2002). Furthermore, they also conclude that total compensation is an integral part of human resource management and a key success element for a company to realize a value-based management approach. This trend has been further encouraged by the development of companies that are increasingly eager to align compensation with function flexibility, whilst also aligning compensation with the overall success of the company or unit for which the manager is responsible. This means moving the individual from simply being an employee to being instead an entrepreneur within the organization. There is a desire therefore to provide reward not only for short-term successes or performance achievements, but also for the longer-term achievement of objectives. This longer-term perspective also supports the idea of sustainability for the objectives and performance achievements.

This transition in Germany is being realized through aligning company strategies and targets with variable compensation, as well as with the help of the long-term compensation, benefit and perquisite elements for different management and executive groups.

The overall prevalence of long-term incentives offered in Germany is increasing. This is especially the case with internationally active companies and those that are publicly listed, which have established these types of competitive compensation programmes. These long-term programmes are usually stock option plans. Over 80% of the DAX 30 companies now have stock option plans, which were initially established in 1996 through the initial option programmes (*Wandelanleiheprogramme*) launched by Deutsche Bank and DaimlerChrysler (Bursee and Schawilye, 2003; Anderson and Klasen, 2003). Other programmes that are prevalent include the stock appreciation rights (SAR) and performance units and shares. The KontraG law ('*Gesetz zur Kontrolle und Transparenz im Unternehmensbereich*'), established in 1998, eased the granting of options to employees and for the first time also permitted the granting of options to board members (at a time when there was euphoria over the developments in the New Economy). This resulted in a wave of programmes being developed and implemented (Bursee and Schawilye, 2003). The central problem in Germany at present remains two-fold: the initial experience period is only very short and as such not very successful, as the majority of programmes or individual granted option tranches remain under water or do not fulfil the performance criteria to be exercised. Nevertheless, alternative programmes (e.g. performance shares or cash-based long-term bonus plans) are continuing to be developed which combine individual compensation with long-term company strategy and target realization.

Beyond the monetary compensation elements, non-monetary elements or benefits and perquisites are an essential component of the total compensation perspective. It is important to consider that benefits and perquisites are seldom the driver for incumbents in management or executive positions to enter, stay or leave a company. Standard benefits and perquisites in Germany's leading companies are company cars and pension plans. Few companies are aware that they can often represent 30–50% of the personnel costs (Ullmann, 2003), which therefore makes it necessary for them to be market aligned as well as effective for the employee. Being market aligned in Europe from 2005 requires the publicly listed companies to provide valuations according to the international accounting standards (IAS) for the offered benefits and perquisites. This is presently further stimulating a greater consciousness with respect to these total compensation components and will swiftly increase further market transparency.

The company car remains the most prevalent benefit offered to senior management functions (approximately 80% of senior managers). The eligibility for a company car is generally not determined by job requirement, but rather is seen as a possibility to offer management employees something that is tax effective. The type of company car remains a status symbol in Germany, and therefore for managers the Mercedes-Benz, BMW and Audi are the most prevalent and preferred automobile manufacturers. Company car budgets offered to managers are most often based on hierarchical levels within an organization and range from list prices from 35 000 up to 75 000 Euros. Private use of the company car is handled generously in most instances, with three-quarters having unlimited private use of the car. For the individual manager, normally the only associated cost is the payment (subtraction from the monthly salary) of the tax for the monetary benefit received (for private use it is presently 1% of the list price plus 0.03 Euros/kilometre between the home and the workplace).

Company pension schemes are the other most prevalent component within the total compensation package. In general, slightly over 80% of managers are provided with a company pension scheme or a pension scheme that is supported by the company. While the prevalence has decreased over the last 20 years, it remains an essential benefit and is increasingly popular. The attractiveness for managers in Germany stems from the present public debate regarding the publicly funded pension scheme and the decreasing future payouts that may be received on the basis of a smaller group of active workers supporting an ever increasing number of pensioners. Retirement, disability and survivor benefits are covered under one pension plan in Germany. Over the past couple of years there has been a clear trend among larger companies to move away from a defined benefit to a defined contribution pension scheme.

Traditional German companies normally offer a defined benefit plan with a flat amount of pension per year of service. The majority of defined benefit plans offer benefits that are calculated on the final average pay (last year annual pay or average of the last three to five years – for more senior functions). The average contribution up to the Social Security Contribution Ceiling (SSCC – presently 61 800 Euros p.a. in West Germany and 52 200 Euros p.a. in East Germany) in 2004 remained at 0.2–0.8% and 1.2–1.8% respectively in excess of the SSCC. These types of schemes, which have more recently been implemented or redesigned, provide benefit rates at the lower end of these ranges.

However, increasingly for large German companies and especially those internationally oriented, defined contribution-oriented pension plans have been established for managers. Here the average contribution formula lies between 1% and 5% of contribution up to the SSCC and slightly above 10% in excess of the SSCC. In general, the income on which the pension is calculated is base pay and in some cases the total cash compensation is used. Current (2004) interest rates used for the calculations range between 5% and 10% (often according to the age of the incumbent).

These plans are occasionally supplemented with matching contribution plans. Here, the extent as well as percentage of the match and the maximum amount where matching will be offered by the employer varies from fixed amounts to percentages of an individual's pay. With respect to the financing of pension plans, the most common method in Germany remains via book reserves.

Beyond the company car and company pension, additional benefits and perquisites such as disability insurance, private health insurance, medical check-ups, accident insurance and medical insurance for international travel are used in packages according to the tasks and assignments of managers. However, they are only prevalent for 15–20% of managers in Germany.

## Top executive compensation

The second part of the chapter turns our attention specifically to executive compensation in Germany. Having addressed key trends for compensation and the composition of packages for managers as part of the context, the chapter will now focus on differences or specific elements of the package for the top managers of German corporations. Corporate governance is an important element and therefore will also be briefly highlighted. The overall trends discussed above, the way compensation increases, are now mainly through increasing variable compensation (both short and long term), this being aligned to the company strategy along with a total compensation approach; this applies for top executives as well. Indeed, it is often top managers who are driving these changes and trends.

The sizes of management boards are generally dependent on the size of the company/corporation and its management structure. For companies with less than 1000 employees, the average board size is three members going up to an average of slightly over seven for companies with more than 50 000 employees (Kienbaum, 2003a). The appointment period for German executives on a management board is generally for a five-year term. The first term of office in some instances may be shorter (anywhere between three and five years) and in some organizations, after a certain age, generally 60, the appointments are on an annual basis only. Compensation increases and reviews for executives in Germany are normally undertaken on an annual basis, although in some instances only every two years. The percentage of increases awarded is subject to various factors, predominantly the inflation rate, the development of the terms of the collective bargaining/tariff agreement, overall company and economic performance, the area of responsibility (especially if there is a change due to organizational restructuring) and the executive's overall responsibility.

Members of the management board are appointed by the supervisory board and collectively are responsible for the company's well-being. This is defined in the publicly listed companies law (*Aktiengesetz*, AktG – Paragraph 77, Sect. 1), which also prescribes that a dual board system separating the management board from the supervisory board must exist in Germany. In a multi-person board, the supervisory boards may nominate one executive to have the role of the CEO (*Vorstandsvorsitzender* – Paragraph 84, Sect. 2, AktG) and as such the CEO has greater representational stature with respect to the public, at annual general meetings or with other stakeholders, and this person also co-ordinates the activities of the different board executives, presides over board meetings and is principally concerned in defining company strategy. Over the past 10 years, the CEO function has been increasing for large and for more international active corporations in the direction of US CEOs in terms of their importance, visibility and presence. This has also resulted in this function receiving, on average, a compensation supplement between 50% and 200% when compared to the other executive compensation packages. Otherwise, for more traditional German CEOs or for the management board elected speaker (*Vorstandssprecher*), the supplement is only 15–25% above that of the other executives. In general, compensation levels for all other executives on a management board in Germany are much the same, with the only exception being for 'young' or newly appointed board members. However, their compensation level is generally raised within or directly after their first five years to the compensation levels of the other executives.

Variable compensation is the important total cash compensation element within the main German corporations and large companies. On average, for executives of smaller companies this represents 30–50% and for executives and board functions of large corporations 50–75% of base compensation. In only a minority of the larger companies is any portion of the short-term incentives offered on a contractually fixed basis. This is a practice which, amongst the internationally active corporations, is part of their past practices. The short-term incentive (bonus) is paid to executives on achieving or exceeding their performance targets. Also for this group, short-term incentives or variable compensation are increasingly set on predetermined targets and no longer on any form of discretionary basis. Performance targets for most executives are split between company/corporate targets and individual targets. In some instances, unit or divisional targets or also overall group targets are an additional determinant that are included. The overall company objective is generally set for the CEO. The broader targets that are predominantly used are company-specific economic development criteria, qualitative measures for the operational unit and company/industry- or unit-specific objectives.

Long-term variable compensation, as already addressed in the previous section, is offered by the largest domestic companies and internationally originating or oriented companies in Germany, including those that are publicly listed. For those that have long-term variable systems, the expectation is that these systems will increase the total compensation levels by 20–40%. As a result of this overall potential total compensation increase, non-publicly traded companies are increasingly required to increase the packages of their executives. This has, up to now, not occurred frequently and has resulted in only marginal increases. Nevertheless, it is a trend that will certainly change with an overall and sustained economic upturn. However, the clear effect it has had in the past couple of years is on the willingness of supervisory boards (*Aufsichtrat*) to more readily replace executives who are not achieving the company objectives or who are seen as being unable to deliver the expected performance (Kienbaum, 2003a, p. 26).

In terms of benefits and perquisites, company pension plans are the essential benefit. The amount of company pension granted for executives in Germany lies within the range of 50–70% of the last salary paid before retirement. This percentage range decreases for executives that have been appointed more recently. The regulatory government pension system is not considered in this calculation. In the majority of companies, pensions are granted after 10 years of executive (board) service. Exceptions to this waiting period do exist and in those cases the pension grant is then offered after five years. Survivor benefits amount to 50–60% of the annual base compensation level for the surviving spouse, 10–15% for children with a surviving spouse, and 15–25% for orphaned children up to a maximum of 100% of the pension.

Company cars, in addition to the conditions for managers addressed earlier, are offered at the upper end of the model spectrum (e.g. Mercedes-Benz S-class), with the CEO generally also having a chauffeur at his disposal, while the remaining executives generally have access to a chauffeur pool.

Additional benefits and perquisites that are often offered to executives in Germany include accident insurance, regular medical check-ups, directors' and officers' liability insurance (D&O), legal and financial consulting services.

## Corporate governance

Pressure from institutional as well as broader investor groups, general international pressure and the overall economic trend resulted in the establishment of a corporate governance code in Germany in February 2002, which was amended in May 2003. The code outlines recommendations and suggestions, to which companies should adhere. The code further prescribes that those companies that do not accept a recommendation, determined with the word *shall*, must make this publicly known (in general, through a notice on the company website and a mention in the annual report). Suggestions in the code identified with the words '*should*' or '*may be*' can be deviated from without necessarily having to acknowledge this publicly. All publicly listed companies have accepted the code in principle. The German corporate governance code is wide reaching, as it addresses issues relating to how to conduct shareholder and general meetings, the interaction between management and supervisory boards, the tasks, responsibilities, composition and compensation of management and supervisory boards, as well as the general issues of transparency and reporting/auditing.

For instance, the code clearly stipulates in Section 4, Paragraph 4.2.3: 'The overall compensation of the members of the Management Board shall comprise a fixed salary and variable components. Variable compensation should include one-time and annually payable components linked to the business performance as well as long-term incentives containing risk elements. All compensation components must be appropriate, both individually and in total' (Government Commission, 2003).

Even with adherence or clear explanations given by companies regarding their non-compliance, executive compensation levels and composition remain a hot topic in the German media. Traditionally, only lump sums for management boards were published; now, with individual compensation levels and their composition being more widely known, the question that is increasingly being raised is: does the compensation level correspond to the performance of the board member (generally the

CEO) and the overall company development? While the corporate governance code and associated debate have resulted in a more structured and overall more transparent disclosure of key governance and compensation issues, there remains continued room for improvement on the part of companies. Nevertheless, as one observer noted, the corporate governance code 'is a big step in getting German companies to think the right way' (Kitchens, 2003).

## Conclusion

If the trends and developments outlined here continue, a clear difference from the more traditional approaches to compensation may become more widespread in Germany. Nevertheless, the trends are clear, the developments continue and are reaching slowly further down the company hierarchies, thereby becoming visible for a large part of the organization and inevitably the population at large. No doubt the executives and managers are the front runners in this progression. This trend may see boards focusing more on a total compensation approach, which is more results and performance oriented.

The need for greater flexibility, cost sensitivity and performance orientation are unmistakable and are being addressed. Through increasingly more transparent corporate governance, this may also become more widely seen. Such developments will further underline the close relationship between compensation and the direction a company will be taking in the future.

# 7

# Designing reward packages

Don McClune

## Introduction – the emotional interface

What other people are paid is usually an emotive subject. This is probably because, apart from the exceptionally lucky, we are all participants in the salaried society and possess a 'personal reward benchmark' against which other people's income can be compared. Using this benchmark, we become potential experts in making salary comparisons and classifying them in terms of 'fair', 'unfair', 'exorbitant', 'pitifully inadequate' and so on.

However, this benchmark is not applied consistently. Take, for example, the perceptions held by the different professions. Medical doctors may feel that they perform a much more worthwhile service to society than barristers. The doctors may see top barristers as earning obscene amounts of money for representing criminals. However, barristers feel that they are relatively poorly paid compared to investment bankers who, it would appear, make huge amounts of money on 'windfalls' and through the use of other people's money. Where they all agree is that the clergy are the professional paupers – middle class people, living in upper class houses and earning lower class salaries.

In business, although the members of the board are invariably the minority group, they are also the wealthiest group in their business society and, as such, can become a socio-economic soft target. The press, quite correctly, researches and communicates examples of cases supporting the 'unfair' vote in terms of discrepancies between directors' pay and corporate performance.

Given the number of interested parties who have the potential to volunteer relatively uninformed and generalized judgements about reward, businessmen and businesswomen have a responsibility to adopt a less emotive, more business-led approach to reward design, particularly in terms of performance incentives.

## Performance incentives – for and against

Human performance in business is partially about how people behave given a set of circumstances.

It would be foolish to ignore the body of opinion described by Bevan and Thompson (1991) that performance incentives do not work. Similarly, there are those, described by McGregor (1960), who find it ridiculous to assume that people in our consumer-orientated society are not fired up, are not prepared to work harder and will not try to work more efficiently if given the opportunity to earn more money. Logic would lead us to conclude that the answer must lie somewhere between these two extreme views.

When discussing reward and motivation, it is tempting for organizations to start by asking themselves *'what do we have to pay in order to get our people to perform to the optimum level of their abilities?'* What they should ask first is *'where has the organization decided it wants to be in the next one, two, three or four years, how do we get our people to make that happen and if they do make it happen, how will we recognize their achievements?'*

If the object of the exercise is to answer the *'what do we have to pay'* question, then the focus is on the payment and not the performance. Conversely, if the object is to answer the second question, which is about the conditions of achieving recognition for a specified level of performance, then the focus is on the quality of the performance goals rather than the quantum of reward.

The executive share option plan, currently the focus of a great deal of speculation in newspapers and specialist HR magazines, is a good example of how our thinking about incentives is changing.

## Current thinking about incentives

In simple terms these plans grant employees the option to buy a number of shares in the company that employs them. The option allows them to buy the shares on a specified date in the future and at a specified price. The expectation is that the share price, when the employee is allowed to buy the shares, 'the date of exercise', will be greater than the price when he or she was given the option to buy the shares, the 'date of grant'. If this is indeed the case, then the employee may buy the shares at the price they were granted, sell those shares at their current market price and pocket the difference. Or they may choose to hold the shares and sell them at a future date for an even larger profit. If, on the other hand, the price of the shares at the date of exercise is less than they were at the date of grant, then the shares are said to be 'under water' and the employee simply chooses not to exercise the option. In this latter situation there is no gain to the employees, but there is also no loss.

Shareholders argue that the people who have the job to increase the value of the shareholders' investment in a company, the management, should run the same risks, in terms of the value of the investment decreasing if the share price decreases. Employees argue that they do not have the same choices as the investor and, furthermore, many things can influence the share price of their company, some of which may be outside their direct control. If the share price starts to fall then the investor can sell their shareholding and take their profits at that time. Employees may not have that choice, so they must stick with the shares under option at least until the exercise date and, possibly, if the shares are under water, beyond the exercise date.

The idea of using a similar instrument as a stock market option for generating pay was thought of in the USA back in the 1970s and it is interesting to reflect upon how this concept has changed since it was first introduced. Originally, executive share option plans were conceived as a means for employees to accumulate capital in order to boost their retirement pension. Today, executive share option plans have evolved to become mid- to long-term, tax effective, deferred income plans, quite different from the original intent. Furthermore, one of the advantages of this type of reward, from an employer's point of view, was that until very recently companies were not obliged to account for the cost of providing share options to their employees in their profit and loss accounts.

However, as we are now living in the 'post-Enron' period, accounting standards generally are under review by regulatory bodies in Europe and the USA. Their deliberations about the practice of granting share options to employees started from views expressed in 2002 by both Alan Greenspan, Chairman of the US Federal Reserve, and Warren Buffett, Chairman of Berkshire Hathaway. Buffett and Greenspan argue that if stock options are a form of compensation, then the cost of providing them must come from somewhere and be recorded as such in the employer's profit and loss account. One of the results of this debate is that Microsoft, in July 2003, announced that it would not be granting any more stock options to its employees from September 2003 (Waters and Morrison, 2003). Microsoft employees shared $16.3 billion in option profits in 2000. Instead of share options, Microsoft said it would be granting restricted stock that would vest after five years. Steve Balmer, Microsoft's CEO, said that 'the shift away from share options reflected the unhappiness amongst the company's employees as its [Microsoft's] shares have languished over recent years'.

As can be seen, the arguments for and against whether incentive plans are worth having are not simple, either from the employee or employer point of view. If the share price at the exercise date is less than, or even equal to, the option price, then the share option plan is likely to be seen as a disincentive – particularly if the employee was hoping to sell some shares to offset the cost of exercising the option.

From the considerations above, it would appear that there is no guarantee that having an incentive will produce the behaviours and results the company requires. On the other hand, employees will look for incentive plans when they join a company because, if the company is successful, they will want recognition for their efforts and skill in creating that success. Furthermore, if the company wants to achieve its strategic goals, it will have to actively manage the performance of its people to achieve the goals. Incentive plans, clearly defined and properly controlled, can be very powerful management tools.

## The components of a pay policy

When discussing pay it is helpful to consider the component parts of the 'package' – called 'total compensation' in the USA or 'total remuneration' in the UK. It is generally accepted that there are four elements to the package, these being:

- base pay (guaranteed income or 'come to work' money)
- short-term incentive pay (annual bonuses and the like)
- benefits (medical, pension, life assurance etc.), and
- longer-term incentives (share plans, LTIPs, etc.).

Straight away it can be seen that this simple breakdown is not as simple as it seems. For example, why provide benefits at all – surely employees could look after themselves or their families? Depending on whether they are single, married, have dependent children, both partners are in employment, etc. will lead one to question the sense and indeed the perceived value of a 'standard' set of benefits, regardless of the employees' personal circumstances. This variation in benefit requirement has helped to create a whole industry devoted to the promotion of 'flexible benefits', a system whereby the benefits can be carried within a total budget, according to the needs of the recipient.

## The base pay and incentive balance

We should also consider the balance between base pay, short-term bonuses and longer-term incentives in the package. Why do organizations not pay merely as little base pay as they can get away with and load everything onto incentive payments? The opponents of this policy may well argue that not every one is willing or has a job capable of being paid as if they were a commissioned salesman. Consider a further development on this theme announced by Marks & Spencer (Buckley, 2003), the large UK retailer. From September 2003, Luc Vandevelde, the then part-time chairman, relinquished his current part-time salary of £1.72 million and instead was paid totally in shares (13 500 shares per month, making his annual salary £526 500 at the July 2003 Marks & Spencer share price). Thus, he totally aligned his remuneration to shareholder value.

## The effective remuneration package

Perhaps we should try to find a way through these issues by considering the logic of the corporate aspirations of attraction, retention and motivation, as shown in Figure 7.1.

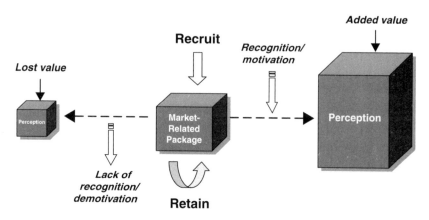

**Figure 7.1** The effective remuneration package.

Going back to the first principles of what we are trying to achieve when we construct a remuneration package, it is possible to see the interplay between fact and perception at work. First of all it is important to have information about what is the 'going rate' for a job or family of jobs in a particular marketplace. This is the 'attraction' part of the equation that allows us to enter the recruitment market in the first place. Many will argue that by researching the salary market and then paying market rates, or even by having a policy that is designed to pay above the median market rate, we may influence inflation. This may indeed be the case, but recruitment is an expensive exercise. Simply to ignore what competitor companies are paying must be weighed up against the possibility of high employee turnover or even an inability to find the right calibre of people.

The market-related package allows the organization to attract people with the appropriate skills and experience, and also to retain them by protecting itself from losing them again to the very market from which they were recruited. This is the 'number crunching' part of remuneration design. However, there is another aspect and this is that human perception enters into the process at a point where good employers, who recognize this aspect, can start to add value to the process.

The concept of adding value to the remuneration policy originates from the fact that the employees, in general, do not have a detailed

125

knowledge of the salary market. Certainly one can read advertisements in newspapers and professional magazines that quote salaries, or consult specialist Internet sites on pay for information applicable to a particular position. This information often only informs us of the salaries that are on offer for people to move from one company to another. It does not tell us what the salaries are for people who are currently 'in position'. Therefore, this salary information is fairly general and relates only to that proportion of jobs that currently are vacant or newly created, or the median rates for jobs for surveys, which may not be comparable.

## Adding value

When people talk to their friends socially and exchange salary information, it us usually of a superficial nature. So the trap that salary practitioners can easily fall into is to believe that the employees in their company have the same knowledge of the salary market as they do – not so. At best they have a perception of the salary market but not a detailed knowledge of it. When quizzed about their salary, a person will usually respond by saying, for example, that they enjoy working for a particular organization because they are reasonably well paid, or there is an opportunity to advance their careers, or the bosses recognize when a good job is being done, or they are well cared for in terms of benefits. These are the add-on factors to the remuneration package. Those who are dealing with the company's pay policies need to work closely with the other parts of human resources to ensure that the optimum value is added to all the hard work entailed in getting the package right in the first place. So the 'value' of the package can become greater than the 'comparative' monetary value.

Although this 'added value' is difficult to quantify, it is possible to get a clearer picture of its effect when one considers the opposite situation. During exit interviews, when people are leaving an organization, often they have a perception that they are not very well paid or even that it is easier to say that they are not reasonably paid rather than to confess that they feel unwanted or undervalued. Often, what they are saying is that, as far as they are concerned, there is a lack of training or development facilities or that there is a lack of simple recognition for the job that they did for the organization. This is what causes them to view their salary package as being smaller than it actually is relative to the market. Words such as 'I am sure I will be better off at another company' are often used.

It is easy to make the mistake of thinking that this phenomenon is restricted to more junior employees. Recently, we were asked to assist a company with a problem they had with the head of their American office. This is a British company and about 60% of their income is derived from the USA. The directors are all British and the boss of the American office, an American, sits on the management committee. However, he was making serious overtures that he was underpaid. The board did not understand how he came to this conclusion so they asked us to look into the situation and form an objective opinion. We found, on paper, that according to his position in their particular business sector in the area they operated in the USA that he was paid above the market median. We discussed this with the company and it was decided that, rather than simply tell him that he was mistaken, we should try to find out why this senior person had come to this conclusion. We spoke to him at some length. It turned out that what he was really worried about was the fact that, since his office's contribution to the bottom line was so significant, he felt that he was insufficiently involved in the strategic planning discussions that occurred regularly in the UK, often without his presence. Because he was not as involved as he felt he should have been, he assumed that he was undervalued and 'undervalue' included his salary. Happily, the board recognized that he had a valid point. They admitted that they had not involved him as much as they should have and they set about putting things right. The outcome was an enormously more satisfied and motivated senior executive and it did not cost the company any more in salary – an example of correcting perception and adding value.

So far, the discussion has been about market salaries and looking at particular markets, but great care needs to be taken that we are comparing like for like. Clearly there is a checklist of the basic factors, commonly known as market comparators, that should be considered. These comparators include the following:

- *The size of the sample.* There is often a misconception that the bigger the sample the better the comparison but, in practical terms, six or eight competitor organizations in a sample is a better comparison than dozens of organizations that bear little resemblance to the organization in question.

- *Financial comparators.* The size of the organizations being compared is an important consideration. Generally, senior positions in very large organizations are paid more than similar senior positions in smaller organizations. However, this might not be true for more junior positions. The size criterion includes looking at market capitalization, sales turnover or total assets. Profit is not usually regarded as a reliable method because of the number of factors that go into arriving at the profit figures.

- *Complexity.* Complexity is often defined in terms of whether the company operates regionally, nationally or internationally and also the complexity of its products and of course, its industrial sector. If the organization does operate internationally then some of the roles will have international accountability, others a local accountability and one needs to be clear that they are being compared to the correct sample.

- *Job matching.* Market salary information based simply on job titles needs to be considered very carefully. For example, the job title of company secretary can be a very important position or almost a status title. Consequently, the salary range may be so wide that if you chose almost any salary number it is likely to be within the range. Again, medians, upper and lower quartile figures will be of little help if the range for a particular position is very wide.

Consideration of these various comparators to arrive at a reasoned view of salary market rates really means that using one comparator such as, for example, company size, is rarely sufficient. Arriving at a consensus of the salary market having looked at the market according to a number of different comparators is usually required. Conversely, if one tries to match too many criteria in the sample matching process, it is very easy to end up with a very small sample indeed. This sample may be too small to be representative.

So it can be seen that an exercise that started out by simply comparing matched data has become much less mechanical and now requires the application of judgement and experience.

There is another aspect or comparator that, if possible, should be considered and that is the operating history of the company. This can

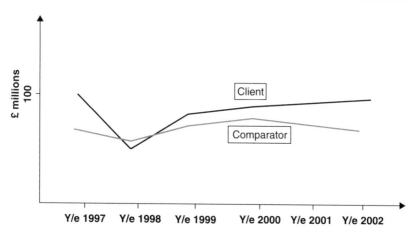

**Figure 7.2** Peer group comparison – five-year profit history.

be seen in the company's report and accounts, and studying these often gives an important indication of whether the company under consideration should be part of the comparator sample.

By way of example, our consultancy was asked to consider the remuneration of the senior managers in a sample of eight competitor companies. The eight companies in the sample were of similar size, using market capitalization, and our client was approximately at the centre of this range. However, when considering the operating history of one of these companies, it was felt that its inclusion in the sample should be questioned. The findings are outlined below.

First of all we considered the profit history over the last five years (Figure 7.2). In terms of the profit history, our client and this comparator organization were very similar.

Next we considered the operating history over the last five years in terms of revenues (Figure 7.3). A wide variation between our client and this sample company was found in that there was a serious tailing off in revenues. It was at this point that some concern started to appear.

Next we looked at the history of size by number of employees (Figure 7.4). It became clear that this particular company was keeping its profit line up by means of downsizing, particularly in terms of the number of people it employed. At this point, it was agreed with our client that this particular company was not a suitable comparator.

This example shows us the importance of looking beyond the plain numbers. Human resource management in general, and remuneration

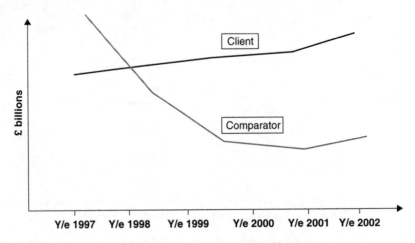

**Figure 7.3** Peer group comparison – five-year revenue history.

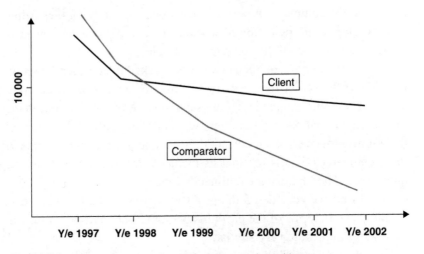

**Figure 7.4** Peer group comparison – five-year employee history.

specialists in particular, should not leave the analysis of financial reports completely to the accountants. One does not have to be a financial guru to derive a great deal of information from a company's report and accounts even when, as in our example, they are examined fairly superficially. When one considers that, for most companies, employment costs range from 40% to 60% of corporate income, then numbers are important and the remuneration policy, through its size and impact, is a strategic consideration. The proper management of this large financial resource is of paramount importance to the proper management of the organization.

## Incentive plans in the twenty-first century

Incentive plans today can be very sophisticated instruments. Some oι the most sophisticated are to be found in the financial services sector, where a high level of understanding in 'financial engineering' is required simply to understand the plan rules. However, these are the exception and most incentive plans do not need to consider matters such as co-investment, carried interest, sweet equity, fund-by-fund or deal-by-deal issues. It is important to strip away the layers of complexity and look at the basic building blocks for a successful, or perceived to be successful, incentive plan.

Over the last few decades there has been a continual search for the Holy Grail of incentive plans and methodologies for measuring performance and work roles have emerged in a variety of forms. For example:

- *Time span of discretion*. Professor Jaques, during extensive research in the Glacier Metal Company, coined the phrase 'time span of discretion', which he defined as 'the longest period which can elapse in a role before the manager can be sure that his subordinate has not been exercising marginally substandard discretion continuously in balancing the pace and quality of his work' (Jaques, 1964).
- *Management by objectives* (Selley and Forman, 2002). Here it was argued that roles were broken down into a number of objectives and that recognizing and managing the objectives was the way to manage the roles.
- *Critical path analysis* (Wall and Proyect, 1997). This borrowed techniques used in project management for managing people and performance.
- *Key performance indicators*. This is an attempt to break down roles and the organization into the key performance parts and thus manage performance more effectively.
- *Job evaluation.* This tries to place a value on a job principally for market salary comparison purposes, but also to calculate internal relativities and the promotional steps between jobs, and the way the jobs can be incentivized or supported through training and development.
- *Economic value added* (Stern, Shiely and Ross, 2001). This is a methodology that attempts to measure the value that is added to the company using such measurements as cost of capital, the value of

R&D, goodwill, etc., in order to arrive at an incentive scheme which encourages value added.

■ *The balanced scorecard.* Created by Kaplan and Norton (1996), in its original format, this attempted to supplement traditional financial performance measures with measures of performance in terms of customers, internal business processes, and learning and growth.

Obviously none of the theories above has become the Holy Grail of performance management and no doubt they will, in time, be replaced by new thinking on the theme. However, they are important developments and one can see an empirical progression that tries to link the management of people to the management of the business entity. What is often overlooked is that the management of people is often as complex and unpredictable as the management of the business. This complexity and unpredictability should not be an excuse to abandon the more complex people aspects in favour of the business considerations.

Not so many years ago, it was common to find HR performance specialists holding the view that pay was an irrelevancy when managing performance. That view is rarely held today, but many HR specialists and line managers do start with the people issues, possibly because they think they need a quick fix solution such as a new performance management scheme, or bonus system. However, the argument should start from the business perspective because improving business performance is the primary consideration.

In our contemporary society the corporate governance legislators require companies to become more transparent about how they justify their performance incentive practices and that this justification be made in business terms such as the returns to shareholders.

Performance plans need a firm bedrock because mistakes in performance management can have a wide effect on the business.

## The logical link

Given the need to start looking at performance issues at the top of the organization, there is then a corresponding need to be disciplined about how to link business performance to people performance – the logical link.

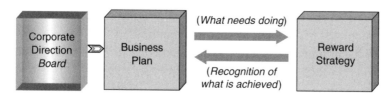

**Figure 7.5** The logical link.

The board decides where the company is headed and they put together a business plan for achieving this. Writing the business plan is not the end objective but is only part of the process, because the company still has to cross what Sir John Harvey-Jones (1994), the former CEO of ICI, calls 'the making it happen gap'.

Figure 7.5 may help to illustrate this point.

What Figure 7.5 shows is that there are two clear activities. The first is a process that allows people to be sure and committed to what needs to be done, and the second is a process that recognizes achievement or success. It is this recognition aspect that is one of the most powerful tools.

The following describes the importance of getting the recognition right.

This example is about a company that operated a discretionary bonus scheme. Nobody understood how the bonus really worked or what it was worth until the bonus cheque arrived at the end of the year. At the end of the year in question, one young man received a bonus which was 100% of his salary. He had worked very hard and was very successful, so he was delighted with his bonus and went off to celebrate. Whilst at the local bar he discovered that another young man, who sat a few desks away and who generally was regarded by colleagues as a failure, was also celebrating the fact that he had received a 100% bonus. On discovering this, our first young man left the bar, went straight back to his desk, phoned up the search consultant who had found him the job in the first place, and told the consultant he wanted to move because he was not appreciated, the company's incentive scheme was rubbish, nobody recognized his contribution and so on. The moral of this case is that it cost the company a lot of money for a bonus that clearly did not have the desired effect. It also cost the company an equal amount to encourage behaviours that they did not want and it would probably cost them even more money to replace the star they had just demotivated. The cause of this unforeseen expenditure was due to the company's belief that throwing money at people was all that was required.

So the argument has progressed a stage further by observing that:

- paying money is a powerful form of recognition
- money is important but not all-important, and
- it is not about how much, but more about how money is used to recognize achievement.

The point here is that simple response/reward behavioural techniques cannot be applied to business, because businesses cannot wait around for the appropriate random behavioural action and then reward it – a kind of 'well done' payment. Most businesses today want to be much more proactive, so that the behavioural or business targets are identified in advance and achievement is incentivized accordingly. This leads us to the business model approach.

## The business model approach

The argument postulated so far is that to design appropriate reward programmes, then first we must consider the business. It would lead on from this that what should be considered is the way businesses work and how this relates to the remuneration policies. To do this, it is not necessary to go into a great deal of business strategy but merely to look at some simple business models that will steer us toward the reward policy solutions.

Figure 7.6 will help to put the basic business activities into place.

First of all, a business needs to have a vision of what it wants to be, how it intends to conduct business and what it will look like in future years. This might seem to be a very obvious statement, but we have all seen businesses that lose their vision and find it increasingly difficult to bring logic to their business plans. Sometimes this 'vision' is called a 'brand image' and this is what successful entrepreneurs hang on to as they develop their businesses with apparent breakneck speed and boundless energy. One of Britain's most successful entrepreneurs must be Sir Richard Branson. Whilst being interviewed by Andrew Main Wilson at the Institute of Directors Annual Convention in April 2003,

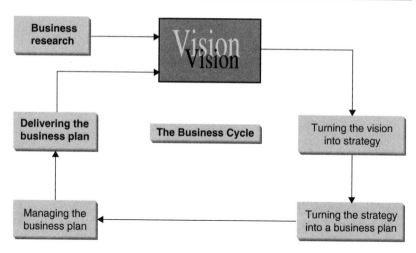

**Figure 7.6** The business cycle.

Sir Richard gave an insight into his operational style. He confessed that he left the finances to the financiers, the marketing to the marketeers, business law to the lawyers, tax to the accountants, but strongly defended his role in maintaining the Virgin brand image for his group of companies, stating that this is one of the most important duties of a head of a business.

Once the image is established and understood (which probably will require considerable market research), then the process of turning the vision into a business strategy is embarked upon. This in turn will result in a more detailed plan of what should happen in future years (the business plan). Finally, delivering the business plan will entail who is going to do what and by when (personal performance plans). So the cycle continues. It is cyclical because by their very nature businesses do not sit still – the old chestnut that goes 'in business if you are standing still you are actually going backwards relative to your competitors' is a truism that we will all do well to remember even in times of recession.

Progressing from the business cycle, the functional effect on the business needs to be considered and to help to do this let us turn to the strategy and look at the strategic business cycle model.

In this cycle examples are given to suggest some of the strategies that might be the result of a business vision. Clearly these strategies need to be defined so that everyone involved in the business has the same

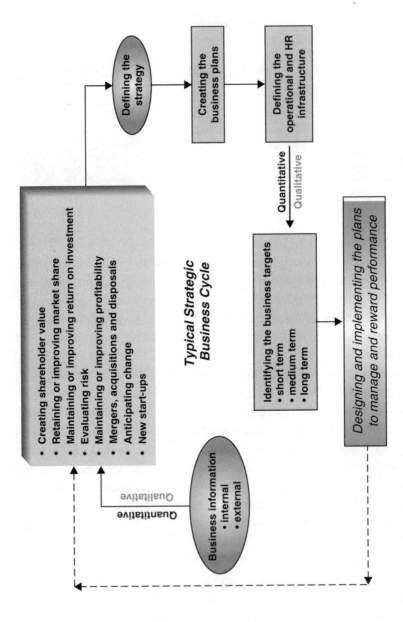

**Figure 7.7** Strategic business cycle model.

understanding of what the strategies mean. This then leads on to the business plan, as previously described, but now we need to turn our attention not only to the availability and organization of the physical resources required in the business, but also to the people resources. This will entail decisions on how many people are needed, how they will be organized in teams, departments, divisions, etc. and what the business wants them to achieve. This will lead to identifying business targets for individual roles. The business targets are already available in broad detail within the strategy and business plans, but now they need to become more specific and ascribed to roles within the organization.

While in this general planning mode, it is also important to think about how we are going to recognize when an individual has achieved his or her targets. It does not necessarily need to be money, although money is usually the recognition currency of business performance. Note that this is the first time in the cycle that money incentives have been mentioned.

However, business is a collective effort and the different parts of the business need to work in harmony – we cannot have everyone rushing around oblivious to what their colleagues are trying to achieve.

There is one more model in this sequence that we need to consider before we can get down to the serious business of setting targets for people and providing incentives for them to achieve their targets. To do this we need to look at the basic functions of a typical business (Figure 7.8).

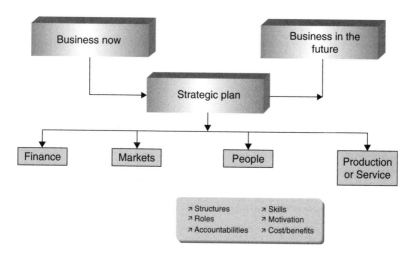

**Figure 7.8** Basic business functions.

Now all this might sound fairly obvious but how often, when we are setting business targets, do we start at the top of the business, consider the interaction between the core functions and set targets accordingly? So often we encourage the production people to concentrate upon production, the finance people to only consider the numbers, the sales people just to sell more, etc. Businesses are required to work in harmony. If that debate has not occurred, then the chances are that the incentive plan may be allowing some people to earn considerably more money, but it is not actually helping the business to achieve its strategic goals. Some of this is about communication and some of it is actually about having the right tools for the job.

In communication terms, let us look at the organization in terms of trust and clarity. The trust/clarity test is a way to see whether the organization is together about where it is going and what it wants to achieve. The results of one such test are shown in Figure 7.9.

Having conducted a climate study, the scores on trust are placed along the a/b axis and scores for clarity along the c/d axis. In this example, point E represents the average employee score and point M the average management score. From this we can see that the employees generally trust the management – they may have come through some tough times lately but they are still in employment so, in general, they have concluded that the management must be doing something right. However, when it comes to clarity they are not very sure about what the

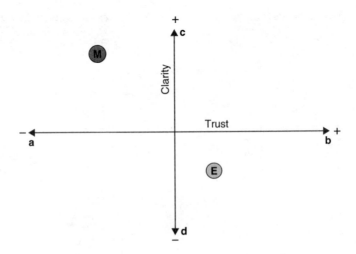

**Figure 7.9** The trust/clarity test.

management's general game plan is – the vision and strategy have not been spelt out particularly well.

As far as the management is concerned, they are clear about the direction of the company but are not very sure that the employees will follow them. This is a fairly typical situation and sometimes, although the incentive plan is in place, it has not been communicated very well or the plan has not been designed in a business-led fashion.

Clearly, had the employees average score been registered in the a/d sector, then some serious repair work to the communication process would have been required and it would certainly not have been the environment in which to introduce a performance incentive plan. Ideally, the c/d sector is where the company should be aiming.

Let us assume that we have achieved the appropriate score in the example above and it is decided to introduce a business-led performance incentive plan. What is needed now is to decide the performance criteria, how to communicate the criteria and how to gain commitment to the targets from all those involved.

This is where a tool-kit of strategic performance instruments is useful. A typical tool-kit would be as outlined below.

## I.   A strategic diagnostic model

The purpose of this model is to carry out an in-depth analysis of the strategic direction of the company and in particular look for the strategic goals that the company wishes to achieve. In other words, it is looking at the company's strategy and business plans in a very performance-orientated manner.

In-depth interviews would be conducted at the highest level – the CEO and perhaps also with his or her close senior colleagues.

## II.   Key business driver diagnostic

From the strategic model the key drivers of the business would be identified and organized into the core functions, typically the:

- financial/commercial function
- production/service function
- sales/marketing function, and
- human resource function.

These key drivers need to be agreed with the CEO and the senior team. Agreement is an important step because the key business drivers are the backbone from which the performance plans will be built and will cascade down the company.

## III.   Defining the key drivers

Having defined the key drivers it is now necessary to ensure that everyone has a common understanding of what each of the drivers mean. At this stage in the process, a group of leading managers and directors would be asked to sit together to define each of the key business drivers that have been identified. For example, what do we really mean by cash flow, what does market presence mean in our organization and what is customer awareness, to quote a few key business drivers that may have been identified. It is important to record these definitions because then everyone has a glossary of terms, appropriate to their particular company, when they are debating who is responsible for what. It is surprising on how many occasions words to describe core business drivers are regularly used without everyone having a clear understanding of their meaning. Hence a great deal of time is wasted debating the meaning rather than spending the time on debating how the key driver can be managed more effectively.

## IV.   Accountability workshops

Accountability workshops operate on a fairly simple yet very effective set of principles. Having identified the key business drivers for the business, and defined them, it is time to decide who is accountable for their delivery.

Clearly the CEO needs to delegate – he or she cannot be responsible for everything but, at the same time, it is ineffective to suppose that the senior management team has collective accountability for everything that goes on in the business. The debate usually starts with the senior team and spreads out and down the organization in a logical and organized fashion.

A matrix is drawn up with the key business drivers along one side, divided into the core business functions, and the team members along the top, as shown in Figure 7.10.

**1. Business Performance (Financial/Commercial):** *Team Member*

*Improving the financial strength and status of the organization; developing and delivering the annual plan; achieving the long-term strategic plan.*

*Business Driver*

| Key Business Results Driver | CC (Div MD) | RW (FD) | KB (Strat) | TG (Cust Serv) | HM (Hol.) | JR (IDS) | AB (BP) | JP (TS) | BC (Inter) |
|---|---|---|---|---|---|---|---|---|---|
| 1.1 Operating profit (i) Divisional | 1/P/C | 2/F/C | 2/T/C | 2/T/C | 3/T/C | 3/T/C | 3/T/C | 3/T/C | 3/T/C |
| (ii) Business unit | 1/T/C | 2/T/C | 2/T/C | 2/J/C | 3/P/Bu | 3/P/Bu | 3/P/Bu | 3/P/Bu | 3/P/Bu |
| 1.2 Operating cash flow | 1/T/C | 2/T/C | 2/T/C | 2/J/C | 3/P/Bu | 3/P/Bu | 3/P/Bu | 3/P/Bu | 3/P/Bu |
| 1.3 Capital expenditure (i) applications | 1/T/C | 2/F/C | – | 2/P/C | 3/P/Bu | 3/P/Bu | 3/P/Bu | 3/P/Bu | 3/P/Bu |
| (ii) approvals | 1/P/C | 2/F/C | 2/T/C | 2/J/C | 3/P/Bu | 3/P/Bu | 3/P/Bu | 3/P/Bu | 3/P/Bu |
| 1.4 Overheads (control) (i) sales and marketing | 1/T/C | – | 2/P/Dp | – | 3/P/Bu | 3/P/Bu | 3/P/Bu | 3/P/Bu | 3/P/Bu |
| (ii) operational | 1/T/C | – | – | 2/P/C | 3/P/Bu | 3/J/Bu | 3/J/Bu | 3/J/Bu | 3/J/Bu |
| (iii) R&D | 1/T/C | – | 2/F/C | – | 3/P/Bu | 3/P/Bu | 3/P/Bu | 3/P/Bu | 3/P/Bu |
| 1.5 Order generation | 1/T/C | – | 2/T/C | 2/T/C | 3/P/Bu | 3/P/Bu | 3/P/Bu | 3/P/Bu | 3/P/Bu |
| 1.6 Sales generation | 1/T/C | – | 2/T/C | 2/T/C | 3/P/Bu | 3/P/Bu | 3/P/Bu | 3/P/Bu | 3/P/Bu |
| 1.7 Management information (i) inputs | 1/T/C | 2/P/Dp | – | 2/F/C | 3/P/Bu | 3/P/Bu | 3/P/Bu | 3/P/Bu | 3/P/Bu |

*Target Analysis*   *Role Specification*   *Accountability Definition*   *Collective Accountabilities*

**Figure 7.10** Matrix of business drivers and team members.

A shorthand method of describing prime accountabilities is as follows: particular key business driver (P), secondary accountabilities (S), accountabilities for key drivers that are shared with other members of the team (SH), accountabilities for a business driver that are delegated to more junior employees (D), etc. are usually shown up as a useful method of managing the information.

At the end of the workshop we have a complete record of who is accountable for what and the foundation for formulating the individual performance targets. The workshops are then repeated down the organization, with each head of department or head of section being present.

## V. Performance plans

Having defined what individual roles are accountable to deliver, it is comparatively simple to draw up the performance plans. First of all, we look at the prime accountabilities against each key business driver and decide on an appropriate performance objective – in other words, what the individual is going to do to support the accountability. Now a target will be assigned and finally we need to know how we can measure when the target has been achieved, so a 'measure' is recorded.

Using this process, one can be confident about a number of key elements that are central to developing an effective performance plan. These are:

1 Starting at the top of the organization to identify the key business drivers means that everyone is using the same method to arrive at the performance measures.
2 When setting targets we need to be sure everyone is pursuing the same goals. It is always suspicious when organizations decide to develop a performance plan which excludes the senior management team, or indeed the middle management team, because it is difficult to identify the source and the continuity of purpose without key players.
3 There is a common understanding and usage of terminology, particularly in terms of the key business drivers, because these terms have been defined for each particular business.

It is the lack of these key performance elements that cause many performance plans to break down and become non-effective.

## Recognizing performance

Having decided upon the performance targets, attention is turned to the development of a means of recognizing the achievement of those targets.

Normally this is in the form of a monetary reward, but care is needed here because reward means different things to different people. For jobs that require a great deal of creativity or are in scientific research and development, a monetary reward may not be the most appropriate way forward. If one is not careful, it is easy to apply oversimplified, generalized targets that are actually counter-productive. For example, the simplest way for R&D people to achieve their operating budget is for them not to do any research. By applying an operating budget achievement target to the R&D people, we can end up incentivizing them to do no work and to put the company out of business five or 10 years hence. However, for the purposes of this discussion, let us consider the more usual performance route.

Previously, short-term incentive bonus design was largely about discretionary bonuses, which really meant that nobody had any idea what the bonus was worth until it was paid and then it was unclear how it was actually calculated. Today, there is an emphasis on transparency.

This means that it is necessary to have an understanding about what the incentive payments are likely to be, in various performance scenarios, before the plan is communicated.

In order to calculate the effect of the various scenarios it is recommended that a financial model be developed, because we need to know the financial resources that may be required. There are many routes to achieving this, but basic principles apply in most, if not all, incentive bonus designs. The cost benefit model illustrated in Figure 7.11 helps to describe these principles.

The corporate performance line, which may be revenues or profits or some other corporate measure, is shown. The target is set and overheads

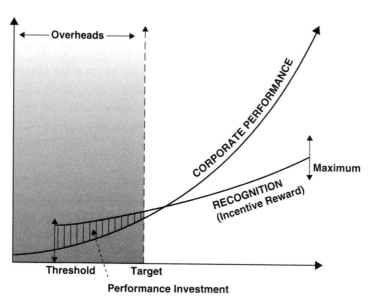

**Figure 7.11** The cost benefit model for the compensation policy.

are included in the target-setting process. The reason that the corporate performance line rises so steeply is because once the company achieves target, the overheads, being largely fixed regardless of corporate performance, have a diminishing effect as the company's performance moves beyond the target.

In the model we can now construct a 'recognition' line, which determines the pool available for performance incentive rewards. In constructing this line there are a number of basic considerations to be made:

## I.  The performance target starting point

The performance starting point is a decision involving whether we are merely going to pay for better than target performance or are we going to encourage individuals to achieve target and beyond? This is a vital consideration because the simple 'better than target' approach can become a disincentive if, fairly early on in the performance period, it becomes obvious that reaching target is going to be very difficult, if not impossible, to achieve.

## II.  The performance threshold

Many organizations today believe that the start point or 'threshold' should be set before the target so that employees are encouraged to achieve target. This is often called 'investing in performance' because the company is taking an investment risk if the target is not reached and yet some performance bonus payments will have to be made. The extent of this risk can be reduced by flattening the slope of the line before the target and making a steeper slope after target is achieved. This is sometimes referred to as the 'gearing effect' of incentive design and serves as a double incentive whereby the further beyond the target line individuals perform, the greater is the ratio of return for their achievements. Another way to reduce the risk is to move the target line to the right to compensate for the performance investment below 100% of target.

## III.  Maximum performance level

Another decision to be made is whether or not to set a maximum performance level. The argument for setting maximum target levels, particularly in financial service organizations, is to avoid paying for windfalls which, by their nature, have not been created by the employees. Here again, decisions on this will depend very much on the corporate style and culture of the organization, showing again that even with incentive design models, decisions involve the message that the organization is trying to put across and are not restricted to the numbers alone.

## IV.  Short-, medium- and long-term plans

Incentive design today is becoming rather sophisticated in the financial services sector, as many of the financial instruments used in investment banking are being adapted for use in incentive rewards. Options, puts, Black–Scholes calculations, deferrals into hedge funds, carried interest, etc. all have their origins in banking and are also to be found in incentive design. The objectives of the organization may be to have a mixture of short-, medium- and long-term plans, and these have to be funded and the risks calculated. Until recently, long-term incentives in the form of share options were considered to be outside the area of direct impact on the company's profits. However, with the increasing volume of opinion that share option plans are a form of remuneration, which have an impact on shareholder value and therefore need to be 'expensed' in the profit and loss account, in future all long-term plans will need to be brought into the cost and risk calculation. Because of this there is today a great deal of interest in deferrals, i.e. how much of the incentive should be paid immediately and how much should be deferred until a later date – possibly based on a medium- or long-term target. The principles of this model are shown in Figure 7.12.

In this model we see the bonus pool being split each year, part of which goes towards an annual payment and part being deferred into a longer-term pool. This longer-term pool then builds up and in year 3 a longer-term formula is applied according to the corporate achievements over the longer-term period.

The advantages of this type of design are:

1  Annual bonus payments can be made in cash and longer-term payments can be made in either cash or equity.
2  The short-term performance can fund or partially fund the longer-term incentive.

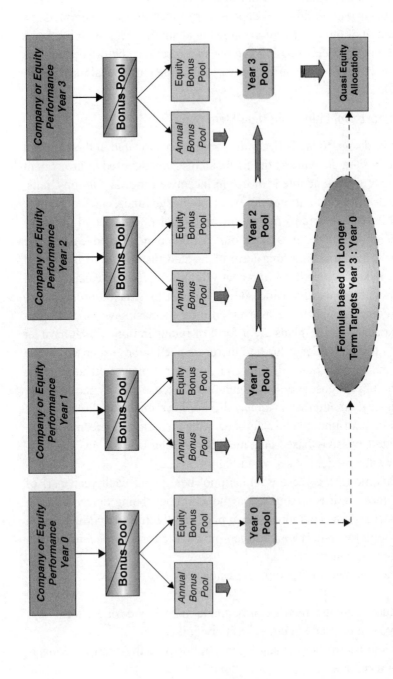

**Figure 7.12** Deferred incentive plan model.

3 Different targets for short-term and longer-term performance can be accommodated.

4 There is a retention period. In this model individuals only receive the deferred part of their annual bonus after year 3. From year 3, when the long-term element kicks in, they receive a double reward based on how they have added value to the company over the deferral period.

5 From year 3 and beyond there is a very strong retention element, because if an employee leaves the company there is a possibility that they may leave behind two years' worth of (yet to be calculated) long-term incentive. It is important therefore that these types of plans set out 'good' and 'bad' leaver conditions from the outset.

This type of arrangement is likely to receive shareholder approval because the short- and long-term aspects of the business are being catered for in the same way that the shareholder would like to protect his or her investment. This approval will be particularly relevant if the reward from the longer-term pool is in the form of company shares.

## Benefits

The final part of the package is the benefits package and at the present time the whole area of benefits is undergoing a sea change. It used to be that the value of the benefits part of the package was not really appreciated. This was probably because everyone received them and it appeared to be a corporate responsibility that benefits such as pensions, healthcare, life assurance, holidays, etc. were provided. However, in the last decade the cost of providing the benefits package has risen so enormously that companies have reviewed, and in many cases cut back on, the benefits they provide.

This has given rise to flexible benefit packages, which means that the employee is offered the choice of cash or benefits, or some mixture of both.

The idea of flexible benefit packages originated in the USA and was driven by the cost of providing healthcare insurance. It was estimated that, in the 1990s, the average American company spent nearly 15% of its payroll on providing healthcare. Many organizations had remuneration policies based on the premise that their employees were all male, their wives did not work, and they had 2.4 children aged 14 and 11. For most companies this 40 years of age profile only applied to about 10% of their employees and, consequently, a range of benefits was being offered that did not apply and was not valued by a large proportion of the employee population. Let us consider a family where both the partners have careers and both are eligible for healthcare. In a flexible situation, this couple would probably gladly give up one of the healthcare entitlements for something like childminder or crèche facilities, even if the cash equivalent were less than the healthcare package value. So the concept of flexible benefits was born and many organizations found that they could reduce the cost of their benefits package if employees were given a choice. The pay-off for employees was that they received the benefits they really wanted, or a cash alternative, at a time in their lives when the benefit or cash was really important to them.

The theory of flexible benefits developed around three models. The original model was a totally flexible one, so the employee could choose from a wide range of benefits or cash. However, this system was found to be very difficult to administer because the advantages of group purchase were lost and employees could trade essential benefits such as pensions.

The flexible benefits package then developed into what became known as the 'modular system', whereby there was a choice of four or five different benefits and cash packages reflecting the various age ranges and lifestyles of the workforce. The employee had a choice of plan, but the choice was limited and the company maintained a greater degree of control than in the total discretionary plan.

Today, most flexible benefits plans are based upon what is now called the 'core plus' plan. In this type of plan, the employee has to accept a core of cash and benefits and then may choose from a selection of non-core benefits. For example, the core may contain single-status medical insurance because if the employee became ill, speedy treatment could be arranged, ensuring a rapid return to work. The plus part may offer a choice of medical insurance for the employee's partner and children. If the employee is unmarried, then family medical cover may not be chosen and instead the choice may be the cash alternative or some other benefit more suitable to the employee's lifestyle.

Although most companies appreciate the value of a flex approach, and the package for directors has typically alwa' ible element, introducing such a plan is not easy and a gi... thought and administrative resources have to be provided in order for it to run effectively. One of the difficulties is dealing with the pension benefits, particularly as many companies have considered their commitment to final salary pension schemes.

Massive changes in the way pension benefits are provided to employees are occurring both in the UK and the USA. For example, in the UK the Pension Fund Partnership in June 2002 surveyed 269 occupational pension plans. This sample contained 220 defined benefits plans, of which 25% have closed their membership – 22% are now closed to new members and a further 3% are closed to both new and existing members. A further 21% reported that it was likely or very likely that their defined benefits plan would be closed to new members during the next 12 months.

Debbie Lovewell, writing in *Employee Benefits* magazine in May 2003, described the idea for a halfway house between final salary plans and defined contribution plans, called 'CARE' plans, which stands for 'Career Average Revalued Earnings' plans. CARE plans are seen to be easier to 'sell' to employees if a company is moving away from a final salary plan because of the way that they are calculated. Typically there is an annual calculation on average career earnings, which can be linked to an inflation index (such as the Retail Prices Index). CARE plans are viewed as plans in which employees and employers share the investment risk.

## Conclusion

Designing a reward package is clearly not the relatively simple exercise of putting some salary numbers together in such a way that they roughly equate to similar businesses in similar industries. As we have seen from the discussion above, the fact that we need people to run our businesses and institutions, and that their behaviour, motivation, loyalty and perceptions are not totally predictable, makes the whole subject of pay and performance fascinating and frustrating, possibly in equal measure.

However, there are a number of tenets that can safely be followed in reward design:

1 The reward design cannot be created without due regard and in harmony with the organization's strategic aspirations.
2 Reward design is not just another human resource department task. It is a managerial requirement that should involve the active input of all the functions of the business.
3 There must be a logic to setting performance targets for individuals and that logic should be demonstrated through a direct path back to the overall corporate goals.
4 Effective targets are not just about single ratios such as profits.
5 Reward packages *and* performance targets are dependent upon the individual's key tasks, job level and job discipline.
6 Team work as well as individual contribution are usually required and should feature in the plan.
7 Whereas management must act as champions for the reward policy, employees need to feel involved.
8 Middle management also must be involved so that they become facilitators not bottlenecks.
9 Like the creation of corporate strategies, reward design must involve research so that financial and attitudinal risk is fully understood by the management team.

## Case studies

The two case studies below, taken from two different companies with very different needs, are included to demonstrate:

- the need to understand the requirements of the business
- that achieving 'buy-in' from the participants is an essential part of a successful plan
- how sensitively designed performance incentive plans can be a positive tool for senior management for the achievement of corporate business goals, and
- how it is possible to combine short- and longer-term targets within one plan.

## Case study 1: An investment bank

### Situation

Whereas the mainstream activities of an investment bank are fairly clear and easily measured for performance purposes, the support services such as legal, finance, human resources, etc. are not as transparent in business terms. This bank had no doubts about the fact that effective support services were important to the success of the organization as a whole. However, there were some concerns about how these activities could be actively rather than passively managed. It was argued that if these activities were not capable of being actively managed, then they could not be part of an incentive reward plan. The incentive reward plan was based on the principle that greater success in the achievement of targets (that could be traced back to the strategic goals of the business) resulted in higher incentive payments for those involved in support functions.

### Project scope

Design and implement a strategically aligned performance management plan and incentive plan for the bank's major support departments and link this to an incentive plan.

### Key project activities

1 Conduct a strategic alignment exercise – this involved analysing the bank's strategic strategy and goals.
2 Key business driver analysis – this involved identifying and defining the key business drivers arising from the strategy analysis and, in particular, identifying those drivers that were associated with support functions.
3 Accountability identification matrix – in a workshop environment provide the support function executives with the opportunity to discuss and create a matrix of their individual and collective accountabilities for the key business drivers.
4 Personal performance plans – from the agreed accountability matrix, discuss with each executive how they are to deliver their

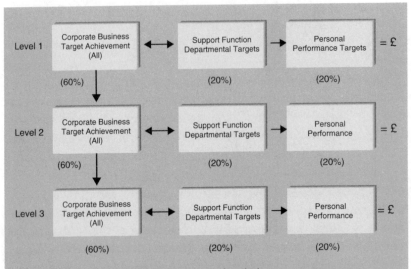

**Figure 7.13** Support function – incentive plan design.

prime accountabilities in terms of objective, measurement and target.

5 Design a performance incentive plan for the support functions based on the delivery of their collective and individual performance plans (see Figure 7.13).

The cascade shown above works as follows. Senior management or the board sets the overall corporate target. This target is determined at the beginning of the performance period and is communicated to all participants. The 'support function departmental targets' are related to the corporate target and these targets facilitate the achievement of the corporate targets. For example, a target for the finance department might be to have all the financial budgeting completed by a specific date each year. Similarly, the marketing department might be required to complete all its market analysis and forecasts in a specific product area by a defined time target. In the same manner, the personal targets can be those that have been agreed through the performance appraisal process.

## Case study 2: Project management company – Middle East

### Situation

Discretionary performance incentive plans can operate successfully in small companies, where communication lines are relatively short. However, there comes a time when the company becomes too complex or too large for the management to retain control of such discretionary plans.

Reluctantly, this organization found this to be the case and decided to adopt a more formal approach to their performance management policies. Furthermore, the promise of a job for life was no longer a viable proposition, so some sort of longer-term incentive that could eventually be linked to an equity acquisition plan was also required.

### Project scope

Design and implement a performance management and incentive plan incorporating both short- and longer-term elements.

In these plans we were to take into account the traditional role complexities, wherein some executives and management had responsibilities across a number of different divisions in the organization.

### Result

1. *The short-term bonus design.* Figure 7.14 shows how the annual bonus was designed, taking in the corporate, divisional and personal targets. The financial model that underpinned this scheme was able to calculate how much was available for bonus distribution. The source for the bonus pool was through the achievement of a profit target. To guard against windfalls, the maximum bonus pool was set at 15% of PBIT (profit before interest and taxation).
2. *Combining the short- and longer-term incentive elements.* This company decided to follow the current trend of using an incentive plan methodology that combined both short- and long-term invectives within the same incentive model. Figure 7.15 demonstrates this model.

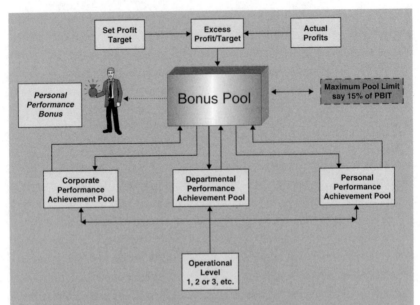

**Figure 7.14** Short-term bonus design.

In this model, in year 1 the proportion of profit target achievement earmarked for the incentive plan is paid into the 'company bonus pool'. In this case, 40% of the pool is paid out as an annual bonus and 60% is retained or 'deferred' within a 'long-term bonus pool'. Similarly, annual bonus payments are made in year 2 and 60% of the money available for the pool is retained and the 'year 2 pool' now has accumulated 60% of year 1 and 60% of year 2 incentive payments. The same occurs in year 3. However, in year 4 two incentive payments are made. The annual bonus is paid again, but in this year a long-term payment is also made. This long-term payment is calculated as 33% of the accumulated long-term bonus pool. In this model, both a short-term annual bonus and a long-term incentive payment will be made in year 4 and in each year thereafter.

The advantages of this type of incentive are:

■ Short- and long-term target achievements are rewarded separately but according to the same general principles.

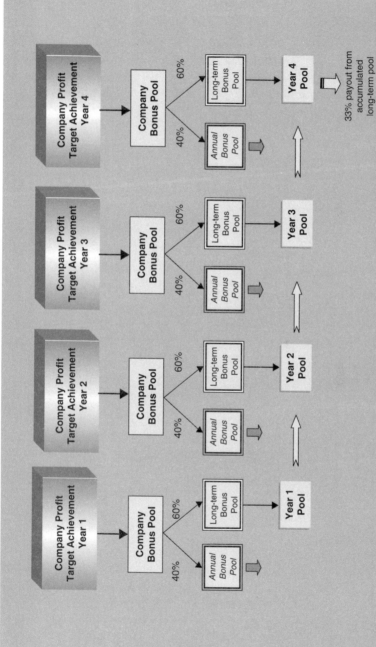

**Figure 7.15** Example of an incentive plan combining short- and longer-term elements.

- If 'good and bad leaver' conditions are applied, then someone leaving to join a competitor will be likely to forfeit at least two years of accumulated long-term incentives.
- Financing the incentive is relatively simple.
- Long-term payments can be made in the form of cash or shares. If they are made in the form of shares, then careful design of share allocation within a tax-effective plan may well be possible, giving an added financial incentive to the plan.

# 8

# Equity incentives

Wayne Guay, David Larcker and John Core

## Introduction

Equity incentives are the measure of economic motivation created by the shares, stock options and restricted stock held by an executive. Equity incentives are an increasingly important feature of the contracting environment between shareholders (as represented by the board of directors) and executives. For example, Hall and Murphy (2002) report that, in 1998, the median values of stock and options held by Standard & Poor's Industrial CEOs and Standard & Poor's Financial CEOs were $30 million and $55 million, respectively. Similarly, Core et al. (2003) report that over the time period from 1993 to 1998, the average ratio of equity portfolio value to annual total pay was 30.3 for CEOs. Our goal in this chapter is to highlight some of the controversies surrounding equity incentives and to provide a synthesis of the academic research on these topics.

## Equity incentives and organizational performance

Despite extensive research, there is little theoretical or empirical consensus on how stock options and/or equity ownership affect firm performance. Early studies such as Morck et al. (1988) argue that, on average, observed CEO equity ownership and incentives are 'too low'. If this is true, one expects to observe that firm performance is an increasing function of CEO equity incentives. Morck et al. (1988) find some evidence consistent with this hypothesis, except among CEOs with very large equity ownership. McConnell and Servaes (1990) find consistent evidence of a positive relation between increases in ownership and firm performance so long as managerial ownership is less than 50%. More recently, researchers have begun exploring the performance implications of stock options. Sesil et al. (2000) find mixed evidence of a positive relation between firm performance and option use intensity. Ittner et al. (2003) find that the relation between option grants and firm performance varies across organizational levels within a sample of new economy firms, and Hanlon et al. (2003) argue that their results indicate stock option grants to executives increase future operating performance.

In contrast to studies that view equity incentives as being 'too low' and that expect a positive relation between firm performance and stock option grants, Demsetz and Lehn (1985), Core and Guay (1999), and Himmelberg et al. (1999) develop an alternative prediction about the relation between equity incentives and performance. These authors conjecture that firms and managers contract optimally, and that managerial ownership levels are set at the value-maximizing level based on firm and manager characteristics. For example, higher (lower) ownership is predicted in firms where more (less) monitoring of executives is required. From this perspective, no simple ex-ante relation between ownership and firm performance is expected. That is, low ownership firms are not necessarily expected to perform poorly, since it might be the case that these firms do not require high-powered equity incentives to ensure that managers take appropriate actions. Similarly, high ownership firms use high-powered equity incentives to resolve serious monitoring problems, not because they expect that high incentive levels will allow them to achieve positive abnormal performance.

Perhaps a more realistic scenario is that firms choose optimal managerial equity incentives when they contract with executives, but that transaction costs prohibit continuous recontracting. Since contracting is not continuous, firms' ownership levels can gradually deviate from the optimal level. This means that a subset of firms always has misaligned incentives and that recontracting for these firms (subject to transaction costs) should produce performance improvements. Core and Larcker (2002) explore this approach in the context of target ownership plans and find that these plans cause executive ownership to increase and that this increase in equity incentives is associated with improvements in subsequent stock market and operating performance.

Despite considerable prior research and rhetoric in the business community, the performance consequences of equity ownership remain an open question. In large part, this lack of conclusive evidence stems from the difficulty in conducting powerful tests of this relation. Larcker (2003) discusses many of the methodological issues that make it difficult to provide empirical tests for the relation between equity and stock option grants and firm performance. Clearly, the need for 'high-powered' incentives varies across firms, and thus greater equity ownership by a particular executive does not necessarily imply that managers have appropriate incentives or that organizational performance will be stronger. Overall, there is no simple theoretical or empirical relation between equity incentives and organization performance.

## Efficiency of equity compensation

Lambert et al. (1991) point out that, to understand the equity incentives, one must consider the manager's entire portfolio of wealth, which consists of both firm-specific wealth such as stock and options, and outside wealth that is likely invested in diversified assets. Their model illustrates that when a firm uses equity compensation to impose additional risk on a risk-averse and undiversified manager, the manager will value the compensation at less than the risk-neutral firm's value of the compensation. For example, the manager's valuation of a stock option can be less than 50% of the Black–Scholes value when the manager is constrained to hold 50% of his total wealth in firm stock. The central insight of Lambert et al. (1991) is that shareholders (or the board of directors) must consider the entire structure of the manager's wealth when determining the optimal contracting arrangement.

Hall and Murphy (2002) replicate and extend Lambert et al. (1991) to make some prescriptions about the structure of current equity compensation. In particular, they argue that stock and options are an inefficient means of providing executive compensation. The intuition is that paying compensation to a risk-averse executive in stock or options can be more costly to the firm than delivering the same value to the executive in cash. This is unquestionably true if the effect of the compensation is solely to increase the amount of risk imposed on the executive and incentive effects of the stock options are ignored (Core and Guay, 2003; Lambert and Larcker, 2003).

As an example, consider an executive with total wealth of $20 million and with only two investment choices: firm stock and the market portfolio. Assume that the executive would prefer to hold only the market portfolio, but is required via a contract to hold $10 million of firm stock. Further, assume that the executive is constrained from selling any existing holdings and cannot rebalance portfolio holdings when the executive receives a compensation payment in the form of an option grant with Black–Scholes value of $1 million (in other words, the firm gives the executive compensation and simultaneously increases the risk imposed on the executive by not allowing portfolio rebalancing).

Now consider how the executive values the $1 million option grant in this setting. After the grant, the executive has $11 million in equity, which is further away from the executive's preferred level of stockholdings. Because the executive cannot implement any portfolio rebalancing and is not provided with a compensating risk premium, the executive values this option grant at less than its Black–Scholes value of $1 million. Since the value perceived by the executive can be substantially below the cost to the firm, Hall and Murphy (2002) conclude that equity grants are an expensive (and inefficient) form of compensation.

Although this conclusion may seem straightforward, Core and Guay (2003) demonstrate that the logic of Hall and Murphy (2002) is open to debate. Core and Guay note that empirical evidence documents that firms grant stock and options to executives for many reasons unrelated to risk-level adjustments, such as to conserve cash and reduce financing costs, to reduce constraints on reported earnings by taking advantage of the non-deductibility of stock option expense, and to manage taxes. Empirical evidence also suggests that the level of executives' equity incentives are determined as part of an employment contract, and that executives engage in portfolio rebalancing in response to stock and option grants (e.g. Janakiraman, 1998; Core and Guay, 1999, 2001; Heath et al., 1999; Ofek and Yermack, 2000).

To see the importance of these distinctions, assume that the executive's holdings of firm equity are not exogenous, but are instead part of an optimal employment contract that motivates the executive to exert the optimal effort and take the optimal actions by imposing risk on the executive. Specifically, assume the contract imposes the optimal incentives by requiring the executive to hold exactly $10 million dollars of firm stock. Further, assume that the executive is allowed/required to rebalance portfolio holdings over time to maintain the agreed level of incentives. This is an efficient policy from the firm's perspective because it is costly to impose more than the optimal level of risk on the executive.

Under this alternative scenario, consider how this executive values a $1 million grant of options. Because the executive is allowed to implement portfolio rebalancing and sell $1 million of existing stock holdings at their market value and still maintain the contracted level of firm equity, the executive will value the option grant at its market value (less transactions costs). Using similar logic and assumptions, Core and Guay (2003) show that the executive also values an increase in the value of his stock and option portfolio at its market value. This conclusion again follows from the assumption that the risk-averse executive can rebalance his portfolio following an increase in its value back to the contractual, optimal level of incentives given the contracting environment. Thus, under these assumptions, the value and incentives inherent in the Black–Scholes model may be a reasonable approximation for the executive's valuation of stock and option grants and his portfolio incentives to increase the stock price.

We see two key unresolved issues in the debate over the valuation and efficiency of equity compensation. One issue is developing a better understanding of the extent to which the benefits received by the firm from imposing risk on executives meet or exceed the cost of imposing this risk, i.e. the extent to which observed contracts are optimal. As discussed in a recent paper by Lambert and Larcker (2003), one can make reasonable assumptions about the incentive effects of stock and stock options, and show that simple prescriptions, such as less options are better or more options are better, are clearly false. A second issue is exploring the extent to which contracting costs, transactions costs and other frictions limit executives' ability to rebalance their stock and option portfolios in response to equity grants and changes in equity portfolio value.

## Relative performance evaluation

A widespread concern among both practitioners and academics is that executive portfolios lack 'relative performance evaluation' (RPE) or, equivalently, that stock and stock options gain value not only because the firm performs well, but also because the stock market rises. For example, Abowd and Kaplan (1999, p. 162) remark:

*Stock options reward stock price appreciation regardless of the performance of the economy or sector.* Why should CEOs be rewarded for doing nothing more than riding the wave of a strong bull market? *[emphasis added] If the exercise price could be linked to measures like the S&P 500, or an index of close product-market competitors, then executives would be rewarded for gains in stock price in excess of those explainable by market factors outside their control. If market-wide stock movements could be netted out of executive incentive schemes, then equivalent incentives could be provided while reducing the volatility of the executives' portfolios.*

A central tenet of agency theory is that compensation contracts filter out systematic noise through relative performance evaluation. Janakiraman et al. (1992), Antle and Smith (1986), Gibbons and Murphy (1992), and others have found relatively little evidence that the annual bonus portion of executive compensation exhibits RPE. However, given that most of a CEO's incentives come from his or her equity portfolio, the lack of *explicit* RPE in a bonus payment does not imply the lack of *implicit* RPE in the overall contract. Casual empiricism observes large stock and option portfolios, and assumes there is no RPE. That is, if firms use RPE, one might expect to see explicitly indexed CEO contracts, where the CEO holds securities that only expose him or her to idiosyncratic firm performance and effectively remove systematic risk from the CEO's performance evaluation. However, while there may be no *explicit* RPE in CEOs' stock and option portfolios, there is considerable *implicit* RPE in these portfolios (Core and Guay, 2003).

To see how implicit RPE arises, note that CEOs hold equity portfolios that reflect the terms of their employment contracts, not the portfolios they would choose in the absence of constraints. Portfolio theory predicts that a rational, risk-averse CEO would hold *no* stock in their firm (in the absence of private information), and instead would have *all* of their wealth invested in a diversified portfolio.[1] That is, a CEO will generally hold a substantial quantity of stock in his or her firm only if required to do so as part of the compensation contract (e.g. for incentive reasons).[2]

Now imagine that a firm hires a new CEO who owns $100 million in outside wealth that the executive prefers to hold in the market index with return $R_m$. For simplicity of exposition, we assume the CEO prefers to hold 100% of his outside wealth in the market index, but the same argument goes through if the CEO prefers to hold a combination of the risk-free asset and the market index. Suppose that the employment contract requires this new CEO to purchase $50 million of the firm's stock, which the executive finances by selling $50 million of market holdings. Under the simplifying assumption that the firm has systematic risk of beta equal to one, the stock return is $R_m + R_i$, where $R_i$ is the idiosyncratic component of the firm's return. Accordingly, after fulfilling the contract, the executive owns $50 million in the market portfolio with return $R_m$ and $50 million in firm stock with return $R_m + R_i$. This new portfolio is equivalent to the $100 million market portfolio that was originally held, plus a new $50 million exposure to the idiosyncratic component of the firm's return $R_i$. The executive's wealth is no more correlated with market movements after the contract than that preferred in the absence of the contract. The only aspect that has changed is that the executive now holds a $50 million exposure to firm idiosyncratic risk, which is consistent with the RPE prediction that the optimal contract

---

[1] By 'no' stock, we mean no stock other than the small amount of stock the CEO owns by owning the market portfolio. If CEO stock ownership was primarily driven by private information, one would expect to observe that some CEOs hold large quantities of stock (those CEOs with positive information) while other CEOs hold no stock (those CEOs with negative information). Furthermore, one would expect to observe large swings in ownership as private information is generated and disseminated. These features are not commonly observed, and laws against insider trading seem to preclude this behaviour.

[2] Another exception to this point is the case of a founding CEO. In this case, it may be difficult for the CEO to sell all of his or her stock immediately without incurring substantial 'signalling costs'. However, programmes such as those employed by Bill Gates, in which the CEO announces regular sales at certain times in the future, allow founding CEOs to gradually reduce their equity holdings without incurring information costs.

requires the CEO to hold more than his preferred exposure to the firm's idiosyncratic (non-market) return. The implicit indexing of his holdings of firm stock is not observed because the structure of his outside wealth and executive preferences are not observed (Jin, 2002; Core et al., 2003; Core and Guay, 2003). This analysis suggests that executive contracts are likely to be more consistent with RPE than might be observed by casual empiricism or by previous empirical RPE research that has not considered the structure of executives' other wealth.

The explicit use of RPE in executive compensation contracts (e.g. indexed stock options) is quite uncommon. Johnson and Tian (2000) note that firms face several potentially costly implementation issues with respect to indexed options. For example, an observable, non-manipulable benchmark index must be specified that well captures common uncertainty beyond the executive's control (e.g. Dye, 1992). Indexed options can also create greater incentives to increase risk than standard options. Further, as discussed below, indexed options require the firm to use variable financial accounting that results in compensation expense for options. If the recognition of accounting expense is important to the firm, this will be a disadvantage of indexed stock option contracts.

## Repricing stock options

Stock option repricing, the practice of resetting the exercise price of previously granted options that are significantly out of the money, has attracted considerable attention in recent years, and is an area of particular concern for institutional investors and the business press:

*Heavy criticism has come from the financial press and from large institutional investors such as the State of Wisconsin Investment Board, who argue that resetting is tantamount to rewarding management for poor performance and that, more importantly, it destroys incentives present in the initial contract.*

(Acharya et al., 2000, p. 66)

The typical argument against repricing is that firms provide options to employees as a form of equity incentives, and that these incentives are intended to encourage employees to take value-maximizing actions.

When the stock price rises, employees are rewarded through the increase in the value of their options. However, if options are repriced after the stock price falls, the repricing effectively removes the risk originally imposed on the executive for incentive purposes, and may be seen to be a 'reward' for poor performance.

Thus, critics argue that repricing is an inappropriate aspect of the compensation contract. Critics also question whether repricing is actually necessary in many cases. In support of this criticism, Chance et al. (2000) examine a sample of repricing firms and find that if the firms had not repriced, over half of their sample would have stock options that were at the money within two years after the repricing event. Of course, two years is a long time if you lose valuable employees to competitor firms in the interim.

As a counter-argument, Saly (1994) and Acharya et al. (2000) point out that it is generally optimal to allow a long-term contract to be renegotiated, and an ex-ante strategy of repricing options following bad outcomes dominates a commitment not to recontract. Intuitively, if the outcome is bad and is known to be the CEO's fault, he or she can be terminated. If the firm wishes to keep the CEO following a bad outcome, it will want to assist him or her with optimal incentives, and doing so involves recontracting.

Arguments against repricing also fail to consider the retention incentives that options are likely to provide. Employee stock options generally have vesting requirements that encourage employees to remain with the firm until the options are exercisable. Furthermore, employee stock options are not tradable or portable. This means that employees must exercise any vested options when they leave the firm, thereby forfeiting the time-value of the options (i.e. the employees are forced into suboptimal early exercise of the options). As an employee builds up an option portfolio over time, these retention incentives increase, thereby making it more costly for a competitor firm to hire away the employee. That is, not only would a competitor firm have to pay the employee his or her market wage, the firm would also have to compensate him or her for the value foregone from forfeiting unvested options or suboptimally exercising options prior to maturity. When the stock price falls precipitously, these retention incentives are largely eliminated and the probability of employee turnover increases as it becomes less costly for competitors to lure employees away. Repricing options can serve to reinstate the retention incentives. Obviously, repricing is costly from the perspective of the firm, but this cost may be substantially smaller than the cost of employee turnover (Acharya et al., 2000; Carter and Lynch, 2001), and thus repricing can be seen as a value-increasing action by the board of directors.[3]

Empirical research on stock option repricing provides insight into several issues. First, for most firms and most industries, the frequency of repricing is low. Brenner et al. (2000) find an incidence of repricing of less than 1.5% per firm-year (over 1992–1995) and Chance et al. (2000) find an even lower incidence of repricing when they examine 4000 large firms from 1985 to 1994. On the other hand, Carter and Lynch (2001) find that over 260 firms repriced during 1998, but most of these firms are small, high-technology firms. In high-technology, 'new economy' firms, Ittner et al. (2003) find that 63.8% of the firms allow repricing, with shareholder approval required in 35.4% of the cases. Moreover, 59.6% of the firms in their sample have repriced stock options at least once, and 31% have repriced stock options more than once following their initial public offering.

Prior research finds that repricing follows poor firm-specific performance, and some researchers interpret this as evidence that repricings are not being undertaken to protect managers from industry performance. On the other hand, Carter and Lynch (2001) point out that repricings are conditional on bad firm-specific performance *and* on the firm's (unobserved) decision not to terminate its employees. If bad managers are fired and get no repricing, then for the remaining sample of good managers, even if there were no true relation between repricing and performance, a negative relation could be observed because the managers who are punished for poor performance are excluded from the sample.

Brenner et al. (2000) and Chance et al. (2000) provide evidence that repricings reflect governance problems (i.e. that entrenched managers are more likely to do repricings). Brenner et al. (2000) present evidence that option grants and compensation are higher for managers whose

---

[3] This argument ignores the fact that restricted stock or other forms of deferred compensation could be equally or more effective as a retention device. For example, tenure-based restricted stock could have the same expected retention value as an equivalent dollar value of options, but with less risk. Interestingly, although stock options are commonly thought to provide retention incentives, there is little direct empirical evidence that documents these effects.

options are repriced. However, Carter and Lynch (2001), in a study that matches each repricing firm against a control firm with out-of-the-money options, find no evidence of a correlation between repricings and governance problems.

## Manipulation of exercise price and timing of stock option grants

Yermack (1997) finds positive abnormal stock returns after option grants, and presents evidence to support the hypothesis that these returns occur because managers time the option grant so that it is made prior to the release of good news (i.e. the exercise price is set prior to the release of good news). By making grants before good news, the manager effectively awards himself an in-the-money option, which is more valuable than the at-the-money option that he or she appears to receive. Yermack (1997) also presents evidence that the severity of this problem is greater for firms with weaker governance (e.g. when the CEO is a member of the compensation committee). Complementing Yermack's argument that managers time equity grants around fixed information disclosure dates, Aboody and Kasznik (2000) suggest that managers also time the disclosure of information around fixed equity grant dates. Specifically, they provide evidence that firms delay disclosure of good news and accelerate the release of bad news prior to stock option award periods.

While the manipulation effect appears to be statistically significant in prior research, one can question its economic significance and whether rational CEOs would engage in risky behaviour for such a small expected gain. Based on abnormal returns for 30 days after the grant date, Aboody and Kasznik (2000) find that the disclosure strategy increases the CEO's option award value by a mean of $46 700 (median $18 500). The amount estimated by Aboody and Kasznik represents 2.5% (5.1%) of reported total CEO compensation of $1 885 600 (CEO option compensation of $923 400). Given that the average CEO within this sample is likely to have a stock and option portfolio worth over 10 times his or her annual compensation, the typical CEO's wealth gain from this behaviour is much less than 1%. No evidence is reported by Aboody and Kasznik as to whether total CEO compensation for the sample firms engaging in this practice is statistically different than for firms not engaging in the practice. There is also the issue of expected litigation costs in the event of shareholder litigation (discussed below) and the potential decrease in the value of their human capital as it becomes known that they are 'manipulating' corporate disclosure.

Yermack (1997) argues that this type of granting practice would likely be construed as illegal insider trading. If CEOs engage in this behaviour opportunistically to the detriment of shareholders, without the permission of the board, they violate their fiduciary responsibility to the shareholders. If shareholders sue the firm over this behaviour, the CEO is not covered by the firm's directors' and officers' insurance, and thus could lose his or her entire wealth in litigation. Unless the CEO expects the risk of being caught in this behaviour to be extremely low, it seems highly irrational to engage in such risk-seeking behavior to extract relatively small rents from the firm.

Both Yermack (1997, pp. 471–472) and Aboody and Kasznik (2000, p. 98) also entertain the possibility that their evidence is consistent with managers acting in shareholders' interests. For example, because the incentives to increase stock price volatility created by an in-the-money option are lower than those created by an at-the-money option (e.g. Lambert et al., 1991), firms may wish to issue in-the-money options but prefer to avoid the accounting cost of such options. To accomplish this objective, they allow managers to time disclosures. Provided that CEOs' and other employees' levels of compensation are adjusted downward to reflect this extra value, one could argue that this type of behaviour is entirely consistent with firms acting in shareholders' interests by writing efficient contracts that minimize a complex array of contracting costs.

Little is presently known about the extent to which CEOs 'self-deal' with stock options. On one hand, it has been argued that the timing of stock option grants is consistent with a form of opportunistic insider trading. However, the economic importance of this behaviour for the executive and the firm is very unclear. On the other hand, arguments can be made that observed granting behaviour simply reflects efficient contracting between boards and CEOs. This latter argument is bolstered by the seemingly transparent nature of self-dealing with options that should make monitoring this activity relatively easy. In addition, one might question why CEOs use stock options (instead of cash or perquisites) to extract rents given that the pay-off from options is risky and depends on stock price increases. One possibility is that option compensation is favoured over cash compensation because the former is taxed on a deferred basis – that is, income tax is paid only at the exercise date and not at the grant date. A second conjecture is that excess option compensation attracts less unwanted public attention than excess cash pay because option expense is not included in reported earnings (e.g. Bebchuk et al., 2002).

## Accounting for stock options

In a competitive labour market, options are granted to employees as a form of compensation in return for services rendered. Like any other factor in production, corporations use these employee services to earn profits. However, unlike other factors in production, most firms record no accounting expense for compensation that is paid in options (assuming the grant date stock price is less than or equal to the exercise price). It is important for the reader to note that the recognition of option compensation as an expense in firms' financial statements is a separate issue from whether option compensation is an economic cost. Institutional accounting rules are influenced by objectives to produce reliable financial statements as well as by the political process. With respect to option compensation, these forces have resulted in financial accounting rules that allow most firms to avoid recognition of option expense in accounting earnings, and to instead disclose an estimate of the expense in a footnote to the financial statements.

As a side note, the fact that options may provide employees with incentives does not provide a justification for excluding an estimate of the economic cost of granting options from the computation of labour expense. To the extent that options create incentives, they are like any other incentive in that they work by imposing risk on the employee and the firm has to pay the employee extra compensation to accept this risk. The benefits to the firm from such incentives will show up in firm profitability when the employees make better decisions as a result of these incentives, and appropriate financial accounting will attempt to match the benefits from these incentives with the costs associated with these incentives. Evidence in Bell et al. (2001) is consistent with investors' perception that services rendered by employees in return for newly granted options extend beyond the year in which the options are granted. As such, it may be reasonable to view the services received from option

169

compensation as a temporary economic asset to be amortized (expensed) over a few years following the grant date.

Although firms in the USA do have the option of expensing (i.e. reducing reporting earnings) the estimated value of options granted, historically relatively few firms make this choice. Recently, starting in the second half of 2002, some large high-profile firms such as Coca-Cola, American Express and Ford Motors have announced plans to expense employee stock options. However, these firms are in the minority and tend not to be the most intensive users of options. For firms that grant, but do not expense, employee stock options, other things being equal (including firms' economic profits), accounting earnings are expected to be greater than the earnings of firms that use no options. There is a discussion of the UK approach to the expensing of options in Chapter 3. However, regardless of whether firms choose to expense options in income, pro-forma income that includes option expense must be disclosed in the footnotes to the financial statements (and it is quite likely that both the IASB and FASB will require expensing of stock options in the future). Furthermore, there is significant disclosure about outstanding employee options in both the firm's proxy statement and annual report, and evidence in Aboody (1996) and Bell et al. (2001) is consistent with an efficient stock market recognizing and pricing these competing claims to the firm's equity.

Nevertheless, firm managers appear to behave as if they believe their stock prices would suffer if earnings included an expense for stock option compensation. For example, Carter and Lynch (2003) document that firms accelerated repricing activity around the effective date of an accounting rule that required expensing of repriced options. Prior to December 1998 in the USA, repricings did not trigger an accounting expense. After this date, firms are required to use variable accounting for repriced options, thereby incurring an accounting expense. Carter and Lynch (2003) find that firms accelerated repricing activity around the effective date of this accounting rule. Following this change in accounting treatment, Carter and Lynch (2003) observe a sharp reduction in the use of repricings to reinstate incentives. A survey by iQuantic (2001) finds that the majority of high-tech 'new economy' firms with underwater options have switched from repricing underwater options to giving a supplemental grant of options at the lower strike price. If cancelling and reissuing options was optimal from a contracting standpoint, it seems that firms are incurring real economic costs to avoid the accounting expense associated with repricings.

If managers incorrectly perceive that there are real costs associated with expensing option compensation, options may be overused and substituted for other forms of compensation, such as cash or restricted stock. If there is a large real economic cost of expensing options, firms might prefer to grant options even if, as argued by Hall and Murphy (2002), their compensation cost is greater than that of restricted stock. It would be unfortunate if financial accounting requirements were an important motivation for firms to either increase or decrease their use of stock options. Specifically, shareholders presumably want the board of directors to select stock option plans that maximize shareholder value, not short-term earnings. Thus, if indexed options or other stock option designs that require variable accounting provide optimal incentives for executives, why would a board reject such a compensation plan because of 'unfavourable' accounting? Clearly, the role of financial accounting for employee stock options is of considerable importance to firms, but not well understood by economists.

## Conclusion

There is a long history of academic research that examines the managerial incentives associated with stock options and equity ownership. The increased use of stock options and the large payouts from stock option grants in recent years has produced considerable debate among academics, in boardrooms and in the financial press regarding the desirability of using equity compensation in executive compensation programmes. In this chapter, we provide a synthesis for some of the major research findings, as well as the fundamental controversies and unresolved issues around equity incentives.

Recent increased scrutiny of corporate governance practices as well as expected changes in financial accounting requirements for stock options have important ramifications for executive compensation and incentives. The expectation that all firms will be required to expense employee stock options has already prompted many firms to voluntarily adopt this accounting treatment. When this accounting change occurs, it will likely remove some of the perceived costs of implementing restricted

171

stock plans, performance-based stock option plans and other equity-based plans that would previously have been out of favour due to the required accounting treatment. Microsoft Corporation's recent decision to begin compensating employees with restricted stock instead of options suggests that these changes have already begun.

We note, however, that a key finding from our survey of the compensation and incentives literature is that simple normative prescriptions (e.g. restricted stock is a better tool for compensation and incentives than options; repricings are an indication of poor governance; more equity ownership by executives is always better than less ownership) are inappropriate. It is necessary to understand the objectives of shareholders, the characteristics of managers and other elements of the decision setting before drawing any conclusions about the desirability of observed equity-based incentive plans or the level of equity ownership by managers. We conclude that the continued and heated debate about stock option accounting, the appropriateness of option plans, the structure of executive pay and the adequacy of corporate governance suggests that there remain many important issues to address in future research on equity compensation and incentives.

# 9

# Remuneration committees

Keith Cameron

## Introduction

Soon after the inventive powers of individuals and the process of scientific discovery were together in harness, and what we recognize as the
Industrial Revolution had begun, this amalgam produced a number of
other challenges to be addressed.

Increasing technical complexity and larger scale operation necessi-
tated greater investment for companies and the development of standards and skills in the management of these organizations. In simple
terms, the anecdotal Victorian inventor/entrepreneur/owner gave way to
the development of the public company, with separation of ownership
from control and increased protection for the investors through standards
enshrined in legislation.

There are several points where ownership and control come together
in practice. The clearest example is the board of a public company and
the board's attendant mechanisms, such as the remuneration committee.

Although the role of the remuneration committee is, to some degree,
prescribed by the legal framework and public codes, there are substantial variations in the way that remuneration committees function. The
purpose of this chapter is to establish the criteria and conflicts that remuneration committees face; to review the influences that affect their

operation; to assess the implications of the standards set for them; and to consider the optimal approaches to their successful operation.

These issues are discussed in the context of companies operating in the United Kingdom. However, the principles and policy considerations apply to all countries and markets with publicly quoted companies.

## The remuneration committee's criteria and conflicts

There has been a long-running debate between those who argue that money is a motivator and those who hold that money does not motivate people.

Motivation is the force that drives people to behave in particular ways and is occasioned by needs that are translated into behavioural goals. As our needs are not identical, there are individuals who may be motivated by spiritual needs that transcend any material needs. For these people, money could not be seen as a motivator.

These individuals may be thought to be in the minority and money is seen to be a motivator for the majority of people, but with two provisos. First is the understanding that money is a motivator in so far as it represents a means of satisfying a need. Second, money can be a motivator if the process is seen to be achievable. If the goal appears to be unobtainable, then the drive to satisfy the need will not be present. As Armstrong and Murlis (1980, p. 18) point out, 'the degree to which people are motivated will depend not only on the perceived value of the outcome of their actions (the goal or reward) but also their expectations of obtaining the reward. They will be more highly motivated if they can control the means of attaining their goals.'

From a company perspective, the task is to provide a reward scheme that is motivational for individuals and cost-effective for the organization. To satisfy the practical requirement for a reward process that will be perceived as motivational and to have it function economically, there are six operational factors to satisfy. These factors apply to any scheme at any level and certainly function as a critical checklist for any remuneration committee required to assess a new proposal or review the results of an existing scheme. The six factors are: motivation, reward/ performance relationship, value for money, payment timing, simplicity and transparency.

## Motivation

This factor is the first check for the design of any variable reward scheme. The word 'motivation' needs to be translated to form a practical test which is exemplified as a series of questions. Will the scheme encourage participants to strive in order to achieve the goal(s)? Will the participants direct their energies appropriately – without disadvantage to the attainment of other objectives – to achieve the scheme goals? Does the scheme relate the goals of the organization and the interests of the participants?

In essence, this factor is concerned with perception. If the scheme is perceived to be able to pay for performance levels that are attainable, then appropriate behaviours should result, goals will be achieved and the scheme can be seen to have passed the motivation test.

## Reward/performance relationship

In the round, a variable reward scheme may be perceived by participants and sponsors as motivational because it drives achievement behaviour. However, there are practical considerations that may cause difficulties even when there is a high level of commitment.

Schemes with several different goals may be in danger of rewarding achievement of targets which are, at worst, not relevant or which will receive reward disproportionate to performance. For example, a scheme that potentially provides 40% of bonus for net profit achievement, 30% for return on investment attained and 30% for extension of the customer base may be thought to be placing undue emphasis on the third measure – particularly if the company is operating in a marketplace where new customers are easy to obtain.

When inappropriate targets are selected the consequences can be disastrous. One substantial UK hotel chain was nearly bankrupted by a bonus scheme that was too successful. The company introduced a scheme that rewarded hotel managers on the basis of room occupancy. The company's intention was to increase sales revenue and to benefit from increased profits that would have increased proportionately. In practice, the hotel managers reduced the room charges to drive the occupancy and the company made a loss on its occupied rooms.

Similarly, there is the well-known story of the bus company that set up a bonus scheme based on fuel savings and was inundated with complaints from passengers who were being ignored at bus stops as the buses drove straight past. The drivers pointed out to the management that stopping and starting was not fuel efficient!

## Value for money

Assuming that the targeting is appropriate, is the scale of reward for the achievement of the target also appropriate? Should the managers of profit centres receive a bonus of 100% of salary if they achieve their profit targets or is 50% of salary the better maximum reward? It can be argued that a very high variable reward chips away at the first criterion, motivation, by encouraging over-concentration on one element of an executive's responsibilities. On a 'value for money' basis, the company could be seen to be providing too much reward for particular aspects of performance.

A dramatic example of disproportionate reward for customers (rather than employees) occurred when vacuum cleaner manufacturer Hoover offered its customers a free return trip to the United States when they purchased a new vacuum cleaner. Wily customers bought the product to obtain the airline ticket and Hoover was forced to honour thousands of free flight obligations before announcing consequential large losses and, in its weakened state, being bought cheaply by a rival.

## Payment timing

Simply stated, the further away the point of measurement of success (and payment) from the activity, the harder it will be for participants to be incentivized. A sales director, whose only performance measure is sales revenue, who is set a five-year target with resultant reward assessed each year but paid at the end of the five-year period, may not be as motivated to achieve as the scheme's architect may have hoped. Although the bonus scheme convention is that the lower level the job, the more frequent the payment (for example, field sales staff on monthly bonus/commission) and the higher level the job, the longer the interval, there are limits.

This was recognized by the advent of longer-term variable reward methods like share option schemes and long-term share plans, which attempt to reward for performance over the medium to long term. Bonus schemes designed for directors are unlikely to drive behaviour if the interval between performance assessment and payment is more than a year.

## Simplicity

There are plenty of variable reward schemes which have several targets with complex measurement methods and qualifying safeguards which are quantifiable and serve to amend the entitlements. The complexity of such schemes works against the general aim of a variable reward scheme to be motivational. Complicated measurement and intricate application result in the participants, at worst, being unclear about the relative importance of the targets and directing their efforts inappropriately.

In the 1970s, one of the UK's leading computer companies revised its sales bonus plan and developed a scheme that set achievement levels for the following: purchasing commitment; mainframe and peripheral product combinations; financing method; payment arrangements. The scheme was further complicated by the earned bonus being paid at different intervals – a percentage after confirmation of the order, a further payment after delivery (or part-deliveries) and a percentage when the invoice had been paid. The participants, all of whom were graduates, found the scheme so complicated that they ignored, in behavioural terms, the prioritization of goals that the scheme was trying to represent and simply concentrated on the single factor that best suited each of them.

The remuneration committee needs to guard against similar circumstances. Schemes for executive directors are often proposed that have multiple performance targets. The reasoning behind the design is understandable as some of the reward schemes have the potential to pay large amounts, but the company needs to be sure that the performance that is rewarded is exactly what is required, as complexity often results in the loss of goal clarity and, frequently, more scope for argument as the measurement of the variables turns into a negotiation.

## Transparency

'Transparent' is defined by the Oxford English Dictionary as 'open, candid ... easily seen through, recognized or detected'. In the context of senior-level reward, this applies not only to the design of a scheme, but also to the mechanics of a scheme. The confidence of observers and participants increases when all aspects (the purpose, goals, rules, calculation methods, participants' details and results) are open to view. Boards have regarded themselves as 'transparent' when they provide full details of targets and results, and are surprised when they are criticized for not being comprehensively transparent. Typically, the methods of performance measurement are often not open to full scrutiny.

It is worth noting that there is a likely relationship between transparency and simplicity. The International Corporate Governance Network comments, 'transparency is not the same as illumination, with highly complex structures being revealed that baffle almost everyone'.

Listing the criteria for a successful variable reward scheme in the order they were reviewed – motivational, reward/performance balance, value for money, payment timing, simplicity, transparency – it can be argued that this is also the order of importance. Certainly it is a plausible order of importance from a senior management perspective. The first three (motivational, reward/performance balance and value for money) capture the behavioural and economic factors and the remainder (payment intervals, simplicity and transparency) assist the process of operation, acting as support to a well-conceived scheme that satisfies the first three criteria.

The remuneration committee, however, may not share top management's view of the relative importance of these six factors. Assuming that the remuneration committee is properly comprised of non-executive directors, it can be argued that they would arrange the list of six factors in a different order. The foundation for any successful scheme is that its design produces the desired behaviours, so remuneration committees are likely to select the motivational factor as the most important.

The second most important factor from the remuneration committee's perspective could be transparency. The accountability of the remuneration committee to shareholders and, increasingly, the interest of the public and the media in top management reward means that non-executive directors must demonstrate their good judgement in determining the appropriate methods and levels of reward for executive directors.

The International Corporate Governance Network, representing $10 trillion of assets, asserted that executive remuneration schemes must serve two masters, so that they will 'serve the needs of both the company managers and the investing institutions and their clients' (International Corporate Governance Network, 2002, p. 1). The ICGN concludes that 'the fundamental requirement for executive remuneration reporting is transparency'. There is considerable and understandable pressure on

**Table 9.1** Different priorities in design

| Management's priority order | Design factor | Remuneration committee priority order |
|---|---|---|
| 1 | Motivation | 1 |
| 2 | Reward/performance balance | 3 |
| 3 | Value for money | 4 |
| 4 | Payment timing | 6 |
| 5 | Simplicity | 5 |
| 6 | Transparency | 2 |

remuneration committees to demonstrate that decisions are appropriate and reasonable.

After that requirement, the remuneration committee may follow suit with the senior executive view that reward/performance relationship and value for money are next in the order of priority. The two remaining factors, payment timing and simplicity, may be valued differently by the remuneration committee and the executive. From the line management's point of view, payment timing could be more important, as the shorter the temporal link between performance, achievement and reward, the more likely the desired behaviours will result. Simplicity is a virtue, but for those steeped in the operation of the organization, some degree of complexity is manageable.

For the non-executive director the position is likely to be reversed. Simplicity supports transparency. Additionally, non-executive directors are not involved in the operational intricacies of the company and are unlikely to have detailed knowledge or experience of the sector, so complexity embodied in a reward scheme would not be a welcome feature.

So the difference of views can be portrayed as shown in Table 9.1.

These differences may become apparent when a new reward scheme is put before the remuneration committee for review and approval. The scheme design will have been produced by or on behalf of the organization's executive and is likely to reflect their priorities and criteria. Top management may value the six criteria as ranked in Table 9.1, while the remuneration committee's differing priorities result in a different value. The result may be unresolved conflict or submission or compromise. Which of these is the end-result will depend, in part, on the characteristics of the remuneration committee.

## Types of remuneration committee

For any operational body, including a remuneration committee, the influences acting on it are legion. The fact of a remuneration committee's existence, operation and history gives rise to a set of norms that will influence its behaviour. The past affects the future operation.

Remuneration committees' constitutional arrangements, which are written and formally adopted, are only one factor determining their operation. Alongside, there are norms generated over time and cemented by custom and practice.

These norms can be of minor importance or substantial significance. Consider the example of the remuneration committee which meets in the evening (following an afternoon board meeting) before returning to enjoy a dinner with the full board. The chair of the remuneration committee restricts the meeting to, say, one hour, so that the dining arrangements will not be disturbed. This may be a productive way of capturing three events in one span of time and the discussion in the remuneration committee should, at least, be focused. However, the imposed guillotine could result in the loss of effective contributions from members, so that the committee does not achieve its potential.

The circumstances in this example are not likely to be of major significance in any assessment of the remuneration committee's performance, but there are conventions that have far greater influence. For instance, the remuneration committee that includes the chief executive as a participant at all meetings and at all times is not healthy. Good governance requires that the remuneration committee is comprised of non-executive directors. This condition can be formally met while including the chief executive by the simple expedient of inviting the chief executive to attend. Where this practice has become standard it is difficult to alter. In companies where such customs are prevalent, it is not unknown for the chief executive to be in attendance while the details of his remuneration are decided.

The management of the discussions in committee and the format and level of debate can vary enormously. Remuneration committees are often faced with detail or complexity. Whether this is reasonable or not will be addressed later, together with the ways to handle necessarily complicated material, but there are remuneration committees that avoid complexity, emphasizing the non-executive aspect of their role, and adopt the convention of discussing the principles and primary aspects of reward proposals, deliberately avoiding discussion of detail.

The reasoning behind this approach is that the non-executives are not from the same sector as the company and are not close to the operational intricacies of the sector, and should concern themselves with the major issues. Advice on detail which may affect important aspects of practice should be part of the technical contribution they receive before discussion takes place.

So the attitude the remuneration committee takes about its role and its historical and preferred method of operation are going to be a significant influence on the way the committee functions.

The second influence to review has some similarity to the first in that it is born out of norms and values. This time the norms and values are those of the larger organization, which will have some effect on the operation of the remuneration committee. If a company values, shall we say, ingenuity and invention, recognizing the attributes as important elements in its potential business success, then it is likely that the workforce will be recruited using these attributes as criteria for selection. The curious and inventive workforce is likely to be imaginative and ingenious in its behaviour. This behaviour is not necessarily replicated by the members of the remuneration committee if they are non-executive directors. However, during the recruitment of the non-executives, some if not all of the company's values are likely to have been used as criteria for selection. So there is an attitudinal axis that will affect the operation of the remuneration committee. Continuing with the example of imagination, at one extreme where imagination is highly valued the remuneration committee will be receptive to new methods and encourage novelty. At the other end of the continuum, imaginative proposals would not be encouraged and a conservative approach using tested and well-tried methods would be supported.

The next consideration is the influence of the owners or, in more conventional terminology, shareholder interest.

The role of the non-executive director is the same as an executive director in terms of legal liability and public responsibility, but in operational terms the executives control the functioning of the company while the non-executives provide advice and counsel using their individual qualities and experience from a vantage point separate from the machinery of the organization.

In some cases, particularly where there is a substantial minority share-holder, one or more non-executive directors may be direct nominees of the large shareholder. More frequently, the linkage is not direct but the onus is still on the non-executive directors in particular to represent the interests of the shareholders. This representation is often portrayed as a form of curtailment and there are many examples of non-executive directors being accused of failing in their duty to contain the commercially foolish enthusiasms of the executive directors.

The shareholders place great store in their non-executive directors as members of the remuneration committee, where they are expected to provide a perspective that is more appropriate than might be provided by the executive directors, whose views would risk being tainted with self-interest. To ensure that non-executive duties can be met, formal standards have been set by public bodies. Logically, these standards should be a natural extension of shareholder interest. This is the third influence on the operation of remuneration committees. If the interests of the shareholders are legitimately defined, then they will be at one with the requirements laid down by the external authorities. The Combined Code on Corporate Governance has been the clearest example of governance standards set for board operation and remuneration committees, but the statutory rules (largely contained within the Companies Acts) now include the Directors' Remuneration Report Regulations 2002. There is some flexibility in the way companies respond to the Combined Code and the Regulations (which will be discussed later), which is why this factor – public standards – exerts an influence that is not, in practice, the same for all remuneration committees.

The final factor that may influence the way the remuneration committee chooses to behave is public interest – a phrase with at least two meanings. In this context, the term is not an expression of wider responsibility or public good. (The Combined Code and other external standards capture this aspect.) For our purposes, public interest means the public's curiosity and concern about top-level remuneration. This can be a significant influence on remuneration committee members if they are required to make decisions against a background that includes public debate in the media and substantial press interest. Directors on remuneration committees have frequently denied that this form of public interest has had any impact on their decisions. Even if this is so, a high level of public interest will have some effect on their review and decision-making

| VALUES | PERSPECTIVE | |
|---|---|---|
| | Internal | External |
| *Historical* | PEDESTRIAN | TENSE |
| *Contemporary* | SELF-SERVING | ADAPTIVE |

**Figure 9.1** Matrix of remuneration committee types.

processes. The style of communication of their decisions, for example, is likely to be different as a result of significant media attention.

These five influences on remuneration committees (committee operating norms, company culture, shareholder interests, governance requirements and public interest) determine the positioning of committees in a matrix of remuneration committee types, whose two axes are Values and Perspective (Figure 9.1).

Values are either Historical or Contemporary. Ralph Waldo Emerson observed: 'There are always two parties, the party of the past and the party of the future; the establishment and the movement.' Assessment of a remuneration committee against two influences, operating norms and company values (and, it could be argued, shareholder interest), establishes its location on the values axis.

Perspective is concerned with the orientation of the remuneration committee – at one extreme on this axis the reference points are inside the organization as far as is possible for discussion, comparison and evaluation. At the other extreme, the considerations are dominated by an outward-looking orientation, where practices in the external market and ideas promoted by outside agencies, together with reliance on data and evidence from the wider world, are strongly valued. Company culture, shareholder interests and public interests will influence remuneration committees' positions on this scale.

Clearly, neither extreme is practically possible on the Perspective axis. The hermit-like committee cannot exist, simply because the regulatory requirements that bind remuneration committees could not then be met, but there is considerable scope for different positioning on this axis, which describes the orientation of the committee and its balance of interest. Typically, remuneration committees that may be classified as Internal will meet the government's reporting requirement to state performance criteria for performance-related reward, listing comparator companies and publishing a comparative business performance analysis. But these statements can be produced publicly while the remuneration committee in practice places greater emphasis on less publicly quantified elements, and the deliberations of the committee are driven by previous years' reward levels and the relativities between directors.

The matrix of remuneration committee types defines four: Pedestrian, Self-serving, Tense and Adaptive.

Pedestrian describes the remuneration committee that values its traditional approach using history and precedents in its internal process management, and favours well-tried and tested approaches to arranging directors' rewards. This is the committee that sees no virtue in being novel and prefers to be conservative. To many who believe that the remuneration committee should lead the organization and by being the explorer set the approach to reward to be followed for the rest of the company, this is frustrating. Brown (2001, p. 6) comments:

*Proposals for new incentive schemes have been rejected purely on the basis that they are novel and not in evidence elsewhere in the market. In every other aspect of corporate strategy, the aim is to differentiate yourself from the competition, but often not in respect of rewards.*

Turning to the next category, this is exemplified by those companies whose remuneration committees have a balanced membership, with individuals of public note and prestige. They bring experience and values, which mean that the committee is not rooted in its own, or the company's, old values. Despite this, the committee is traditional and precedent based in its reward mechanisms and its reward decisions. At the end of the process, the committee operates in self-serving mode. Cynically, observers of this type of committee accuse the members of 'being asleep on the job'. The view is that the non-executive directors enjoy powerful reputations, but they do not apply themselves to disciplined work to realize the potential of the remuneration committee. There are several UK and US examples of large companies that have appointed prestigious non-executive directors, often with vast international political experience, but subsequent company difficulties have laid open the workings of the remuneration committee, which have been shown to be undiscerning and compliant.

There are likely to be more remuneration committees fitting the description 'Tense' than there would have been several years ago. The increased public and political interest in top-level remuneration has resulted in formal reporting requirements (the Directors' Remuneration Report Regulations 2002) that place an emphasis on market comparisons, which, in turn, draws committees towards the External classification on the Perspective axis. However, many of the companies trying to comply with new public requirements are doing so from a traditional and repetitive style of operating, which is rooted in the organizations' values. Where companies have conservative or insular operating methods, where secrecy and subjectivity have been significant features and these methods have continued to be thought appropriate, the obligation to take a more External perspective with requirements for outside market involvement and openness places remuneration committees under tension, as they struggle with key elements that are, to a large degree, in opposition to each other. Taking a simple example, the chief executive's salary is no longer the result of a discussion between members that the chairman summarizes to produce a committee view, but of a decision based on external market statistics prepared and presented by a third party.

Finally, the remuneration committees that have a contemporary set of values and norms and are orientated towards external reference points of markets and comparators can be seen as those embracing the most recent model of remuneration committee operation. These committees can be described as Adaptive, as they move or have moved to adopt what is conventionally regarded as 'best practice'.

## External pressures

Concern about the effectiveness of remuneration committees has manifested itself in government attempts to produce standards of corporate governance that largely concentrate on the remuneration and contractual arrangements of top executives.

The Cadbury Committee published its recommendations in 1992. Its concerns with corporate governance were broader than remuneration, but it made a number of recommendations that were adopted as appropriate standards for public companies on reward.

The Cadbury proposals included disclosure of the chairman's and directors' total emoluments and identification of the highest paid UK directors' total emoluments. The Committee also proposed that pensions and 'relevant information about stock options', together with separate figures for salary and performance pay (and the basis on which performance is measured), should be published annually.

While the obligations of the Cadbury Committee were met by most companies, there was a public and political view that the requirements were inadequate. Lord Halifax's comment, 'the problem with British Companies is that they mark their own exam papers', reflected the concern that appropriate corporate governance was not yet established.

Two years later, the Greenbury Committee reported and, employing the three themes of accountability, transparency and performance linkage, made the following recommendations:

- remuneration committees to comprise non-executive directors only
- remuneration policy to be published
- market comparisons to determine pay practice
- share option issues to be phased and performance conditions to apply.

The Greenbury Committee also recommended executive director contracts with a maximum notice period of one year.

The proposals were endorsed by government and formally adopted, but a further need to tackle the subject was perceived and the Hampel Committee reported in 1998, three years after Greenbury.

The Hampel Committee proposed that the chairman and chief executive roles should be separate (this was an accepted recommendation of the Cadbury Committee in 1992). Directors' contracts should be one year or less – a repeat of a Greenbury recommendation. Hampel also proposed that non-executive directors should constitute at least one-third of the board; each director's remuneration should be stated in the annual report and all boards should assess their own collective performance and that of individual directors.

The discernible pattern is one of proposals being accepted by the relevant authorities, but only slowly and partially being adopted by companies.

A number of surveys between 2000 and 2002 confirmed that many of the 'best practices' of the Cadbury, Greeenbury and Hampel Committees had not been widely implemented.

In 2000, a National Association of Pension Funds Survey established that only 10 of the top 350 public companies had a vote on remuneration issues at the annual general meeting.

In 2002, the Co-operative Insurance Society (one of the major institutional investors) surveyed the top 100 UK companies and found that over half did not have a fully independent remuneration committee, 20% of companies had a majority of non-executive directors who were not independent and 31% had executive directors who had service contracts of more than one year.

Also in 2002, the Pension Investment Research Consultancy (PIRC) found that fewer than 40% of remuneration committees were fully independent in 523 surveyed companies. Ten per cent of these companies continued to combine the roles of chairman and chief executive.

The code of good practice developed by the three committees did not have the power of law and, without pressure, companies were too slow to meet the expectations of shareholders in improving their corporate governance in relation to employment and reward. In the context of the classification discussed earlier in this chapter, the government and the institutions attempted to instil Contemporary values and an External perspective, which would result in an Adaptive mode being adopted by public companies.

With progress to Adaptive being judged to be too slow, the major fund investment bodies, operating as the Institutional Shareholders' Committee, agreed to become more active on issues of corporate governance and intervene 'where necessary'.

The ISC comprises the Association of British Insurers, the National Association of Pension Funds, the Association of Investment Trust Companies and the Investment Management Association. By virtue of the funds they manage, their influence is substantial. The ISC has, however, felt their views were not sufficiently respected and, in parallel, were concerned that an inflexible code imposed by government statute would curtail their discretion.

## Stakeholder interest

There is a range of stakeholders who affect a board's behaviour. As far as the remuneration and corporate governance is concerned, those interests may be conflicting. Looking at the work of the remuneration committee, we have already seen that the criteria of the non-executive directors and the executive directors may not always align.

Figure 9.2 sets out the internal and external stakeholders' interests, which try to find operational harmony.

From the outer ring of the diagram, the government has, through the committees of Cadbury, Greenbury and Hampel, set standards for company behaviour on executive director employment and remuneration. The ABI, NAPF, IMA, etc., both individually and under their collective industry banner, have tried to exert practical pressure. Institutional investors have, privately, had influence on occasions, although the small

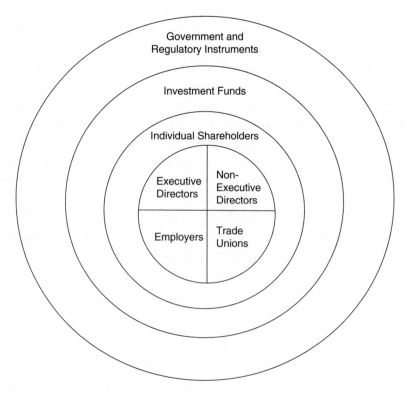

**Figure 9.2** Shareholder influences.

shareholder has had no influence, only the opportunity to embarrass the board at annual general meetings.

Within the organization, the non-executive directors may have adopted an approach that could be classified as Adaptive, which results in operation close to the standards publicly espoused. However, there remain a substantial number of companies that have not operated within the best practice guidelines and the other stakeholders not mentioned so far – the employees and the trade unions – have not been able to effect any changes towards best practice. The trade unions may have some opportunity for embarrassment via the media, but its effect is not significant.

The tardy progress towards best practice and some criticism from the public following media attention made the government resolve to tackle issues differently.

The Secretary of State for Trade and Industry, in a consultative document published in 2001, said:

*More than six years ago, the Greenbury report set out three fundamental principles in this area: accountability, transparency and performance linkage. The government agrees that these are the right principles, but it does not believe that the best practice framework has been successful in achieving adequate levels of compliance. Although many quoted companies have complied fully, this is not an area where so patchy a performance is acceptable.*

(Directors' Remuneration: Foreword)

Following the consultation, the government introduced the Directors' Remuneration Reporting Regulations 2002, which came into effect for listed companies (other than those listed on the Alternative Investment Market) on 31 December 2002.

In order to develop the Greenbury criteria of accountability, transparency and performance linkage, the Regulations require explicit information to be published in the annual report and to be subject to a shareholder resolution approving the directors' remuneration at the annual general meeting. The shareholder vote is not binding on the company, but the results must be published. The government argued that legal complexities discouraged them from making the vote legally binding and that the information requirements and shareholders' views would be sufficiently powerful to engender appropriate corporate behaviour.

The Regulations fall into three parts: the role of the remuneration committee, policy statements on directors' remuneration and reports on directors' remuneration for the previous year.

The role of the remuneration committee in determining directors' rewards must be described and details of consultants retained to advise the committee must be published. This requirement addresses the concerns raised by the International Corporate Governance Network. Quoting Conyon and Peck (2000), the Network comments:

*Remuneration committee proposals to the main board about pay levels and structures are based on information received from the company's human resources department. The information collected by the company is done in conjunction with advice from professional advisers outside the company. In consequence, the remuneration committee does not usually have its own separate advisers, or influence its terms of reference. If a consultancy firm does a large volume of business with the company, and is appointed to those tasks by the executive, is there a danger that the advice given to the independent committee of directors is contaminated in some way?*

(ICGW paragraph 49)

The second area specified by the committee is reward policy. Companies must detail their long-term incentive and share option plans, and the mechanism for measurement and allocation. A statement on the duration of directors' service contracts, notice periods and termination payments is also required.

The third set of requirements covers the directors' reward for the previous year. A full analysis for each director has to be presented, together with details of any termination payments, share option awards or long-term incentive payments made. The report also requires the publication of a performance graph comparing the company's total shareholder return (TSR) over the past five years with that of a group of companies which constitute a named broad equity market index.

Since the introduction of the Regulations there have been a number of cases where the AGM vote by shareholders has defeated or nearly defeated the resolution. The responses of companies in these circumstances has ranged from a commitment to review policies and practices before the next AGM to withdrawing specific proposals in their entirety.

The government's assessment is that the Regulations are satisfactorily performing their intended functions. Alongside these developments, the government initiated a review of corporate governance, which culminated in the Higgs report and produced a number of proposals that regulated and strengthened the role of the non-executive director.

## Remuneration committees in operation

The constitution of a remuneration committee helps to define the optimal way of assisting the remuneration committee to undertake its work.

Assuming the standard model, the chair of the remuneration committee will be a non-executive director, as will the other members. The committee will be serviced by the company secretariat, although information may be commissioned through existing company sources or from an independent agency.

To help the remuneration committee meet its objectives, the individuals and company departments servicing the committee need to provide appropriate information and balanced recommendations. They also need to avoid pitfalls that make the work of the committee more difficult.

### The unexpected

As a standard discipline, papers containing proposals for remuneration committee deliberation are circulated before a meeting rather than tabled at the meeting. However, it is not unknown for addenda to be produced at a meeting. Such supplementaries may be produced to provide additional support for the case contained in the original report. Even if this is so, it does not help the relationship between the provider and the recipients! Producing additional material late puts recipients under pressure – particularly when the subject matter is not in their field of expertise.

### Lobbying

Formally, the process of reward determination is based on written papers and subsequent discussion in committee. (An Institute of Directors survey of 1580 members in 1998 found that 59% arrived at their decisions using this method and 22% also used outside consultants; 11% relied on members' own knowledge of the issues.) However, there are other opportunities to influence views outside the committee meeting. Material for the committee's consideration may be provided through the offices of the human resources department or the company secretariat and may also travel through the chief executive's office before arriving with the non-executive directors.

There are en route opportunities for discussion with the non-executive directors by any of those involved in the process of disseminating information. Views can be put and opinions expressed. How powerful do these views have to be before they are perceived as an attempt to lobby? When there is a clear objective in the mind of the communicator, any opinion is expressed for a clear purpose. These opinions may be interpreted by committee members as a form of pressure (even if the opinions are correct) and the members are likely to react adversely to any pressure. Lobbying is not well regarded by remuneration committee members.

## Technical proposals

Non-executive directors are frequently chosen for their experience in a field that is relevant to the company which is recruiting them. Relevance can include experience of events or processes which the organization may have to deal with or knowledge of a sector which can be translated to the benefit of the hiring company. It is not common for the non-executive directors to have deep and detailed knowledge of the sector in which the company operates. For that reason, reward schemes that rely on highly technical factors are not popular with remuneration committee members. The criteria of transparency and simplicity are difficult to achieve when reward schemes are rooted in complex technical factors.

## Complex proposals

Similarly, complicated proposals are not popular with committee members, as they also make it difficult to achieve transparency and simplicity. Even if the component elements of a variable reward scheme are straightforward, the design can be complicated by the inclusion of too many factors and complex formulae to be used for calculating the results. Once again, straying from the simplicity criterion is not helpful for the remuneration committee.

## Internal measures of success

The Directors' Remuneration Report Regulations 2002 have reduced the incidence of internal reference points being used in preference to external measures, although the requirement for measurement of a company's total shareholder return against a published index or a group of relevant companies only relates to long-term incentives. Nonetheless, this helps to establish the discipline of quantitative external measurement.

Some remuneration committees are undoubtedly presented with proposals that have internal measures of success. The members may also be asked to judge awards against subjective criteria. Using the classification discussed earlier, companies that are Pedestrian display procedural inertia and deep-rooted company cultural influences. They tend to be inward looking and are likely to use internal measures as their scales for assessing performance. Other remuneration committees will be alienated by internal reference, as they recognize their responsibility to approve appropriate reward arrangements is difficult to achieve without independent and objective standards.

There is a clear discipline for those involved in servicing remuneration committees. Although each committee is different and there is no single mode of operation, the in-company managers who supply or advise committees must avoid making the remuneration committee members feel exposed or pressured. Non-executive directors are uncomfortable with unexpected material, lobbying, overly technical material, complexity and the use of internal measures.

## Assisting the remuneration committee

Informed discussion is the essence of the committee's work and for that discussion to be productive, the papers prepared for the committee need to be well structured and comprehensive in scope and depth.

For a discussion about any scheme being proposed, the submission should contain an introduction that summarizes the background to the production of the paper, including a statement of the objective.

The policy position should be addressed next. To establish legitimacy, any relationship to public standards and reporting requirements can be addressed at this stage. The policy proposal can then be outlined.

The specific proposals for the reward scheme should follow. The proposals should meet the design criteria that have been reviewed earlier in this chapter, namely motivational, appropriate perform-ance measures, value for money, payment timing, transparency and simplicity.

The material, which should be comprehensive in scope and depth, includes the extrapolations of potential reward at different levels of performance and the comparative market information used. The most appropriate way to include so much material and meet the criterion of simplicity is to position the comprehensive data in appendices.

It is also helpful for the remuneration committee to receive a sum-mary explanation of a proposed scheme which is written with the expectation of use in the public domain. This summary may be used later in the annual report, as there is a requirement for con-siderable disclosure about remuneration. It may be used earlier, in public, if the company announces revised or new reward arrange-ments. It is helpful to have the summary written as if it was a press release. It is a good test of a scheme to have it summarized in non-technical language and it provides committee members with comfort, knowing that the proposal is communicable and that they can achieve transparency.

At the same time, the architects of the proposal can draft the formal statement, which would be included in the remuneration report contained in the annual report and accounts. This abbreviated but for-mal report can be drafted at the time a scheme is being discussed. Its production is another source of comfort for the remuneration committee.

Another consideration that can helpfully be addressed during the review of the submissions presented to the remuneration committee is the relationship between reward proposals for executive directors and the reward policies and practices in place for other relevant groups, typically the senior management population. This may be a subject for discussion rather than being part of the written proposal, but it is helpful to cover the issue as shareholders are increasingly interested in consistency on reward issues. This does not imply a levelling of reward or pressure for schemes with company-wide application, but it does mean that there should be no contradictions in pay philosophy or practice.

## Summary

There have been changes to the nature of remuneration committees as a result of successive advisory codes and legal regulation. These changes have not resulted in one standard way that remuneration committees operate. There continue to be tensions. It can be argued that non-executive directors (the remuneration committee) and the other board members (the executive directors) have inherently different preoccupations with reward issues and these differences are unlikely to be reconciled. Certainly, the separate expectations of the two types of directors make it difficult to see how they can share an identical perspective.

This is not necessarily a critical or problematic variance. Non-executive directors and executive directors do have the same fiduciary responsibilities under the Companies Acts. The differences have been difficult where remuneration committees have lacked authority, often when the executive has been very powerful. Legislative changes have now strengthened the position of remuneration committees.

Even with a strengthened code, there is still significant scope for remuneration committees to operate in different ways. The typology discussed earlier describes four types of remuneration committees. It is likely that public standards will draw remuneration committees towards the Adaptive category, which endorses Contemporary values and an External perspective.

A heavy responsibility lies with the human resources function and the company secretariat, and it is important that the relationship between the information provider and the decision-makers is one of confidence and trust. If the guidelines, based on an understanding of the needs and sensibilities of the remuneration committee, are followed, a sound and productive relationship should result.

# 10

# Human resource strategy and top-level pay

Shaun Tyson

## Introduction

Rewards for top executives are a significant element in human resource strategies. Indeed, top teams themselves are key stakeholders in both the business strategy and in the reward strategy that underlies their own compensation. For this reason, the integration of human resource strategies into business strategies and the significance of top pay strategies in the organizational context are relevant to our study. In this chapter we will look at the implications of different models of human resource strategy for rewards at the top, and for the management of senior talent.

## Corporate strategy and business strategy

Corporate strategies are concerned with deciding the overall portfolio of businesses and the mixture of businesses, together with managing the corporate relationship with the stock market. A contrast can be made with business strategies which are the ways the organization intends to give effect to the corporate strategy in specific product or service areas. Business strategies can be defined as the attempt by those who control an organization to find ways to position their business or organization objectives so they can exploit the planning environment and maximize the future use of the organization's capital and human assets.

The most significant aspects of this definition are the references to the 'positioning' of the organization in order to take advantage of the planning environment, the notion that those at the top have an objective of long-term positioning, that they seek to shift emphasis and resources according to changes in the business environment. The other important aspect of the definition is the need to maximize the human as well as the capital assets. Seeing people as assets rather than just costs is often described as a differentiator between personnel administration and modern human resource management, where people are used to obtain competitive advantage, through the quality of recruitment, selection, development and other related policies, in accord with strategic business objectives.

However, the relationship between business strategy and human resource strategy is problematic. Strategies, at the level of a large conglomerate with many businesses or at the business unit level, are susceptible to many pressures. Strategy creation is a 'political' process, achieved through negotiation, agreement and discussion around the issues, each of which may appear differently to each director according to his or her mental map (Calori et al., 1994; Huff, 1990; Bailey et al., 2000), and the varying logics upon which different mentalities are based. Strategy is also inevitably a reaction to external events, to political, economic, social and technological changes. Top teams are unlikely to have all the information they need at any one time to make good decisions, and they are unlikely to be aware of all the relevant actions of their competitors. For these reasons we can say that strategy is often emergent, subject to continuous reconstruction and reinterpretation (Mintzberg and Waters, 1985).

Strategy is, in any case, a statement of intent. Strategies themselves may only be statements with varying levels of detail about how the business intends to act in order to achieve certain agreed objectives. Until strategies are realized – that is, put into place by management with actions designed to bring about specific outcomes – they remain only proposals. To move from words and figures on a computer screen or on pieces of paper to become recognizable, coherent activities performed by employees, strategies have to be realized.

We ought to be clear that there are differences between strategic objectives (such as to increase sales by 10% on particular products or services) and strategies or 'stratagems' (that is, the way these objectives are to be achieved). Strategies may well include drivers for improved efficiency and cost reduction, for increased sales revenue from profitable products and services in the example quoted above, and ways to improve the quality and/or the range of products or services. Strategies may include restructuring, training and development, reward structures and policies, redundancies and redeployment, as well as change management and organization development, and many other actions, systems and processes where human resource management is frequently a joint process conducted between specialists and line managers.

The relationship between business strategy and human resource strategy is also contingent upon the stage at which the HR function is involved in discussions about business strategy.

Data from recent CRANET surveys shows that most HR staff in the UK and Europe are involved in the development of corporate strategy from the outset, but the figures do vary considerably (Table 10.1).

As can be seen, the variation between the responses in the most recent survey and the previous survey shows that the HR function is not improving its position. There are also variations between the industry sector, with the greatest involvement at the outset being in the public sector.

From the above discussion we can see that business and human resource strategies are found in policies and actions designed to achieve strategic business objectives over time. Since objectives can usually only be achieved through a combination of functional strategies, the business plan is likely to be a mixture, for example, of financial, marketing, operational, human resources and other functional strategies, depending upon the objective to be achieved. The mixture also makes

**Table 10.1** Involvement of HR in development of corporate strategy (% of organizations responding)

|  | UK average | | EU average (1999) |
|---|---|---|---|
|  | 1999 | 2003 |  |
| From the outset | 54 | 49 | 58 |
| Consulted during process | 32 | 30 | 24 |
| Involved only at implementation | 8 | 9 | 10 |
| Not consulted | 6 | 12 | 8 |

Source: CRANET Surveys, 1999, 2003.

assessment of the unique contribution of any particular functional area difficult.

Human resource strategy has been defined as:

*Those decisions and actions which concern the management of employees at all levels in the business, and which are related to the implementation of strategies directed towards creating and sustaining competitive advantage.*

(Miller, 1987, p. 352)

This definition stresses the relationship between human resource activity and the business need to create and maintain competitive advantage, and sees HRM as an important aspect of the implementation of strategic plans. There is a value in disaggregating the functional strands within strategies. Although to implement strategies a functional mix is usually essential, functional strategies can show how coherent and consistent policies are, and whether or not they are mutually supportive. What has been outlined here is close to the notion of 'external' fit of HR to the business environment and the business needs or objectives, and 'internal' fit between policies as described by Baird and Meshoulam (1988).

In this chapter we argue that reward strategies for those at the top of the organization have a significant influence on the achievement of HR strategy objectives. The basis for this assertion is the impact of pay packages and the performance-related element upon the business; the impact of the mix of base pay and variable pay upon director-level actions and the impact of those rewards upon employer–employee relationships and motivation. We also argue that reward policy influences recruitment and retention, and hence the contractual relationships within which directors relate to the organization and consequently their performance.

There is evidence from a number of sources that reward strategies that are appropriate for the business context are most likely to produce a more effective performance (Rajagopalan, 1996; Bloom and Milkovich, 1998). The context includes the particular legal, structural, products/service market context, as well as the human resource strategy.

For example, Balkin and Gomez-Mejia (1990) examine the relationship between corporate strategy and business unit (SBU) strategy, and compensation strategies, the pay mix, marketing position and pay policies in 212 US manufacturing companies. The corporate strategies were defined according to their diversification strategies, and the SBU strategies were defined as either 'dynamic growth' or 'rationalization/maintenance'. The results showed that corporate strategy influences pay strategies, including pay package design marketing position and pay policies, in such areas as open pay communication, pay for performance, egalitarian pay policies, amongst others. SBU strategy was shown to affect pay package design and pay market strategy (either above or below the market median). Two major strategic patterns were discerned. Each one was associated with a unique set of corporate and SBU strategies that were bundled together. One of these is a mechanistic pattern associated with corporate strategies that have a wide range of products, and SBUs with 'maintenance' strategies. This bundle included a pay mix of base pay and benefits, pay policies reflecting hierarchical position, and centralized, controlled, secret policies without employee participation. The second pattern was 'organic', associated with single-product companies and growth SBU strategies, which emphasized flexibility, an individual pay structure, with more 'at-risk' pay, incentives, a decentralized approach and open communications with opportunities for employee involvement.

Clearly, this study, although limited to the manufacturing sector, shows corporate and SBU effects, but also the interplay between them, '... the effectiveness of the compensation systems (based on the assessments made by the executives in the survey) varies as a function of the interaction between pay and organizational strategies' (Balkin and Gomez-Mejia, 1990, p. 160).

It follows from the above example that to suggest that top pay should be simply designed to give effect to the business strategy objectives may be too simplistic a view of the linkage between reward systems and organizational performance, and that contextual variables will also need to be taken into account (Gerhart and Rynes, 2003). One way to deal with the organizational context and 'internal' relationships between HR policies is to look at the main models of HR strategy in the businesses and to examine the way these can influence and be influenced by reward strategies for senior executives. Arguably then, there is a benefit in taking broad typifications or 'models' of HR strategy from which we can observe variations in practice.

Following Boxall and Purcell (2003), we can discern two main models, to which we would add a third model that is becoming more apparent. These are the 'fit' or 'best fit' model, the resource-based view

(RBV) and the agile organization concept. We will examine each of these in turn.

## Models of HRM strategy

### The 'best fit' model

Of all the generic HR strategies, this is the most commonly quoted. Indeed, its basic tenet of relating HR strategies closely to business strategies is assumed of all the HR strategy models. The famous formulations of different strategic positions (prospector, analyser, defender business strategies) have their related archetypal HR strategies (Miles and Snow, 1978). If HR strategy is critical in driving an SBU strategy forward in the short to medium term, as an integrated part of the strategy, it will be seen as important especially at the implementation phase. HR strategy is often seen as a second- or third-order strategy that follows the business strategy, as a way to make it happen.

There are external and internal pressures on the 'fit' between HR and business strategy. External pressures include the actions of competitors and changes to the social and political environment (for example, change to the law, to social institutions, societal pressures and economic shifts such as the inflation and unemployment rates). Internal pressures include labour force changes – for example, new technical systems and revised organization structures, such as divisionalization. These could all bring about pressures to disrupt the integration of the HR and business strategy. Quite simply, new policies and practices in people management have to be designed to meet the pressures and, as a consequence, the policies cease first to meet business needs and to be integrated with the business plans, and second cease to be coherent with other policies in HRM.

For the 'fit' model of HR strategy to be functional for the organization, the actions of all employees should conform to the desired state in delivering against the businesses strategic goals. Internal and external pressures that distort this requirement prompt frequent adjustments to policies and demand much ingenuity from HR staff and line managers – for example, changes to interest rates which increase costs might require savings to be found from already overstretched salary budgets, at a time when reduction in manpower would be damaging, new product launches from competitors might result in a rapid adjustment to the company's plans, involving new working hours, reorganization, rapid recruitment of new specialist staff, and so on. HR strategy is in a constant dynamic relationship with business strategy, and policies therefore need constant adjustment. However, the assumptions behind the original policies cannot be changed, and some policies are almost inevitably inappropriate given the time lag between developing the policy and the desired results. For example, management development schemes will take several years from inception to changed behaviour for a critical mass of managers, reward programmes cannot be introduced and cancelled or replaced every few weeks, and recruitment plans once activated are costly to change.

The 'fit' model is also highly dependent upon the accuracy of the targets in the business plan, and the effectiveness of the process for translating those targets into departmental, group and individual targets. This is highlighted by the targets used for the incentive plans, such as LTIPs, at director level. The measures selected to be targets have an influence on the earnings of top executives. For example, there are differences between market-based measures within incentive plans and accounting-based earnings in such plans (Gibbons and Murphy, 1990).

Sloan (1993) showed that the use of accounting-type measures such as return on assets (ROA), based on earnings or profits, rather than market-based measures such as total shareholder return (TSR), based on changes in equity values over time, provided a more stable platform for incentives by top executives:

*Overall the evidence suggests that shielding executive compensation from market-wide fluctuation in equity values is one reason for the use of earnings in top executive compensation contracts.*

(Sloan, 1993, p. 92)

Other researchers had already noted that top executives were paid according to their relative performance compared to their peer group or industry comparators (Antle and Smith, 1986; Gibbons and Murphy, 1990). According to the theory of relative performance evaluation, companies 'filter out' the common risks in the industry sector as a whole by reference to the comparative measures found in industry averages and/or through special exercises with a comparator group (see Chapter 7), thus measuring the specific contribution of the individual when assessing performance for the incentive scheme.

This approach would certainly be consistent with the 'fit' model as a device for ensuring and rewarding alignment with the company's particular context and circumstances. However, one of the dominant assumptions behind the 'fit' model is that directors' actions and interests are aligned to those of the shareholders, through compensation plans where targets are set. The type of target and the target-setting process may make a difference to the alignment, and may well influence the degree of risk shared by the directors, and influence the focus of their efforts.

Typically, profit or accounting earnings type measures reflect previous organizational performance, rather than current or future performance, whereas market-based measures could be said to reflect the potential of the business, assuming market analysis and investors have taken into account any knowledge of marketing plans, new products or services and the quality of senior management, amongst other factors.

We should also be aware that in the 'best fit' model the business strategy always comes first, but there is evidence that the directors and their reports will also influence the business strategy. The arrows go both ways in Figure 10.1, allowing the impact of managerial discretion on the business strategy. Managers must be expected to act and therefore to close off some options for actions, and also open up other lines of action if this suits them, such as research and development, or opportunistically entering into what seemed like a great advantage – such as an alliance, or merger, or new product and service lines. The relationship between HR strategy and business strategy is likely to be constantly realigning itself.

To summarize, the 'best fit' model is most suitable in stable businesses, at the business unit level, where HR can be used to drive the

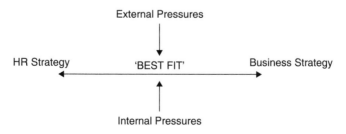

**Figure 10.1** The dynamics of HR strategy and business strategy relationships.

business forward by integrating HR strategy with business strategy, which requires sophisticated planning and policy development.

## The resource-based view

The resource-based view of organizations originated with the ideas of Edith Penrose, the economist, in the 1950s in her theories of the firm. The conception that organizations are resource rich – with human, physical and organizational assets to deploy – also brings the realization that these resources can be configured in a variety of ways (Boxall and Purcell, 2003). This brings greater opportunities for managerial discretion, but also the limitations of path dependency. The history of previous decisions and the way in which resources are actually deployed suggests a specific approach to doing business, meaning that certain business models have typically been preferred over others in the past (Barney, 1991, 1999).

The resource-based view (RBV) argues that, to achieve a competitive advantage, firms need to possess valuable, rare, inimitable and well-organized resources (Barney and Wright, 1998); these are systemic and interdependent in their operation within the organization. Therefore, the difficulty for competitors entering the same industry sector as an established business would be to imitate their entire way of working. Capacity in the organization means more than the quality of the employees, and incorporates production, logistic, marketing and sales methodologies, and all the HR systems that the organization has developed through a lengthy process of learning how to be effective when faced with many different challenges.

The significance of this approach is firstly that the RBV offers a theoretical basis to the study of HRM which had been lacking – that is, a theory which showed the potential business value in treating employees as assets rather than just costs. Secondly, the basic ideas were capable of further development, in particular to show that the people management practices create the human, social and organizational capital – in other words, the overall intellectual capital of the enterprise, and thence of society (Wright et al., 2001).

The RBV gives us new insights into the pay of senior executives. First, it suggests we should look at reward systems for whatever level of employee as systems integrated with the long-term development of the business. This prompts us to examine the long-term aspects of reward policies and to ask whether or not these policies produce the necessary degree of integration with long-term business aims. The characteristics of LTIPs have already been described earlier (see Chapter 7). LTIPs, unlike stock option schemes, typically apply only to senior executives.

The RBV of HR strategy would be expected to encompass the entire reward structure in the organization; there is therefore the question of what relationship normally exists between the pay structures for directors and those other employees. Institutional shareholders are sensitive to this point. The Association of British Insurers guidelines on executive remuneration (issued 19 December 2002) include within their list of principles, at point 6:

*Remuneration committees should have regard to pay and conditions elsewhere in the company. They should pay particular attention to arrangements for senior executives who are not board directors but have a significant influence over the company's ability to meet its strategic objectives.*

(p. 3)

The evidence on how structures work through the hierarchy indicate that, whatever alignment may exist at the top, this diminishes as we go down the hierarchy, where rewards have little direct relationship to organizational performance (Baker et al., 1988). Werner and Tosi (1995, p. 1686) go on to show that, at whatever hierarchical level, in management-controlled firms managers received higher pay than 'owner-managed firms', irrespective of organizational performance:

*In firms controlled by their management, there was no relationship between changes in pay and changes in firm performance for any executive level. In these firms, pay for lower level management groups is decoupled from firm performance and not aligned with owners' interests, leaving them with less compensation risk than their peers in owner controlled firms.*

In its recent survey of board-level pay in the UK following the changes to reporting required in the January 2003 regulations in the UK, Incomes Data Services noted that over 100 of the latest annual accounts included statements showing that pay awards and levels of salaries throughout the organizations were taken into account when deciding executive director-level pay (IDS, 2003, p. 13). The survey goes on to give examples of companies such as Debenhams and International Power that followed this practice. The reporting regulations have created greater transparency in reward policy, so it is probable that most organizations will have to show consistency between policies for directors and the remainder of the employees.

This aspect of the RBV could be to the detriment of another feature of the approach to strategy, the need to attract and retain talented people. There is a long-standing debate about the relationship between director-level pay as a ratio of average pay in the organization. We know, for example, that directors in the USA earn a much higher multiple of average earnings than in the UK (see Chapter 2). There is also strong evidence that director-level compensation reflects the strategic significance of the job, the scarcity of the skills, the level of talent available and the competitive labour markets from which these directors are recruited. For example, in the UK, finance directors typically received salaries at higher levels than other directors, except for CEOs (IDS, 2003). The problem is how to sustain internal relativities whilst remaining competitive for talented executives.

Attraction and retention are often explicit aims of stock option schemes. Share option schemes, unlike LTIPs, are often extended to other employees besides directors, thereby reinforcing the reward policy in the company as a whole, supporting the same needs for retention, together with the potential benefits that share schemes may encourage wider involvement and participation amongst employees. One solution to the apparent problem that top executive talent must be rewarded, whilst top executives' salaries may now be seen as a part of the reward structure throughout the firm, is that by differentiating rewards in base pay, and offering some similar elements to the package, as in share schemes, both the needs may be satisfied.

There is evidence to support the notion that the various types of all employee share schemes have a positive effect on organizational performance. This shows that firms in the UK in which employees have a financial stake do perform better (Freeman, 2001). On average, those with approved schemes give employees more information about business performance, more decision-making opportunities and enjoy improved productivity. Joint consultation and company-level communications with workers are more widespread in such companies, a result the author showed exists also in the USA (Dube and Freeman, 2000).

Research for the European Foundation found that financial participation was greatest in the UK (45%) and the Netherlands (45%) with France at 41%, and its lowest in Portugal and Austria. Around one-third of all organizations were shown to have share ownership schemes, profit share being more common than share ownership (Pendleton et al., 2001). These developments, which spread during the 1990s, were due to some extent to government attempts to build all employee schemes. This study also showed that increased communication about corporate strategy and finance occurred amongst share scheme companies, and showed also that those companies with share schemes invested more in training.

Perhaps what is happening here is that encouraging specific behaviours alongside company communication and more local-level decision-making, reinforced by the use of share schemes and profit-related bonuses, does produce superior performance rather than either of these two compensation mechanisms in isolation. Support for this also comes from the work undertaken by Watson Wyatt on the Human Capital Index, which seeks to show that a high figure on Tobins Q is associated with specific HR practices, including widespread share ownership amongst the employees.

In spite of these positive pointers to the use of financial participation strategies, we should be cautious in our conclusions on this point. Most of the studies were undertaken during the long 'bull' market on the stock exchange in the UK and USA. Executives and employees alike may not maintain the same enthusiasm when share prices are falling. These results also relate to all employee share and profit-sharing schemes. Stock options for executives or variants in these schemes are unlikely to bring the same corporate-wide benefits.

Furthermore, there is evidence that employees (including directors) frequently sell shares shortly after receiving them, thus negating the intended effects of retention and participation. In the case of performance conditions, found in LTIPs and often in share option schemes, there is the question of whether directors seek more chances to meet the criteria, and the problem that share values have fallen to the point where they are 'under water', so making shares not worth selling. On this basis, the motivational element in share schemes may be missing.

The classic response to the question on the balance of variable pay to base pay is to reward the long-term value of the individual with base pay, whilst rewarding performance with variable pay (Zingheim and Schuster, 2000). This is entirely in line with the RBV. Given this is the most likely approach for top executives, the RBV relies on a long-term strategy of development, and suggests that directors should be part of a team, with a long-term commitment. Reward strategy, in this view, is to embed the system with the business model, requiring the directors' targets to be those that sustain the business objectives.

The quality of the top level of managers will be judged by institutional investors, where issues of how good the company is at attracting and retaining talent, the quality of its strategy, the expertise of management and management credibility are examined when making investment decisions (Low and Siesfield, 1998). This allows the organization to be differentiated based on the competencies and the capacity to leverage resources, its capacity to offer a system for finding, retaining and rewarding the best senior executives in the industry sector being a part of that process.

## Agile organizations

Most organizations have changed, adapted or restructured their operations in the last two decades. Mergers, acquisitions or demergers have received a boost from the need to globalize, and to keep down costs in the face of competition. In addition to downsizing, pressure on costs, and the resulting redundancy and outsourcing, organizations have moved away from plans over five years to shorter-term planning horizons, around two to three years (Tyson and Doherty, 1999).

In their famous study on the 'boundaryless organization', Ashkenas et al. (1995) use their experience in engineering a major transformation at GE and other organizations facing change to describe what they call a revolution, where hierarchical distinctions are disappearing, functional silos are removed, and external boundaries between organizations and their suppliers and customers are less distinct, as are geographic boundaries, which no longer hold good in the new global economies. They describe the new success factors for organizations as speed, flexibility, integration and innovation, but with an emphasis on process internally and a concentration on organizational learning and interorganization relationships.

The 'white-water' era where continuous change is the norm produces a need for a different approach to both business and HR strategy. The notion that organizations should develop a long-term capability to be change oriented, flexible and adaptable to fast-moving shifts in the business environment is central to the idea of organizational agility. The strategic human resource implications from this business strategy are located in the style of working where innovation, collaboration and robustness in the face of continuous change and developmental approaches, with the accent on learning, team development and flexibility in response to challenges, are seen as the way forward. The HR policy implications would then be found in the flexibility of job design, rewards for appropriate behaviours and learning built into the work itself (Dyer and Shafer, 1999).

The case of the Albert Einstein Healthcare Network (AEHN), as described by Shafer et al. (2001), illustrates how an agile organization strategy can be developed through the HR strategy. In this case, a private healthcare organization, located in Pennsylvania, USA, sought to become a nimble, change-oriented, fully integrated healthcare network. The CEO sought to move the organization from being a traditional, stable, acute care hospital by developing three strategic capabilities: to be able to initiate new services and exploit opportunities, to be able to adapt by improving its capacity to anticipate external threats and to deal with these effectively, and to be able to deliver by enhancing its efficiency, through strategic alliances, improved economies of scale and similar improvements to effectiveness. The HR strategies were all concerned with achieving these capability creation goals: 'achieving contextual clarity' (by communications and training), 'embedding core values' (by objectives, communication, selection), 'enriching work' (through flexible assignments, job design), 'promoting personal growth' (by needs assessment and on the job learning) and 'providing commensurate returns' (by recognition, celebration, position revaluation) (Shafer et al., 2001, p. 200). This latter capability emphasized non-monetary rewards, partly because the employees in the health sector were supposed to be less instrumentally attached to their work. However, broad banding was introduced, some positions were re-evaluated and 'the pay levels of a few high performing individuals with rare technical skills were significantly adjusted by pegging their rates to the 75th rather than the 50th percentile of the market' (Shafer et al., 2001, p. 206).

From the above brief description of this case, we can see that the virtues of the agile organization reside in its change capability and its flexibility in the face of uncertainty. One way to deal with a highly uncertain future is to create a capability to respond quickly whatever the future brings. This is not the same as managing change, which implies that change is moving from one steady state to another. Rather, it is more like developing the capability to dance, to dodge, weave, flex and to move all the time.

One could argue that the agile organization concept is another variant of the RBV. Agility is a strategic capability, a critically important competence of the human resource. However, there are some important differences. In addition to the built-in capacity to change and flex, agile organizations need a core of high-quality staff, to maintain organizational learning. There is frequently a need for dual strategies in the context of organizational renewal, where efficiency in running the existing operation is necessary alongside the creation of adaptability and innovation (Dyer and Shafer, 1999).

For reward strategies generally, and for top executive pay specifically, flexibility is one aspect of the agile organization. Flexibility is found in the above case – for example, broad banding and responsiveness – by setting targets that relate to business aims, which would be reviewed frequently. The retention of strategically important staff by a preparedness to pay above the average is another example of responsiveness. Flexibility may also be possible where new reward schemes can be introduced; this would also be where senior executives in the fast-changing industry sectors might be expected to share a high proportion of the risk – for example, through the balance of reward being in variable pay, such as bonus or stock options, with stretch performance targets.

Fay and Thompson (2001) surveyed successful and unsuccessful reward initiatives in 231 US organizations and 69 Canadian organizations, around 65% of which employed less than 5000 employees. This showed that, of the new and modified reward programmes initiated between 1995 and 2000 in these organizations, the average organization had 6.5 new or modified reward initiatives and that 59% of the initiatives were considered not successful or only somewhat successful. These included 183 out of 300 new short-term incentive schemes and 76 out of 104 long-term incentive plans. Even modified plans showed 150 out of 231 short-term incentive plans were not or were only somewhat successful, and

48 out of 66 long-term incentives were not entirely successful. These were, of course, programmes for more of the organization than just the board, but the long-term incentives were mostly for senior executives.

There are several lessons from this study. First, there are a very large number of new and modified initiatives, even if these organizations were not entirely representative of all companies in the USA and Canada. A surprisingly large number of these initiatives fell short of achieving their aims. We may conclude, therefore, that agile organizations should not seek to introduce large numbers of new schemes, and flexibility should perhaps come from setting targets frequently and reviewing performance with the intention of rewarding high performance accordingly. In the Fay and Thompson study quoted above, financial targets were seen as the most useful measures.

LTIPs in agile organizations are problematic. The need for a dual strategy, to ensure continuing operational efficiency during change, is an objective that suits the principles of LTIPs. However, given the long-term nature of LTIPs, typically three, five or even ten years, they may be thought to perpetuate the more bureaucratic, stable, but eventually unresponsive business. The difficulty resides in maintaining line of sight when organizations change rapidly.

But, as we have argued in this book, the evidence on how much risk senior managers take is ambiguous. For example, from their major study on CEO wealth, Jensen and Murphy (1990, p. 240) state 'the data suggests that CEOs bear little risk of being dismissed by their boards of directors'. These data were taken from an earlier period than the present, but a study of the turnover of bank CEOs in the 1980s showed that compensation growth corresponds to the changes in expected marginal product, but the labour turnover of CEOs is connected to the comparison the organization makes of the existing CEO with alternative executives (Barro and Barro, 1990, p. 477). The use of different levels of risk-bearing by executives as represented in their compensation plans and employment contracts is believed to vary according to the risk in the business, and this is also mediated by monitoring executive performance, as a more acceptable alternative (Beatty and Zajac, 1995). In a study of managerial turnover, there is some further support for the effects on managerial turnover of circumstances such as the renewal context (Kesner and Dalton, 1994). This research shows that, where CEOs are from outside, there are high levels of managerial turnover, but that organizational performance prior to the succession is the main factor relating to managerial turnover.

Data from a Recruitment Confidence Index survey (2004) showed that a high proportion of directors are promoted from within, whilst the data also showed lack of the formal succession planning. This study examined how directors were recruited in over 1000 companies in the UK according to HR director respondents; results are shown in Tables 10.2 and 10.3.

One conclusion we could draw from these data is that, for appointments at the top, contacts, friendships and the 'network' are a vital source of candidates. This might explain the high proportion of both internal promotions and successful word-of-mouth applications, and the low level of formal succession planning. These results are compatible

**Table 10.2** Which methods are used to recruit executive directors?

|  | Overall (%) | Public (%) | Private (%) |
|---|---|---|---|
| Internal promotion | 39 | 41 | 39 |
| Search consultants | 35 | 39 | 35 |
| Informal networks | 22 | 16 | 24 |
| Nominations from investors | 3 | 2 | 3 |
| Nominations from professional advisors | 2 | 2 | 2 |
| National newspapers | 21 | 34 | 17 |
| Local newspapers | 6 | 10 | 5 |
| Commercial websites | 6 | 8 | 5 |
| Corporate websites | 11 | 18 | 8 |

**Table 10.3** Which methods are successful at recruiting executive directors?

|  | Overall (%) | Public (%) | Private (%) |
|---|---|---|---|
| Internal promotion | 35 | 37 | 35 |
| Search consultants | 28 | 32 | 28 |
| Informal networks | 17 | 11 | 19 |
| Nominations from investors | 2 | 1 | 2 |
| Nominations from professional advisors | 2 | 2 | 1 |
| National newspapers | 17 | 28 | 13 |
| Local newspapers | 4 | 7 | 3 |
| Commercial websites | 3 | 5 | 3 |
| Corporate websites | 7 | 12 | 5 |

with the agile organization concept in two ways. First, the networks used by top executives are not only within but are also between organizations, where relationships between former colleagues, friends, suppliers, customers and other influential people within the industry sector offer opportunities for information gathering, for rapid response and a support system for dealing with uncertainty. Second, informality and personal relationships are prerequisites of a strong culture at the heart of the organization, even in the public sector, enabling rapid changes and a fertile ground for organizational learning. The internal network becomes a central feature of organizational life for the top executive, what Art Kleiner (2003) calls the 'core group'. The paradox of modern organizations is that more fluid formal structures mean more influence deriving from personal relationships.

In these circumstances, rewards take on a symbolic value and, as the AEHN case revealed, the non-monetary, lifestyle aspects to rewards, the culture and style of working, the excitement from innovation and the strength of comradeship flowing out of the team relationship provide the main motivational drivers. Formal reward systems should support these elements and, we have argued, should reflect the change capability value to the business.

## Conclusions

Our discussion of the three main approaches to HR strategy and the likely implications for rewards has shown three typical strategic approaches that are nevertheless related. The 'best fit' model is based on the fundamental premise that the HR strategy should give effect to business goals. If competitive advantage is to be achieved, according to the RBV this will come from the special capabilities (competencies, knowledge and processes) the organization possesses, and these rare, inimitable and valuable capabilities should therefore be the focus of the HR strategy. The RBV takes a pride in the development of human, social and organizational capital, but in a change-oriented environment the capabilities perhaps most prized are those that give rise to agility in the organization.

The discussion in this chapter has centred around the themes of how do we recruit, retain, develop and motivate talent at the top, and what reward mechanisms are appropriate to each strategic model. Many aspects of the employment relationship for top executives go beyond the financial pay-off from their actions. However, in larger companies the reward quanta are so large that we cannot ignore the design or corporate governance issues that give rise to the reward package. The trend towards shifting the balance of the package to high amounts of pay at risk, in LTIPs and incentive bonuses, may reflect the move towards a more agile HR strategy approach in general. The use of targets and multiple objectives via the balanced scorecard might also show the felt need for greater alignment, as one would expect from a 'best fit' model. The RBV requires stability. Many of the mechanisms designed for rewarding senior executives have supported this approach: LTIPs and stock options, top hat pensions and golden handcuffs of various kinds, for example. However, the trend may now be shifting to a more flexible approach. Corporate governance rules favouring one-year contracts and performance comparisons based on TSR are examples of how a new 'best practice' is emerging.

If we believe a 'free' market determines price, then the high price of executive labour is thought to represent its scarcity, and this is then easily transposed to be the 'intrinsic' value of the executives themselves. Most large businesses report difficulty in recruiting high-quality senior executives, which no doubt encourages them to develop and promote such people from within. As the rewards for executives increase, whether or not through fat cat pay rises, so the status of executives might be expected to rise. This will likely be the case if top executives share more of the risks of business. Higher risk-taking puts the director into the role of the principal, rather than the agent.

The difficulty here is that recent history has shown that there is a strong desire, given their lofty status, to reduce the risks and to ensure they are financially compensated irrespective of the business outcome. The recent scandals at Enron in the USA and Parmalat in Europe are new in terms of scale, but not new in substance – previous scandals were arguably just as serious. The new corporate governance initiatives designed to improve communication and transparency may well result in a more sophisticated and powerful role for shareholders, and a more public discussion about top executive rewards.

The majority of top executives are not likely to be adversely affected by these new rules. At the top, reputation, to be seen to succeed, to be a successful individual in one's network and to compete and win, both in external and internal relationships, are the really powerful motivators.

# Bibliography

Aboody, D. (1996). Market valuation of employee stock options. *Journal of Accounting and Economics*, **22**(1–3), 357–391.

Aboody, D. and Kasznik, R. (2000). CEO stock option awards and the timing of corporate voluntary disclosures. *Journal of Accounting and Economics*, **29**(1), 73–100.

Abowd, J.M. and Kaplan, D.S. (1999). Executive compensation: six questions that need answering. *Journal of Economic Perspectives*, **13**(4), 145–168.

Abrahamson, E. and Park, C. (1994). Concealment of negative organisational outcomes: an agency theory perspective. *Academy of Management Journal*, **37**(5), 1302–1334.

Acharya, V., John, K. and Sundaram, R. (2000). On the optimality of resetting executive stock options. *Journal of Financial Economics*, **57**(1), 65–101.

Anderson, P.A. and Klasen, K. (2003). Management compensation at the Daimler Chrysler Corporation. *Personal Führung*, **11**, 46–49.

Angbazo, L. and Narayanan, R. (1997). Top management compensation and the structure of the Board of Directors in commercial banks. *European Finance Review*, **1**, 239–259.

Antle, R. and Smith, A. (1986). An empirical investigation of the relative performance evaluation of corporate executives. *Journal of Accounting Research*, **24**(1), 1–39.

Armstrong, M. and Murlis, H. (1980). *A Handbook of Salary Administration*. London: Kogan Page.

Ashkenas, R., Ulrich, D., Jick, T. and Kerr, S. (1995). *The Boundaryless Organisation*. San Francisco: Jossey Bass.

Bailey, A., Johnson, G. and Daniels, K. (2000). Validation of a multidimensional measure of strategy development process. *British Journal of Management*, **11**(2), 151–162.

Baird, L. and Meshoulam, I. (1988). Managing two fits of strategic human resource management. *Academy of Management Review*, **13**, 116–128.

Baker, G.P., Jensen, M.C. and Murphy, K.J. (1988). Compensation and incentives: practice versus theory. *Journal of Finance*, **XLIII**(3), 593–616.

Balkin, D.B. and Gomez-Mejia, L. (1990). Matching compensation and organisational strategies. *Strategic Management Journal*, **11**, 153–169.

Barney, J.B. (1991). Firm resources and sustained competitive advantage. *Journal of Management*, **17**, 99–120.

Barney, J.B. (1999). How a firm's capabilities affect boundary conditions. *Sloan Management Review*, **40**(3), 137–145.

Barney, J.B. and Wright, P. (1998). On being a strategic partner: the role of human resources in gaining competitive advantage. *Human Resource Management*, **37**(1), 31–46.

Barro, J.R. and Barro, R.J. (1990). Pay, performance and turnover of banks CEOs. *Journal of Labour Economics*, **8**(4), 448–481.

Bartlett, S.A. and Chandler, R.A. (1999). The private shareholder, corporate governance and the role of the annual report. *Journal of Business Law*, September, 415–428.

Beatty, R.P. and Zajac, E.J. (1995). Managerial incentives monitoring and risk bearing in initial public offering firms. *Journal of Applied Corporate Finance*, **8**(2), 87.

Bebchuk, L., Fried, J. and Walker, D. (2002). Managerial power and rent extraction in the design of executive compensation. *University of Chicago Law Review*, **69**, 751–846.

Bell, T., Landsman, W., Miller, B. and Yeh, S. (2001). The valuation implications of employee stock-option accounting for computer software firms. Working Paper, UNC Chapel Hill.

Bender, R. (2003). How executive director remuneration is determined in two FTSE 350 utilities. *Corporate Governance*, **11**(3), 206–217.

Bevan, S. and Thompson, M. (1991). Performance management at the crossroads. *Personnel Management*, **23**(11), 36–39.

Black, A., Wright, P. and Bachman, J.E. (2000). *In Search of Shareholder Value: Managing the Drivers of Performance*, 2nd edition. Financial Times/Prentice-Hall.

Black, F. and Scholes, M. (1973). The pricing of options and corporate liabilities. *Journal of Political Economy*, **81**(3), 637–654.

Bloom, M. and Milkovich, G.T. (1998). Relationships among risk, incentive pay and organisational performance. *Academy of Management Journal*, **41**, 283–297.

Boxall, P. and Purcell, J. (2003). *Strategy and Human Resource Management*. Palgrave: Macmillan.

Bournois, F. and Roussillon, S. (1998). *Préparer les dirigeants de demain*. Paris: Editions d'organisation.

Boyd, B.K. (1995). CEO duality and firm performance: a contingency model. *Strategic Management Journal*, **16**, 301–312.

Brenner, M., Sundaram, R. and Yermack, D. (2000). Altering the terms of executive stock options. *Journal of Financial Economics*, **57**(1), 103–128.

Brickley, J.A., Bhagat, S. and Lease, R.C. (1985). The impact of long-range managerial compensation plans on shareholder wealth. *Journal of Accounting and Economics*, **7**, 115–129.

Brown, D. (2001). *Reward Strategies*. CIPD Publishing.

Buckley, S. (2003). Vandevelde to be paid with shares in M&S. *Financial Times*, 9 July.

Bursee, M. and Schawilye, R. (2003). Stock options – und was kommt danach? *Frankfurter Allegemeinen Zeitung*, 24 March, p. 30.

*Business Week* (1999). France: a CEO's pay shouldn't be a secret, 9 August, p. 47.

Caby, J. and Hirigoyen, G. (1997). *La création de valeur de l'entreprise*. Paris: Économica.

Calori, R., Johnson, G. and Sarnin, P. (1994). CEO's cognitive maps and the scope of the organisation. *Strategic Management Journal*, **15**(6), 437–457.

Carter, M. and Lynch, L. (2001). An examination of executive stock option repricing. *Journal of Financial Economics*, **61**(2), 207–225.

Carter, M. and Lynch, L. (2003). The consequences of the FASB's 1998 proposal on accounting for stock option repricing. *Journal of Accounting and Economics*, **35**(1), 51–72.

Chance, D., Kumar, R. and Todd, R. (2000). The 'repricing' of executive stock options. *Journal of Financial Economics*, **57**(1), 129–154.

Charreaux, G. (1991). Structures de propriété, relation d'agence et performance financère. *Revue Économique,* **42**(3), mai, 521–552.

Cheffins, B.R. (2003). Will executive pay globalise along American lines? *Corporate Governance,* **11**(1), 8–24.

Clarke, T. (1998). The stakeholder corporation: a business philosophy for the information age. *Long Range Planning,* **31**(2), 182–194.

Commission des Opérations de Bourse (COB) (1999). La transparence du marché, Bulletin no. 338, September.

Conyon, M.J. and Peck, S.I. (2000). The structure of executive compensation contracts: UK evidence. *Long Range Planning,* **33**(4), 478–504.

Co-operative Insurance Society Survey (2002). *Financial Times,* 21 October.

Core, J. and Guay, W. (1999). The use of equity grants to manage optimal equity incentive levels. *Journal of Accounting and Economics,* **28**(2), 151–184.

Core, J. and Guay, W. (2001). Stock option plans for non-executive employees. *Journal of Financial Economics,* **61**(2), 253–287.

Core, J. and Guay, W. (2003). When contracts require risk-averse executives to hold equity: Implications for option valuation and relative performance evaluation. Working Paper, University of Pennsylvania.

Core, J. and Larcker, D. (2002). Performance consequences of mandatory increases in CEO stock ownership. *Journal of Financial Economics,* **64**(3), 317–340.

Core, J.E., Holthausen, R.W. and Larker, D.F. (1999). Corporate governance, chief executive officer compensation and firm performance. *Journal of Financial Economics,* **51**, 371–406.

Core, J., Guay, W. and Verrecchia, R. (2003). Price versus non-price performance in optimal CEO contracts. *Accounting Review,* **78**, 957–981.

Cosh, A.D. and Hughes, A. (1987). The anatomy of corporate control: directors, shareholders and executive remuneration in giant US and UK corporations. *Cambridge Journal of Economics,* **11**, 285–313.

Couret, A. and Hirigoyen, G. (1990). *L'actionnariat des salariés.* Que sais je?, no. 2507, PUF.

CRANET Surveys (1999, 2003).

DAFSA Desfossé (1996). *Dictionnaire des sociétés* 1997. Paris.

Davis Global Advisors (2000). *Leading Corporate Governance Indicators 2000.*

Demsetz, H. and Lehn, K. (1985). The structure of corporate ownership: causes and consequences. *Journal of Political Economy*, **93**(6), 1155–1177.

Department of Trade and Industry (2001). Directors' remuneration, a consultative document, URN 01/1400, December.

Department of Trade and Industry and Pricewaterhouse Coopers (1999). *Monitoring of Corporate Governance Aspects of Director's Remuneration.*

Desbrières, P. (1991). *Participation financeére, stock-options et rachats d'entreprise par les salarié.* Paris: Économica.

Desbrières, P. (1997). Stock-options. In *Encyclopédie de gestion* (Simon, Y. and Joffre, J.P., eds), p. 169. Paris: Économica.

Dube, A. and Freeman, R. (2000). *Shared Compensation Systems and Decision-making in the US Job Market.* Commission for Labour Cooperation, USA, May.

Dye, R. (1992). Relative performance evaluation and project selection. *Journal of Accounting Research*, **30**(1), 27–52.

Dyer, L. and Shafer, R. (1999). Creating organisational agility: implications for strategic human resource management. In *Research in Personnel and Human Resource Management, Supplement 4: Strategic HRM in the Twenty-First Century* (Wright, P., Dyer, L., Boudreau, J. and Milkovich, G., eds). Stanford, CT.

Elliot, J. (1976). *A General Theory of Bureaucracy.* Heinemann.

Emerson, R.W., in Hamel, G. and Prahalad, C.K. (1994). *Competing for the Future.* Harvard Business School Press.

International Governance Network (2002). *Executive Remuneration – The Caucus Race.* A report to the International Governance Network (2002).

Fagnot, O. (1999). Les plans d'options sur actions *(stock-options)*: un complément de rétribution adopté par la moitié des entreprises françaises cotées en bourse. *Premières Synthèses*, 99-03, n° 10-1, DARES.

Fay, C.H. and Thompson, M.A. (2001). Contextual determinants of reward system's success: an exploratory study. *Human Resource Management Journal*, **40**(3), 213–226.

Femppel, K. (2002). Vergütungspolitik – ein statischer oder dynamischer Entwicklungsprozess? *Personal Führung*, **11**, 10–13.

*Financial Times* (1999). Salary disclosures in France: transparency or 'voyeurism'?, 26 July, p. 2.

Fox, A.F. and Opong, K.K. (1999). The impact of board changes on shareholder wealth; some UK evidence. *Corporate Governance*, 7(4), October, 385–396.

*Frankfurter Allgemeine Zeitung* (2003). Europa soll eine Aktionärsdemokratie schaffen, 19 April, p. 11.

Freeman, R. (2001). Upping the stakes. *People Management*, 8 February, pp. 25–29.

Garr, D. (2000). *IBM Redux: Lou Gerstner and the Business Turnaround of the Decade*. Harper Business.

Gerhart, B. and Rynes, S.L. (2003). *Compensation. Theory, Evidence and Strategic Implications*. Thousand Oaks, CA: Sage.

Gibbons, R. and Murphy, K. (1990). Relative performance evaluation for chief executive officers. *Industrial and Labour Relations Review*, **43**, 30–51.

Gibbons, R. and Murphy, K. (1992). Optimal incentive contracts in the presence of career concerns: theory and evidence. *Journal of Political Economy*, **100**(3), 468–505.

Giddens, A. (2000). *The Third Way and its Critics*. Cambridge: Policy Press.

Gillan, S.L. and Starks, L.T. (2000). Corporate governance proposals and shareholder activism: the role of institutional investors. *Journal of Financial Economics*, **57**, 275–305.

Gooderham, P.N. and Nordhaug, O. (2003). *International Management. Cross Boundary Challenges*. Oxford: Blackwell.

Government Commission (2003). German Corporate Governance Code. German Government.

Grötzinger, M. and Hohmann, R. (2003). Variable Vergütung in der Krise? *Personal*, **10**, 16–20.

Hall, B. and Murphy, K. (2002). Stock options for undiversified executives. *Journal of Accounting and Economics*, **33**(1), 3–42.

Hanlon, M., Rajgopal, S. and Shevlin, T. (2003). Are executive stock options associated with future earnings? *Journal of Accounting and Economics*.

Hardes, H.-D. and Wickert, H. (2002). Aktienoptionspläne für Führungskräfte: Effiziente Anreizinstrumente? *Personal Führung*, **11**, 22–27.

Harvey-Jones, J. (1994). *Making it Happen – Reflections on Leadership*. Profile Books.

Hauser, H.-E. (2000). *SMEs in Germany: Facts and Figures 2000*. Bonn: Institute für Mittelstandsforschung.

Heath, C., Huddart, S. and Lang, M. (1999). Psychological factors and stock option exercise. *Quarterly Journal of Economics*, **114**(2), 601–627.

Heidrick & Struggles (1999). Is your board fit for the global challenge? *Corporate Governance in Europe*.

Herz, C. and Hofmann, S. (2003). Manager-Bezüge bleiben krisenfest. *Handelsblatt*, 9 April.

Higgs, D. (2003). *Review of the Role and Effectiveness of Non-executive Directors*. The Department of Trade and Industry.

Himmelberg, C., Hubbard, G. and Palia, D. (1999). Understanding the determinants of managerial ownership and the link between ownership and performance. *Journal of Financial Economics*, **53**(3), 353–384.

Hirigoyen, G. (1987). Transmission des PME et participation des salariés. *Revue Banque,* **472**, 482–487.

Hodgson, P., Kirkwood, D.A. and Smith, T. (1999). *Directors' Remuneration in the Privatised Utilities*, Paper No. 11. London: Centre for Reform.

Holland, P., Dowling, P. and Innes, P. (2000). Principles, policies and practices of CEO compensation in Australia: is there a relationship? Working Paper 20-05, University of Tasmania.

Holthausen, R. and Larcker, D. (1993). Board of directors, ownership structure and CEO compensation. Working Paper, University of Pennsylvania.

Holthausen, R. and Larcker, D. (1996). The financial performance of reverse leveraged buyouts. *Journal of Financial Economics*, **42**(3), 293–332.

Huff, A. (1990). *Mapping Strategic Thought*. London: Wiley.

Hwang, C. and Anderson, C. (1993). Boardroom back scratching in setting CEO compensation. Working Paper, University of Pittsburgh.

Incomes Data Services Limited (2003). *Directors' Pay Report 2003*. London: IDS.

iQuantic (2001). *Responding to Underwater Options and Volatile Stock Market Conditions*.

Ittner, C., Lambert, R. and Larcker, D. (2003). The structure and performance consequences of equity grants to employees of new economy firms. *Journal of Accounting and Economics*, **34**(1–3), 89–127.

Jackson, N. and Carter, P. (1995). Turning light on the concept of corporate governance. *Human Relations*, **48**(8), 875–882.

Jackson, T. (2002). The management of people across cultures: valuing people differently. *Human Resource Management Journal* (USA), **41**(4), 455–476.

Jacobi, O., Keller, B., Müller-Jentsch, W. (1998). Germany facing new challenges. In *Changing Industrial Relations in Europe* (Ferner, A. and Hyman, R., eds), pp. 190–238.

Jaques, E. (1964). *Time-span Handbook*. London: Heinemann.

Janakiraman, S. (1998). Stock option awards and exercise behavior of CEOs: an empirical analysis. Working Paper, University of Texas at Dallas.

Janakiraman, S., Lambert, R. and Larcker, D. (1992). An empirical investigation of the relative performance evaluation hypothesis. *Journal of Accounting Research*, **30**(1), 53–69.

Jensen, M.C. and Murphy, K.J. (1990). Performance pay and top management incentives. *Journal of Political Economy*, **98**(2), 225–263.

Jin, L. (2002). CEO compensation, diversification, and incentives. *Journal of Financial Economics*, **66**(1), 29–63.

Johnson, S. and Tian, Y. (2000). The value and incentive effects of non-traditional executive stock option plans. *Journal of Financial Economics*, **57**(1), 3–34.

Jürgens, U. and Rupp, J. (2002). The German system of corporate governance: characteristics and changes. Working Paper, Wissenschaftszentrum Berlin für Sozialforschung, Berlin, May.

Kaplan, R.S. and Norton, D.P. (1996). *The Balanced Scorecard: Translating Strategy into Action*. Harvard Business Press.

Kesner, I.F. and Dalton, D.R. (1994). Top management turnover, and CEO succession: an investigation of the effects on performance. *Journal of Management Studies*, **31**(5), 701–713.

Kienbaum Management Consultants GmbH (2001). *Compensation and Benefits Survey 2001*.

Kienbaum Management Consultants GmbH (2003a). *Vergütungsstudie 2001/2002 – Vorstands- und Aufsichtsratsmitglieder*, p. 26.

Kienbaum Management Consultants GmbH (2003b). *Vergütungsstudie 2003 – Band 1 Leitende Angestellte*, p. 41.

Kienbaum Management Consultants GmbH/Hewitt Associates GmbH (2003). *Top Business TCM™, Deutschland 2003*.

Kitchens, S. (2003). *Tricks of the Trade*. Forbes.com, 9 January.

Kleiner, A. (2003). *Who Really Matters? The Core Group*. London: Nicholas Brealey.

Knebel, H. (2002). Entgeltpolitik in bewegten Zeiten. *Personal Führung*, **11**, 14–17.

KPMG Deutsche-Treuhand-Gesellschaft (2003). Value Based Management – Shareholder-Value-Konzepte – Eine Untersuchung der DAX 100-Unternehmen.

Lambert, R. and Larcker, D. (2003). Options, restricted stock, and incentives. Working Paper, University of Pennsylvania.

Lambert, R., Larcker, D. and Verrecchia, R. (1991). Portfolio considerations in valuing executive compensation. *Journal of Accounting Research*, **29**(1), 129–149.

Larcker, D.F. (2003). Discussion of 'Are executive stock options associated with future earnings?' *Journal of Accounting and Economics* **36**(1–3), 91–103.

*Le Monde* (2001). Seuls huit PDG acceptent de révéler leur fortune, 8–9 July, p. 15.

*Le Monde* (2002a). Le salaire du PDG a progressé de 80% en 2001, 17 April.

*Le Monde* (2002b). Vivendi Universal paie la facture de son expansion, 7 March.

*Le Monde* (2002c). Ce que gagnent vraiment les grands patrons, 13 July.

Lejoly, K. and Moingeon, M. (2003). *Gouvernement d'entreprise: débat théoriques et pratiques*. Paris: Ellipses.

Lippert, R.L. and Moore, W.T. (1994). Compensation contracts of chief executive officers: determinants of pay – performance sensitivity. *Journal of Financial Research*, **XVII**(3), 321–332.

The London Stock Exchange (1998). Committee on Corporate Governance. The Combined Code.

Lovewell, D. (2003). Organisations take care. *Employee Benefits*, May.

Low, J. and Siesfield, T. (1998). *Measures that Matter*. Boston: Ernst & Young.

Lozano, J.F. (2001). Proposal for a model for the elaboration of ethical codes based on discourse ethics. *Business Ethics: A European Review*, **10**(2), 157–162.

Lucier et al. (2002). Why CEOs fail: the causes and consequences of turnover at the top. *Strategy and Business*, Third Quarter.

Malik, F. (2002). *Die neue Corporate-Governance*, 3rd expanded edition. Frankfurter Allgemeine Buch.

McConnell, J. and Servaes, H. (1990). Additional evidence on equity ownership and corporate value. *Journal of Financial Economics*, **27**(2), 595–612.

McGregor, D. (1960). *The Human Side of Enterprise*. New York: McGraw-Hill.

Merchant, K.A., Van Der Stede, W. and Liu Zheng (2003). Disciplinary constraints on the advancement of knowledge: the case of organisational incentive systems. *Accounting, Organisations and Society*, **28**, 251–286.

Miles, R.E. and Snow, C.C. (1978). *Organisational Strategy, Structure and Process*. New York: McGraw-Hill.

Miller, D.J. (1995). CEO salary increases may be rational after all: referents and contracts in CEO pay. *Academy of Management Journal*, **38**(5), 1361–1385.

Miller, P. (1987). Strategic industrial relations and human resource management, distinction, definition, recognition. *Journal of Management Studies*, **24**(4), 347–361.

Mintzberg, H. and Waters, J.A. (1985). Of strategies deliberate and emergent. *Strategic Management Journal*, **6**(3), 257–272.

Monks, R. and Sykes, A. (2002). *Capitalism Without Owners Will Fail*. UK and New York: Centre for the Study of Financial Innovation.

Morck, R., Shleifer, A. and Vishny, R. (1988). Management ownership and market valuation: an empirical analysis. *Journal of Financial Economics*, **20**, 293–315.

NAPF Survey (2000). *Financial Times*, 21 October.

Newman, H.A. and Mozes, H.A. (1999). Does composition of the compensation committee influence CEO compensation practices. *Financial Management*, Autumn, 28. p. 3, 41 et seq.

Nichols, D. and Subramanian, C. (2001). Executive compensation: excessive or equitable? *Journal of Business Ethics*, **29**, 339–351.

Norris, P. and Mills, N. (2002). Accounting for share-based payments – can the past be a guide to the future? *Benefits and Compensation International*, **32**(5), 5.

Ofek, E. and Yermack, D. (2000). Taking stock: equity-based compensation and the evolution of managerial ownership. *Journal of Finance*, **55**(3), 1367–1384.

Oyer, P. and Schaefer, S. (2001). Why do some firms give options to all employees?: An empirical investigation of alternative theories. Working Paper, Stanford University.

Pendleton, A., Poutsma, E., Brewster, C. and Van Ommeren, J. (2001). Financial participation in Europe: an investigation of profit sharing and employee share ownership. Report prepared by Cranfield University for European Foundation for the Improvement of Living and Working Conditions, Dublin, Ireland.

Pension Fund Partnership. *2002 Survey of Occupational Pension Schemes (UK)*.

Pension Investments Research Consultancy Survey (2002). *Financial Times*, 25 October.

*People Management* (2002). Top rewards under scrutiny, 7 February, p. 19.

Pigé, B. (1996). Les marchés constituent-ils un organe externe de contrôle des dirigeants? *Journées internationales de l'AFFI*, 24–26 June.

Prevost, A.K. and Rao, E.P. (2000). Of what value are shareholder proposals sponsored by public pension funds? *Journal of Business*, **73**(2), 177–204.

Rajagopalan, N. (1996). Strategic orientations, incentive plan adoptions and firm performance: evidence from electric utility firms. *Strategic Management Journal*, **18**, 761–785.

Rappaport, A. (1997). *Creating Shareholder Value: A Guide for Managers and Investors*. Free Press.

Rosengart, A. and Wetzel, D. (2003). Die maßlosen Manager. *Die Welt*, 25 June, p. 10.

Saly, P.J. (1994). Repricing executive stock options in a down market. *Journal of Accounting and Economics*, **18**(3), 325–356.

Schwertfeger, B. (2003). Mitarbeiter werden zu abgerichteten Hündchen. *Personal*, **2**, 62–63.

Seibt, C. (2003). Crommes Knigge. *Financial Times Deutschland*, 2 September, p. 29.

Selley, M. and Forman, E.H. (2002). *Decisions by Objectives*. World Scientific Publishing Co.

Sesil, J., Kroumova, M., Kruse, D. and Blasi, J. (2000). Broad-based employee stock options in the U.S.: company performance and characteristics. Working Paper, Rutgers University.

Shafer, R.A., Dyer, L., Kilty, J., Amos, J. and Ericksen, J. (2001). Crafting a human resource strategy to foster organisational agility: a case study. *Human Resource Management Journal*, **40**(3), 197–212.

Skapinker, M. (2003). CEO: a greedy liar with personality disorder. *Financial Times*, 2 July, p. 12.

Sloan, R.G. (1993). Accounting earnings and top executive compensation. *Journal of Accounting and Economics*, **16**, 55–100.

Stern, J.M., Shiely, J.S. and Ross, I. (2001). *The EVA Challenge: Implementing Value Added Change in an Organisation*. John Wiley.

Stilpon, N. (2001). Corporate governance trends and developments in the OECD area: where do we go from there? *International Financial Law Review*, Supplement, 11–20.

Storck, M. (1986). Définition légale du contrôle d'une société en droit fiançais, *Revue des Sociétés*, pp. 385–404.

Tosi, H.L. and Gomez-Mejia, L.R. (1989). The decoupling of CEO pay and performance: an agency theory perspective. *Administration Science Quarterly*, **34**, 169–189.

Tosi, H.L. Jr and Gomez-Mejia, L.R. (1994). CEO compensation monitoring and firm performance. *Academy of Management Journal*, **37**(4), 1002–1011.

TUC (2000). Top cats: the last closed shop. Online report, 9 September. Available at http://www.tuc.org/em_research/tuc-2212-f0.cfm (date of access 2 November 2002).

Tufano, P. (1996). Who manages risk? An empirical examination of risk management practices in the gold mining industry. *Journal of Finance*, **51**(4), 1097–1137.

Tyson, S. (1999). *Human Resource Strategy*. London: Pitman.

Tyson, S. and Doherty, N. (1999). *Human Resource Excellence Report*. Financial Times/Cranfield.

Ullmann, F. (2003). Nebenleistungen sind alles andere als nebensächlich. *Handelsblatt*, 24 September.

Vernier, E. (1996). Que vaut une entreprise sans son dirigeant? *Banque*, **566**, January, 34–36.

Viénot, M. (1995). Le conseil d'administration des sociétés cotés, Rapport du groupe de travail CNPF/AFEP.

Von Preen, A. and Blang, H.-G. (2003). Der Einstieg in den Umstieg ist erfolgt. *Personal*, September, pp. 64–66.

Wall, D.K. and Proyect, M.M. (1997). *Critical Pathways Development Guide*. Bonus Books.

Waters, R. and Morrison, S. (2003). Microsoft ends stock options for employees. *Financial Times*, 9 July.

Watson Wyatt (2000). Human Capital Index. European Survey report, http://www.watsonwyatt.com.

Weil, Gotshal and Manges (2002). Comparative study of corporate governance codes relevant to the European Union and its member states. January.

Werner, S. and Tosi, H.L. (1995). Other people's money: the effects of ownership on competitive strategy and managerial pay. *Academy of Management Journal*, **38**(6), 1672–1691.

Westphal, J.D. and Zajac, E.J. (1994). Substance and symbolism in CEOs' Long Term Incentive Plans. *Administrative Science Quarterly*, **39**, 367–390.

Whitley, R. (1992). The social construction of organisations and markets: the comparative analysis of business recipes. In *Rethinking Organisations* (Reed, M. and Hughes, M., eds). London: Sage.

Williams, S. (2001). *Emotion and Social Theory*. London: Sage.

Winstanley, D. and Woodall, J. (eds) (2000). Introduction. In *Ethical Issues in Contemporary Human Resource Management*. Basingstoke: Macmillan.

Wright, P.M., Dunford, B.B. and Snell, S.A. (2001). Human resources and the resource based view of the firm. *Journal of Management*, **27**, 701–721.

Yermack, D. (1997). Good timing: CEO stock option awards and company news announcements. *Journal of Finance*, **52**(2), 449–476.

Zingheim, P.K. and Schuster, J.R. (2000). *Pay People Right*. San Francisco: Jossey Bass.

# Index